JENSON BUTTON

LIFE TO THE LIMIT

JENSON BUTTON

LIFE TO THE LIMIT

MY AUTOBIOGRAPHY

BLINK
bringing you closer

Published by Blink Publishing
3.08, The Plaza,
535 Kings Road,
Chelsea Harbour,
London, SW10 0SZ

www.blinkpublishing.co.uk

facebook.com/blinkpublishing
twitter.com/blinkpublishing

Hardback – 978-1-911600-34-3
Trade paperback – 978-1-911600-35-0
eBook – 978-1-911600-37-4

A CIP catalogue of this book is available from the British Library.

Designed and set by seagulls.net
Printed and bound by Clays Ltd, St. Ives Plc

1 3 5 7 9 10 8 6 4 2

All images are from private collections except those that appear courtesy of Getty
Images, Bath in Time, Sutton, PA Images, LAT Images, and Darren Heath.

Blink Publishing is an imprint of the Bonnier Publishing Group
www.bonnierpublishing.co.uk

For the old boy. Simply put I couldn't have done any of it without you. Not just because you're my dad, who I love dearly, but also because you were my best friend, my confidant and my inspiration then, now and for ever. Together every step of the way, we made our dream a reality. I love you and I miss you.

CONTENTS

PROLOGUE

8.30am

Finding my peace starts with a shot of coffee.

'Ready, JB?'

That's Mikey, my physio, and he means for a run, although calling it a run flatters what we do. It's more like a little jog. Fifteen or twenty minutes' worth just to get everything pumping that should be pumping. After that it's time for a shower, get dressed, and then a hearty breakfast in McLaren hospitality before the serious stuff begins.

It's race day.

10am

I join the engineers and chief mechanic for thirty minutes of strategy talk about our pit stops, how many we're going to make and when we plan to make them; our tactics; our qualifying pace compared to other teams'; the successes and failures of the race before. There's a buzz about the team, of course, a feeling of tension and a sense of heightened expectation. Me, I've perfected the art of being relaxed but excited, a state of mind that I've acquired with age and experience. It tends to descend on me during that first meeting and I greet it with the relief and gratitude of a dog greeting its master.

Qualifying is a different matter. No relaxed excitement on the Saturday, just nerves – probably because I'm not very good at the whole one-lap-fast-time demands of qualifying. Give me a race any day. Ninety minutes of planning, strategy and concentration, that's what I like.

After the first meeting, we have a second one, about the set-up of the car. An hour of that and I get dragged away to the paddock club. Every team has a paddock club, where sponsors and possible future sponsors mill around a hospitality area overlooking the circuit. I meet those guys, do a little speech, answer some questions about qualifying, press the flesh, and then return downstairs to meet fans in the pit lane.

And if you were to say that meeting sponsors and fans isn't the best preparation for a Grand Prix, then I'd probably agree with you. But it's part of what we do. Without sponsors and fans you don't race, simple as that. Either you suck it up, do your job and enjoy it, or you're Kimi Räikkönen.

Midday

With the race just two hours away, Mikey and I have an early lunch. Honestly, we do everything together. We're like Ant and Dec, except you can tell us apart.

Lunch is chicken breast with dark-green salad and quinoa. It's the only meal of the weekend that's high in carbs – the quinoa – which I need to sustain me through the race. It's got to be food I know well so I don't risk an upset stomach.

After that I take part in the drivers' parade, where we perch on the back seat of road cars and are driven around the circuit, waving at the crowd. When that's over someone sticks a microphone in your face so you can say a few words for broadcast to fans at the circuit.

Up until now I would have been wearing the normal team gear of trousers and shirt, but after the parade I go into the tiny driver's room, where I pull on fireproof long johns, followed by a fireproof top (with the sponsor logos on, in case your suit is only zipped halfway), followed by the suit itself (which I only zip halfway) and then my boots.

12.30pm

Back upstairs, Mikey's ready in the massage room with some tunes playing: Rage Against the Machine, Kings Of Leon, Pharrell Williams, whatever we fancy for the next forty-five minutes of warming-up and stretching.

Mikey and I are usually pretty chatty, but it's about now that the conversation dries up, and I start to get my focus on, thinking about the race, especially the start of it, and looking forward to getting in the car. Everything before that is just build-up. I'm not saying it's tedious, but it's duty-stuff; it's what you must do as part of the privilege of racing in Formula One. There comes a point when you just can't wait to get in the car. And that point is now.

1.30pm

After a trip to the toilet I go to the garage, where the car awaits, the real star of the show, a temperamental prima donna tended to by mechanics and engineers in bulbous headphones.

I collect my earplugs, balaclava, gloves and helmet from the top of a toolbox at the back. The earplugs are not the normal earplugs you'd wear to block out the sound of your partner's snoring; they have several functions. First, yes, they're earplugs, to prevent hearing damage; second, they're earphones so I can hear instructions over the team radio, and third, they're a G meter, which allows the team to check the level of G-force you've been subjected to. If you've hit something, for example, they can check the data and be better able to make a judgement on whether or not you should compete in the next race.

Next comes the balaclava. I run a wire from the earplugs out of the balaclava and then, when I put my helmet on, plug the lead from the earplugs into it. The mic for the talkback is in the helmet. I'm wired for sound. My visor's up.

Next I grab the gloves but don't put them on just yet. I climb into the car. My only superstition is that I always get in from the right-hand side. Don't ask me why I do that.

Strapping-in is quite an operation. We use a six-point harness, which means you have two straps that come up between your legs, two around your waist and then two over your shoulders, all clicking together into a middle piece. The two between my legs I do up myself; the other four a mechanic does for me.

'That feel all right?' he says. I wriggle, adjust and give him a thumbs up.

Now the headrest goes in. It has a quick-release mechanism so they can get me out fast if something goes wrong. After that comes the wheel. It slots on, solid like a Tonka toy. I pull on my gloves. My visor's still up.

'Okay, JB, we're going green in one minute,' says my race engineer, which means they're waiting for the all-clear to start the car. Around me the crew are ready to remove the tyre warmers.

We go green, they start the car, and a noise like World War III breaking out batters the garage walls. Now we are subservient to the engine. All of us are at its mercy.

'*Go*,' yells the engineer, and my number one mechanic walks backwards, checking to make sure the pit lane is clear and indicating for me to pull out at the same time. *Rip*. Off come the tyre warmers. I edge forward. The wheel has a button on it to trigger the pit-lane limiter, which keeps the speed of the car to below 60kmh, and I make sure it's active.

And then, I flick my visor down. And right away I'm there, in the most peaceful place I or any other driver knows, where all other concerns withdraw and it's just you, alone with the car and at one with it, knowing that however loud and bumpy it gets, however much G-force you pull, nothing can shatter the bond between you and your car.

That feeling of peace is the best thing – the best, most perfect and pure thing about racing.

Coming to the end of the pit lane, I do a practice start, which involves pulling over to the right of the track, checking there's nothing coming, getting the revs up and then pulling away, just to give myself a feel for launch.

Now I'm off on my installation lap, talking to the engineer. 'Turn one, radio okay?' 'Check.' 'Turn two.' 'Check.' All the way around the lap. During the race itself I prefer the engineers to keep schtum unless it's important. But that lap we stay in touch, confirming that everything is working; that our temperamental prima donna is happy.

1.50pm

When I reach the dummy grid, I shut off the engine. There are people all over the grid, TV crews, mechanics, VIPs, God knows who else, so I roll to a stop and let mechanics wheel me into my space. Don't want to risk hurting someone. Or, worse, damaging the car.

Out come the wheel and the headrest and I get out, take off my helmet to chat to the engineer and give him feedback on the installation lap.

Mikey's nearby. He'll have an umbrella if it's hot or raining – and it's usually one of the two – as well as a drink, and then we'll leave to find the nearest toilet. I'm lucky in that I've never needed to wee in the car – it's only an hour-and-a-half race and you're sweating buckets so you shouldn't really *need* a wee – but it's best to be sure.

Once that's done I nip to the front of the grid and stand to attention for the national anthem. There's a fine if you miss it, and besides, it's rude, so I make sure I'm there. Then I get the kit back on and clamber into the car.

At this point they feed a drinks tube into the helmet so I can get fluid during the race. It's not water but neither will you find it in Tesco: it's a high-salt mix of minerals, proteins and carbohydrates developed exclusively for me. The headrest goes in, then the wheel. All around me on the grid other teams are doing the same. The TV crews and VIPs are ushered away.

They start the car. The engineer counts down the mechanics and the tyre blankets come off. The chief mechanic gives me a thumbs up and leaves and now we're off on a green-flag lap.

The green flag lap takes us from the dummy grid on to the real grid but as far as drivers are concerned it's all about getting heat into the tyres. That's why you see drivers weaving, just to get that temperature up. In addition to doing that I brake on the throttle to generate warmth in the brakes. That puts heat into the wheel, which in turn puts heat into the tyre.

By the time of the second-to-last corner I'll start my preparation for the start by doing burn-outs, timing it so the last burn-out takes place just as I roll into my parking space for the race start.

I put the car into neutral, check my mirrors and wait for the grid to form up behind me. So close now. So close to the moment.

'All cars in position,' says my engineer when the grid is in place, the only contact we're allowed to have before the start.

And now the red lights come on. One, two, three, four, five. I take first gear, get the clutch to a position where it's about to bite and then get on the throttle. In the middle of the steering wheel are the rev lights. When they reach 8,000rpm, the throttle is poised for a good launch.

The noise is immense. The sound of twenty drivers revving at 8,000rpm is enough to flatten forests, but it's a sound we all love, drivers and fans alike; it's part of the reason we're here, that roar that you don't so much hear as *feel*, like it's a physical event.

And again, that peace exists. I am the calm in the eye of the storm as I hold the throttle at 8,000rpm, controlling it at the same time as I try to surf the wave of adrenalin that builds and surges through me, aware of the involuntary movement in my foot that trembles with excitement and nerves and the physical strain of holding the throttle still and trying to master it, thinking, *God, foot, stay still*. Just stay still. Keep the revs to 8,000. And then…

2pm
Lights out.

PART ONE

'All you need to know about racing you
can learn from *Super Mario Kart*.'

1

You'll think I'm making this up, but it's true: my first memory is of cars. Toy cars. Corgi. Matchbox. Hot Wheels. Our landing at home was a long one, and I used to set up tracks complete with corners – turn one, turn two, turn three – where trucks raced Lamborghinis, they both raced Formula One cars, and sometimes the trucks even pulled off an unlikely victory. From downstairs wafted the smell of cooking, maybe the sound of music drifting from one of my sisters' rooms. And me on the landing, creating a world where a truck could outpace a Lamborghini if that's what I wanted it to do. I was born in 1980, so for me those are the sights and sounds and smells of the decade. This was home.

Home was Northcote Crescent in Frome, which is pronounced 'froom' or, if you're using your best Somerset accent (which I'll do on request), 'frohm'. It was literally the first street you came across as you drove into town. It curved up and away from the main road, changed its mind and then went back again, the way crescents do, with bungalows on one side and two-storey detached houses on the other, modern for the time.

First on the right in one of the detached houses (technically the first house in Frome), was where we lived, the Button family. Mum, Simone:

half South African, blonde and glamorous, having made the transition from stop-the-traffic gorgeous when she was young to an even more rarefied beauty in middle age. My memory of her back then is in the kitchen, cooking and baking, bathed in light and wreathed in aroma.

She'll probably have a go at me for saying that ('I wasn't *always* in the kitchen, Jense, why did you say that in your book?') but that's how I remember the early eighties version of her. She thought frozen food was the devil's work so we had 'proper' food every night, and for Sunday lunch she'd really go to town – a full-on roast complete with potatoes cooked in duck fat and all the trimmings. She was so caring, so affectionate, hardly ever lost her temper or raised her voice. It's only relatively recently that I've heard her swear – and even then only when she's talking about other drivers in Formula One.

Later on, when I moved into F1, she used to come to the races. The British Grand Prix was her favourite. That was 'her' race. When I retired she said, 'I won't watch Formula One when you're not racing, Jense.' But she does, she watches it all the time. 'I just can't not watch it. I don't know why, because it frustrates me. But I still watch it.'

I wonder these days if I might have taken advantage of Mum's good nature when I was younger. Which is another way of admitting that I know full well I did. I think we were all guilty of it. We'd be a bit ruder to her than was right; we didn't show her as much respect as we should have done. I'd say something to her that I knew would hurt her feelings and then afterwards think, *Why did I say that?* I guess it's common with families. It's because you're blood and the things they say annoy you more, or in a different way, than other people, so you snap at them, and then afterwards feel really bad about it. You're like, *Why did I get stressed out about something so small?*

These days, I try to spend as much time with Mum as I can but that isn't much, to be honest, given the fact that she lives alone in Somerset and I live in Los Angeles with my girlfriend. It's sad in a way, because obviously me and my sisters have all moved away and my sisters have their own families (I'm a bit of a disappointment in that regard) so Mum can get lonely, living by herself.

Then there were my three older sisters. The eldest, Tanya, was proper fearsome. She flew the nest when I was five. She was eighteen by then. That left my middle sister, Samantha, who's quite punchy, again you probably wouldn't mess, and Natasha, who's very sweet, very soft, maybe too soft for her own good, both of whom had left school by the time I started. So fat lot of good they were.

Still, they made up for it by behaving like three young, devilry-making mums, being great fun and spoiling me rotten. Honestly, between my sisters and my mum I was totally doted on. Years later I'd be called the golden boy of Formula One but I was the golden boy of Northcote Crescent way before that.

My sisters liked dressing me up. And there was one time – just one time, mind you – they got me really dolled up in girls' clothes and then insisted on calling me 'Jennifer'. I'm not sure what my dad thought of it – not much, probably – but Mum found it hilarious. She always said I looked like a girl anyway. One of her favourite tales is about the time someone in the street asked the name of her 'little girl', despite the fact that at the time I was wearing a check shirt, braces and dungarees. The reason was my hair, she says. My hairstyle growing up was a blond bob that she'd insist on styling at every available opportunity, and for especially long and tortuous periods just before school. She did it to us all, fussing over us like a mother hen. Even if we went to my auntie's house we'd have to stop the car just before we got there, get out and stand in a row so that she could do our hair and make sure we looked presentable.

One thing you'd have to say about an environment like that is that it taught me a lot about women. I had an affinity with the opposite sex from an early age. My mother likes to tell the story from my playschool days when there were several little girls who refused to go in until I'd arrived. On the minus side, however, my mum and sisters may have been over-protective at times. As a result, it's fair to say that I probably grew too fond of the security of home, making life harder for me when it eventually came to school.

Then there was my dad, John Button. Weathered features, a glint in his eye and a smile never far from his lips, he looked like a cross between Rod Stewart and Crocodile Dundee and, now I come to think about it, had the twinkly personality to match.

He was a big deal in Frome, partly thanks to the fact that he owned various car dealerships, but mainly down to his career in rallycross, which is a circuit race for souped-up and modified road cars. It's not a big sport, or at least it wasn't back then, and his only success was limited to runner-up places in the Embassy RAC-MSA British Rallycross Championship and the TEAC Lydden Hill Rallycross Championship in 1976. But the old man made a name for himself anyway with his choice of car, a modified VW Beetle nicknamed 'the Colorado Beetle' because of its distinctive black, yellow and red paintwork. That was him all over. Well known around town, always in the local paper with his racing or for something he was doing at the dealership, he just couldn't help but stand out.

An East End lad originally, Dad was born in 1943 and so was around when the Kray Twins were at their peak. As a young man he worked at a local garage detailing cars, which is cleaning and polishing them but to a very high standard, so everything's gleaming and crisp. Along the road was another second-hand car dealership owned by a young man called Bernie Ecclestone. Admiring the good work my dad was doing Bernie offered him a job doing the detailing at his place but the old man turned him down. This was in the late fifties, early sixties, but later when I entered F1, and Bernie had become the ringmaster of the sport, he remembered it well. Him and Dad always used to have a laugh about it in the paddock.

So he was a proper East End boy, the old man: a car dealer who used to manage bands as well, always trying to find an angle. He had all the best lines about his cars. He'd be selling to a guy and say, 'It might not be the quickest, it might not be the best-looking…' and then he'd pause and look lovingly at the car, 'but it's reliable.' And like all second-hand car dealers, he'd always find a way to spin a car. One of his favourite tricks was to add an extra stripe along the side, claim the car was a limited edition and bump the price up by another grand. 'You won't see many of those on the roads,' he'd say. 'That much I can promise.'

For a while he had a franchise selling for a Polish manufacturer called FSO – probably the ugliest cars on the road – and he'd do a deal: an FSO and a holiday. The holidays cost something like £100 but he'd mark the car up by another two grand and pitch it as a once-in-a-life-time deal. To promote the offer he'd create a special display by pouring sand around the front of the car, adding a bucket, spade and beach ball for effect. Ta-da! A beach in a car showroom. It worked as well. 'Here, have the ugliest motor this side of a Lada Rivas, plus a holiday that I've marked up by almost two thousand per cent.' 'Great! Where do we sign?'

Crazy stuff but he could pull it off because he had that cockney charm, gift of the gab. Whatever you want to call it, the old man had it – in buckets (and spades).

He could be strict (well, compared to Mum, who I wrapped around my little finger) but he never, ever got angry, although occasionally he'd get strange ideas in his head and do things I didn't understand. There was one time, when I was little, that I had a pedal go-kart, the sort that had a handbrake in the middle, between your legs. I went everywhere on it. Loved it. And then one day he just threw it away.

Whether he'd got it into his head that I was too old for it, or it was a punishment, I can't remember, but it was a perfectly good go-kart, and no way had I outgrown it, so it was an odd thing to do, whichever way you look at it.

He was diabetic, so thinking back it's possible he was affected by mood swings. To be fair, incidents like that were very few and far between. Mainly he was just brilliant. I was in awe of him.

So that was us. The Buttons. We weren't wealthy, but on the other hand we were by no means poor. We could afford our annual family holiday to Majorca and we didn't want for much, if anything. To be honest, it should have been idyllic.

And it would have been idyllic, but for one thing. Individually my parents were great: Mum, the archetypal earth mother, always ready with hugs and kisses; Dad, a tiny bit more strict and mercurial, but both of them like superheroes to me growing up.

The problem was they couldn't stand each other.

2

Mum and Dad never agreed on why I was called Jenson. According to my dad, I was named after one of his rallycross rivals, Erling Jensen, only with the E changed to an O so people wouldn't think of the sports car, Jensen. According to Mum, however, she'd been toying with – wait for it – 'Jordan', but having caught sight of a Jensen sports car decided to call me that instead, again with the E changed to an O, which she said sounded 'more mannish'.

That was by far the least of their disagreements though. They did their best not to show it, but there were plenty of arguments. And even during those periods of relative peace, there was that awkward atmosphere that descends when an unhappy couple has no option but to be in the same room together. No amount of false courtesy or stitched-on smiles can quite dispel it. It just sits there, stinking up the place like yesterday's fish in the kitchen bin.

As an adult you can process it. You're armed with experience and more than likely in possession of the facts too. But I was just small – we're talking the very early years of my life here – and I was left in the dark, 'shielded' was probably how they thought of it, but of course you can never really do that.

They'd met at a dance in Newquay when they were young, spending the rest of the holiday together. Home time came and they went their separate ways, My mum to Frome and Dad to London, probably thinking they'd never see each other again. But one night Mum went to see the Rolling Stones at Longleat and when her father came to collect her he said, 'We've got a surprise visitor for you.' Guess who?

Lookswise they were made for each other. Mum used to dye her hair jet black and there are all these really cool black-and-white pictures of the pair of them, usually posing on the bonnet of a car. Mum was never into motor racing like Dad – she couldn't even drive – but her own father had also been a racer. His passion was autocross, a different class of racing altogether – often a doorway into rallycross. Where rallycross uses a purpose-made circuit, in autocross they literally stick a load of pegs in the ground to make a track then race against the clock, rather than other drivers. Small world – it turned out that my dad and my granddad had actually competed at the same time, although not against each other. I only found that out about five years ago.

Anyway, so my parents met and fell in… well, was it love or was it lust? I'm not sure. But to be fair, and when you consider that Tanya's thirteen years older than me, they'd already been together a while before I came on the scene, so there must have been something between them once. You can see from the pictures that there were happy times. The trouble was they were just two very different people. Like I say, my mum is very caring and with that comes a certain over-protectiveness, which in turn can lead to jealousy.

My dad was the wrong person to be in a relationship with if you're jealous. I'm not saying he was unfaithful; in fact, I'm 100 per cent sure he wasn't, because I remember being very young and him telling me, 'Just so you know, Jense, I never played around,' and that's good enough for me.

But still, the fact remains. He was good-looking and he was flirtatious and he was well known in Frome. He was the guy who used to sell holidays with cars. Any swanky do in town, he'd be there. And, of course, he used to race as well. Rallycross was a niche sport but it was televised – Murray Walker was a commentator – so Dad moved in some pretty cool circles. Put it this way: Tanya used to play with a young Damon Hill who, as the son of the legendary Graham Hill, was pretty much racing royalty.

All of which meant that my parents occupied two different worlds. My mum, not tied to the kitchen but there by choice or at least a sense of duty; my dad being, well, my dad.

Still, life goes on, and with that in the background, I busied myself with the important matter of being a small boy. I wasn't interested in football (never had any time for ball games) but I loved to be active and still do. I hate rest days. I get headaches and I feel like a slob and get grotty. I hate to be indoors.

It was the same back then, and the key to my freedom was my bike. My first was a Raleigh racer. I remember Mum taking the stabilisers off, me falling off and crying, being a right wuss, and her having to comfort me.

After that I had little silver Marin mountain bike, which I absolutely loved. Recently I moved to California and had a real penny-dropping moment when I realised that Marin mountain bikes come from Marin County in California. I used to ride that Marin around the estate and to secondary school.

The layout of our house was such that you could run around the whole of the ground floor, from the hallway into the kitchen, dining room, lounge and then back to the hallway again, and one of my favourite things to do as a really small kid was run this circuit, round and round, round and round, which seems crazy now, as if I'm making it up just to be cute for the book. But it's the truth, I promise you. It used to send my sisters mad, the constant thump-thump of my feet, in and out of the lounge as they sat trying to watch *Dempsey & Makepeace* or *Just Good Friends*.

It took me a long time to get bored of that game, but when I did I came up with another one. I had long piece of rope, washing line maybe. I held one end then ran around the circuit trying to catch the other end, like a dog chasing its own tail.

I got into scrapes. Northcote Crescent was on an incline looking down upon the main street into Frome, with the art college on the other side of the road. One day I found myself in the drive, looking down the hill, and then into the garage where my dad stored a whole lot of spare wheels and tyres, a little light bulb going on over my five-year-old head.

Moments later a tyre was thumping down our drive and across the road. Fascinated, I watched as it hit the low wall of a house opposite, bounced, gained a bit of height and then bounced again, each *boof* giving it more height as it made its way to the main road, teeming with cars.

It flew across the road, by some miracle missing everything. I watched it finally come to rest on the opposite pavement.

Tanya had seen everything. 'What did you do that for, Jenson?' she said.

'I just wanted to see what would happen,' I replied.

She shook her head. Not long after that she left home, but I don't think the two incidents were related.

Another time, I jumped in Dad's Jaguar XJS (white with a black vinyl roof, very swanky) and did what I normally did, which was to pretend I was driving, yanking the steering wheel hard in one direction and then the other – no steering lock, obviously – pretending to change gear, all the usual moves. Only this time I decided to have a fiddle with the handbrake as well, and somehow managed to let it off.

So, I mentioned the house was on an incline. The car, facing up the drive, began to roll backwards. From inside the house came Samantha, who must have seen what was happening, waving her arms and shouting, 'Stop! Stop!'

Of us all, Samantha was the messiest. Samantha being so messy was the reason I never got told off about being untidy myself, although, to be fair, I didn't get told off much about anything.

That, however, looked in danger of changing. The car took no notice of Samantha telling it to stop. Nor did it respond to me frantically jamming my feet on the pedals. It just kept rolling back towards the road of Northcote Crescent and then, if it made it across the road, into the very same neighbour's wall that had launched my tyre into space.

Selflessly, Samantha threw herself at the car and tried to hold it back. But if you pit a scrawny teenage girl against a Jaguar XJS with a black vinyl roof there's only ever going to be one outcome, and after several moments of effort and impressive bravery she had to admit defeat and scuttle out of the way, allowing the Jag to continue its inevitable journey across the road and into the wall.

Upshot: one very bent Jag.

I did get told off for that little escapade but I can't remember if there was a punishment. Probably not, to be honest. I wouldn't be at all surprised if Dad was secretly pleased that I was playing around in the Jag. He had never deliberately instilled in me a love of cars or motor racing, but I consider myself lucky that it was already there, written into my DNA. I think it would have disappointed him if his only boy had turned his nose up at it.

As it was, I'd already fallen – hook, line and sinker. There was no eureka moment. No single event that changed me from normal average Jenson Button into 'Jenson Button, Car Fanatic', it just sort of... happened, like learning to walk and talk. It was just in me.

3

Scalextric. I bloody loved Scalextric. Playing it was probably the first time I began to grasp the dynamics of racing. It's all about throttle control, managing corner entry and exit. That's where I first started to learn about racing a car rather than simply moving it from point A to point B. I began to realise that it wasn't just about getting on the accelerator and reaching a top speed. You had to know when to lift off and when to get back on it.

I had a garage for my toy cars. I used to copy what my dad did in his garage. I had one of those Hot Wheels loop-the-loops as well. Come to think of it, I must have had the loop-the-loop before the Scalextric, which would have been a step up in the world. I used to spend hours on the loop-the-loop, happy to have something new to do with what was a fairly vast collection of toy cars. Both parents used to buy them for me and I spent entire days pushing them around the house. A while back I had some nieces and nephews visit and I let them play with my Formula One miniatures, the exquisitely detailed collectable ones. That turned out to be a mistake because when I next looked they were all in bits. Their game was to smash the cars, but I was never like that when I was their age. I wasn't OCD about it, but even so, I was careful with my cars. I used to set them up on the landing, loads of them, integrate them into mad stories.

Same with TV. I think back to my favourite shows and there was *Thomas the Tank Engine,* of course, but he was quickly usurped by *Airwolf* and, even better, *Knight Rider.* I used to love the Herbie films, *Chitty Chitty Bang Bang.* Anything with a car was like catnip to me. It was an obsession that had bitten hard and bitten deep. On my wall was a poster of a Ferrari F40, and as I grew older it was joined by posters of Pamela Anderson and Bart Simpson. My tastes changed over the years (sorry, Pam), but I never grew out of the F40. I ended up buying one. One minute I'm an eight-year-old kid with a poster of an F40 on my wall, the next I've got one. One thing you've got to say for my child-hood car obsession – it wasn't just a passing fad.

Neither was it just cars. It was *racing.* By five or six I was watching Formula One with my dad, pointing out to him when I thought a car was getting ready to overtake and being right most of the time.

Back then I watched Nigel Mansell tussle with Nelson Piquet in 1986. That was good, but the rivalry that really caught my imagination came later and was between Alain Prost and Ayrton Senna when they were teammates at McLaren.

I didn't realise it then but looking back that's the greatest battle Formula One has ever seen: Ayrton, the Brazilian, who was very open, very emotional, and Alain, who they called the Professor, because he was so methodical and dedicated, working with the team and building the car to suit his style. For Alain, it was about winning, not by a huge margin, just winning. He would rather win by a tiny margin and do it safely.

Ayrton was very different. He was about destroying the opposition. He wanted Alain eating his dust. Just beating him wasn't enough. He needed more.

There was a great race in Monaco in 1988, where Ayrton was leading Alain by a massive amount, but he still kept pushing and pushing, only to end up putting his car in the wall. Prost won and Ayrton was so devastated he didn't even go back to the paddock, just left the car and went home, back to his apartment.

And it didn't end there, because a couple of years later Alain went to Ferrari and the battle resumed with Ayrton in the McLaren. Same thing. They'd do anything to beat each other. They were always driving each other off the circuit (twice, I think, but you get the picture).

Alain Prost once said, 'He never wanted to beat me, he wanted to humiliate me, to show the world that he was much stronger, much better – and that was his weakness.'

Prost was right. Ayrton didn't have any other flaws as a driver, but that was his Achilles heel: that need, not just to win, but to do it so emphatically that his opponent was ground to dust.

Of the two, my favourite was Alain. I just liked his personality, how he came across on TV, very calm, nowhere near as emotional as Ayrton. I still had respect for Ayrton, but even so, I chose Alain as my driver to follow and you've got to choose one, you can't have two. Looking back now, Ayrton was very quick, a faster driver than Alain over one lap. But Alain was very calculated and very intelligent and would do everything he could to win. He knew that it's not about being quick on one lap, it's about being quick over the whole distance. He really understood that. Every pit stop, he would make sure that it was perfect on the entry, perfect on the exit.

I liked Nigel, of course. Our Nige. Nigel Mansell with the big bushy eyebrows. And it was great to have a British driver to follow. Even so, I wasn't the sort of guy that had to follow the British driver just because they're British. Our fans are very much like that. Spanish fans follow Spanish drivers. South American fans follow South American drivers. But Brits are different. They pick and choose drivers, and it doesn't matter if they're British or not, which I like.

Either way, the Formula One drivers were like gods to me, growing up. You always look up to your heroes and your dream is to race in Formula One but you don't think it will ever happen. They seemed like superheroes. Little did I know, they're not.

Meanwhile, back in the mid-eighties and I'd started primary school, Vallis First School, and it was pretty awful.

As I said before, my problem was being too fond of my home life. Northcote Crescent, with the rest of the Buttons and my toy cars, was where my heart lay. That was home to the restless, boisterous kid I knew myself to be. The thing was that he stayed there when I left. Outside of home I was an almost painfully shy, nervous kid.

It would begin before I'd even left the house. With Mum fussing over my hair I'd start to worry about the day ahead before Dad took me in the car. Things weren't so bad once I arrived. I'd always feel a bit more comfortable when I was there. It was the nerves beforehand that used to get me.

These days I do all sorts of public engagements, and even the smallest thing, like doing an interview or being on stage, gives me the same feeling of apprehension beforehand. Then you do the thing and it feels great and you get off and think, *Well that was okay. Why was I bricking that?* And that whole parcel of feelings sends me right back to my schooldays. I wish I could get rid of it, but it's embedded somehow.

The kids at school couldn't get a handle on my name. These days everyone's got a weird name; it must be a bloody nightmare for teachers.

But back in the early 1980s all the boys were called Michael or Christopher and the girls were Amanda or Sarah. 'Jenson' was impossibly exotic for Somerset so they settled either on JB, which has stuck, or 'Jason', which was probably just a mishearing now I come to think about it. Not forgetting, of course, the inevitable nicknames that I had to pretend I thought were funny: 'Zipper', 'Jennifer' (bit late with that one), and my personal favourite, 'Genitals'.

Don't get me wrong, it wasn't *that* bad. I'm not saying it was a bitter time of loneliness and hardship, it was just… *okay*, I suppose. Like if you could illustrate my time at school with a bodily movement, it would be a shrug. A line graph would show no highs or lows, just a continuous straight line.

There was one thing I did find out about myself at school, though, and that came when I left primary and went to middle school, Selwood, where I continued to lead an undistinguished, disengaged and bordering-on-lonely scholastic life.

In my first or second year I was made to play rugby for the school team. God knows why. Something to do with the first team being off in France. Maybe I was the only boy with two legs available. I don't know. Either way, I got forced to play rugby, and what I remember most about that experience is the misery. I turned up knowing nothing about the rules (and years and years later, I still know nothing about the rules of rugby), took one look at what was happening on the pitch and thought, *You have got to be kidding.* Our opponents all had beards. We were twelve, and although I was reasonably tall, I was a proper skinny kid, and not at all built for scrums

So anyway, they put me on, and despite my best attempts to fade out of the game, I somehow got the ball. No idea what to do with it,

I thought I better run, so I ran. From the corner of my eye I saw one of the bearded opponents hulking over so I threw the ball. Not to anyone. Just threw it rather than get tackled. My team were disgusted with me and I didn't get the ball for the rest of the game. I knew then that team sports weren't for me, the reason being I didn't want to let the team down.

Now, you might say, 'But, Jenson, you were a Formula One driver. No sport offers a greater potential for letting the team down than Formula One.' And you would, of course, be right. The difference is that I never believed in my ability to play team sports, whereas I've always had confidence in my skill as a racer. I always knew that I'd earned my place on the team and on the grid. If I crashed, then of course I'd be upset for the team and I'd go round saying sorry, but I don't think I ever felt the same way I did on the rugby pitch that day. I never thought I'd let the side down; that I shouldn't be there. I'm not sure if it's an especially admirable way to live your life but there you have it: from that moment on, I made sure to stick to what I was good at.

4

I always got way more presents than my sisters, which should have been a source of friction but never was, mainly because they're such a lovely, even-tempered bunch. Nor did I suffer from the celebration fatigue that affects people who have a birthday close to Christmas (mine's 19 January). I just got a whole bunch of presents at Christmas and then a load more a little under a month later. It was brilliant.

It's the same nowadays. Mum literally showers me with gifts. It's hilarious. At Christmas everybody's finished opening their presents and I've still got a massive pile to unwrap. (I like to think I'm fairly generous in return, mind you. Put it this way, nobody's driving around in an old FSO.)

True to form, my seventh birthday delivered the goods, pick of the prizes being a Yamaha 50cc bike, nicknamed the 'Piwi 50'. Brand new, and a new design as well, it wasn't crazy money, and there's every chance my dad used his contacts to get a deal, but even so, it was a pretty mega present for a seven-year-old kid.

'Shall we start it up?' said Dad. We were in the drive of Northcote. No doubt Mum, Samantha and Natasha were watching, too, but to my shame I don't remember. I was transfixed by my shiny new Piwi.

He cranked it up and it was like sensory overload. This was different somehow from cars. I can remember the sound and smell of it like it was yesterday; it'll stay with me for ever.

I jumped on, ready to go. It was a freezing cold day, and right away I was struck by the warmth of it beneath me. The sense of being so close to the engine, all that power. A whole 50cc of it. 'No, no, you can't ride it here,' Dad told me.

One short trip later and I was on a little tarmac path in a nearby park, Dad watching me like a hawk as I went up and down, gradually getting a feel for the bike. It occurred to me that I wasn't scared. My crash helmet saw to that. And that's the stupid thing about all forms of motor racing. Or it is with me anyway. As soon as I'm wearing my gear, and especially the helmet, then for some reason it stops being scary. It's daft because it's a total illusion, but there you go.

'No full throttle,' warned Dad, but I was getting right on it anyway. I was beginning to feel in control of it, as though me and the bike had ceased being two separate things. Like being on a bicycle, the Piwi had become an extension of my body, controlling it came as naturally to me as moving an arm or a leg. Besides, the bike was fitted with a restrictor to stop you opening the throttle all the way.

It preyed on my mind, that limiter. Right away I was unhappy with the idea that I was being prevented from getting the bike to anything like full speed. The thought nagged at me so much that when we got home and Dad asked, 'How was that?' I swallowed hard, and at the risk of sounding ungrateful, replied, 'It was really nice, Dad, but I got a bit bored.'

'Bored?' he said, looking amused and taken aback at the same time.

'It's a bit slow,' I said.

Slow was 20mph, the restrictor's limit. I knew it was capable of at least 30mph.

'Right, well, we can do something about that,' he said, not angry at all. Thinking back now, he was probably secretly delighted.

The next day was sunny and dry when Dad removed the restrictor – simple job, just undoing a bolt – and we returned to the little park.

'Go easy,' he said, as I climbed on and cranked it up. Once again I thrilled to the warmth of it, gripping the throttle and bursting with confidence after yesterday's successful session. I set my eyes front, feeling the weight of the helmet, sensing the bike below me straining to be set free. I opened it up.

I came straight off the back. Fell with a nasty but painless thump to the deck and watched as my beloved bike careered off and came to rest against a wall.

My dad shook his head. 'I told you to take it easy,' he frowned, which was about as cross as he ever got with me.

The rider was unhurt. The bike was undamaged. It hadn't even toppled over. So I got straight back on and God's honest truth, that is the one and only time I ever came off that bike.

Off I went, successfully this time, and I loved it, having that extra power to play with was just, like, *oh my God*, and in short order I was thinking, *Now I've got to try and find its limit*. I've been the same since that moment, always trying to find the limit of whatever I'm driving. Push it as hard as I can.

Dad wasn't so keen. He could see the way my mind was working and, using the power of common sense, decided that we should probably cease further biking activities, what with it being a public park.

So we ended up going to an airfield near Bridgwater. That was better. We laid rocks to make a little circuit but even so, after thirty minutes I was returning to him. 'Dad, I'm bored.'

How spoilt did I sound? *God.* But Dad understood. And was probably thinking, *Great. Chip off the old block.* Perhaps at some deep subconscious level I even understood that myself: that hearing me want to push the bike and challenge myself was music to his ears. This wasn't about me. It was about *us.* We didn't know we were taking the first steps on a racing career, didn't even dream of it then. We just knew we were in it together.

'Bored, are you?' he said. 'Right, there's a circuit down the road, a little scramble track. We'll go there.'

Now this was a different kettle of fish. Arriving, what we saw were squadrons of older kids on bigger 80cc bikes. They were drifting, skidding, getting airborne over jumps. The noise was immense. The sight of it all made me gulp.

I went out, feeling intimidated and out of my depth, the sensation increasing after a few laps. *No,* I thought, *this isn't for me,* and I went back to where he stood and admitted that I'd bitten off more than I could chew.

'All right, Jense,' he said, indicating a van selling greasy burgers and the like, 'let's have a bite to eat then see how you feel after that. Sound fair?'

He was in two minds, I could see. On the one hand he was pleased I'd developed a taste for racing, but on the other he didn't want me getting ahead of myself. The memory of me coming off in the park was still fresh and the last thing he wanted was for me to break an arm or leg.

We stood munching bacon and egg sarnies on white bread, the staple food of all weekend racers, and I watched other guys do their circuits, feeling the urge gradually return. Perhaps that was the first time I'd felt that particular sensation but I've certainly experienced it since, never more so than since retiring from F1. At the end of my career, I was quite happy if I never sat in another F1 car, but then I'm there watching Silverstone qualifying and I'm thinking, *Oh my God, they're so cool.* Formula One cars are so cool. It's coming past you at 200 miles an hour, and it's like, *Ah, I think I want to drive one again.*

Same back then. By the time I finished my sarnie I was gagging for another go and went back out with renewed confidence, racing around with the bigger boys, drifting the ride, throwing out the back wheel, foot sticking out, copying all their moves.

There was a guy giving me advice, saying, 'You need to carry more speed into the corners, son, so you can drift, otherwise you're never going to get the back out,' so I tried out some new moves. I was even making a few tentative jumps. Check out Evel Knievel.

And on the sidelines, Dad watched me like a hawk, chewing his lip with worry and no doubt wondering what on earth he'd got us into.

5

My parents' arguments continued, the relationship crumbling into ruin, until at last they accepted defeat and did what they should have done several years before. They got divorced.

I don't remember it well. There was no big blow-out, no emotional goodbyes. Dad just took his stuff and that was it. From that point on I shuttled between the two parents, who for a long time absolutely hated each other's guts, which obviously didn't help

But to be honest, I can't remember being all that bothered about the divorce. I recall telling someone it was brilliant because I'd get two sets of birthday and Christmas presents from now on, presumably trying to rationalise it in my own seven-year-old way. Even so there's no point pretending that it scarred me. It was probably harder for my sisters, but for me I'd never really thought of Mum and Dad as a couple anyway. As far as I was concerned, his moving out meant that the arguments would cease; the sour atmosphere that had hung around in Northcote Crescent would at last be absent. The good far outweighed the bad.

Dad's new home was a little studio in the yard of a farm just outside Frome. It was tiny. I took my girlfriend, Brittny, to see it not long ago, just on a whim as we were nearby, and I couldn't believe just how small it was. I don't suppose I noticed it at the time.

Still, the new location offered brand-new and exciting possibilities for a seven-year-old kid. By that time, 1987, Dad's Colorado Beetle had gone to the great rallycross circuit in the sky, replaced by a VW Golf. To warm it up and check it over before races, Dad used to start it up at the farm, and I can distinctly recall the sound it made, the full-throated *vroom* of its modified racing engine, tuned to perfection, too loud for my young ears no doubt – someone call Health & Safety – but supremely thrilling all the same. Yet more fuel for my racing obsession.

Another advantage of him moving out was that I was with him more. Weird how that works: your parents split up and you get to spend more time with them. But that's the way it was. Things calmed down between them and for a while were civilised enough that Mum was relaxed if I wanted to spend more time at the farm. But when Dad started seeing someone – Pippa, who he'd later marry – Mum stopped being so relaxed. The battle lines were redrawn and she'd insist that he only had me at prescribed times.

Even so, it meant all sorts of trips with him – we went to the seaside and to funfairs – and we did a lot of biking. For about eight months or so we were happy with the Piwi. We took it to Longleat forest, where we'd create little circuits and I'd ride through the trees. Great fun. Again, I can summon the smell of it, the wood chippings and cut wood. It was always wet, I remember, never dry at Longleat – but once again I was starting to feel, well I don't want to say 'bored' again, but perhaps limited. I wanted something more.

On a return trip to the scramble circuit, we got talking to an older kid and his dad. The kid was riding an 80cc and I was eyeing it jealously in between circuits of my own.

'You should get him one of those bikes,' said the guy, giving my dad a nudge. 'He's knows what he's doing now. He could start racing.'

At that, the old man had a vision of the future. He could see that I was pushing the bike and pushing myself. It wasn't about competition – at that point, I hadn't raced anyone – it was about trying to go quicker than the last lap, trying to take that corner that little bit faster, getting the back end out a bit more. Maybe my determination had taken him by surprise; perhaps he hadn't expected that competitive urge to surface so quickly. But it had, and it gave him serious pause for thought. He'd seen too many broken arms and legs, too many near-misses. The bike was supposed to be a fun thing we could do together, not the agent of my injury or death. A 50cc Piwi was one thing, but an 80cc Kawasaki? (It was green. So was I.) And what about after that? And after that?

One thing you'd have to say about my dad: he was protective. All through my career he'd leap to my defence if anybody bad-mouthed me, and this protective instinct manifested itself then as well.

He put his foot down, much to my dismay. No, I wouldn't be moving up to 80cc. And that was that. No amount of pleading worked. He wouldn't budge.

Nevertheless, he still had a problem, one faced by weekend dads the world over: what on earth am I going to do with the kid? The answer came thanks to a visit he paid to a car show, where he bumped into an old pal, Keith Ripp, who owned Rippspeed, a London shop that specialised in tuning parts and accessories for Minis. They got talking, as you do, and the subject of keeping me occupied came up.

'Ah,' said Keith, 'I might have just the thing…'

6

Christmas 1987 was the first since my parents had gone their separate ways. Also my dad's business had done well that year, which meant that it was a bit of a bumper season for presents. Natasha was given a great stereo and Samantha got a VW Polo. (Tanya, sadly, wasn't present. She'd fallen out with Pippa.)

And me? I got a Zipkart from Rippspeed, specially developed for a new karting category, Cadets, which was aimed at kids aged between eight and twelve. I was a month away from my eighth birthday, it couldn't have been better timed.

It looked great as well. It was yellow, with yellow wheels, and a 60cc, two-stroke Comer engine that you started with a cord like a lawn-mower, and it had a centrifugal clutch, the same system as a scooter. Because it was two-stroke you had to buy the fuel and the oil and mix it together yourself. Which, of course, would be Dad's job. In fact, for almost the whole of my career in karting, Dad was the one who looked after it. He was my pit crew and race engineer in one.

We fired her up. I jumped in. I'm pretty sure I was still wearing my pyjamas at the time. Bear in mind the only experience I'd previously had on four wheels was the kart that Dad threw away (that's if you don't count rolling his Jag down the drive) but even so, I don't remember feeling in the slightest bit nervous. Partly because, well, you don't at that age. You think you're indestructible. I see kids hurling themselves down ski slopes and my heart's in my mouth. And secondly because straight away I felt right at home in it. Just like the bike, I had sense of this machine below me, of power awaiting my command. I wasn't nervous of it because I instinctively felt that I could control it.

And I did. After a fashion. I drove it around a pub car park, almost hit something, and that was enough of that, we went to enjoy the rest of our Christmas Day.

Next day, Boxing Day, Dad and I took the kart to the disused airfield near Bridgwater. What a revelation. Now I had a vast open space to play with and I was opening it up, starting to get a real feel for it, whizzing up and down what had once been runways.

'I'm bored,' I told him, twenty minutes later. *Déjà vu.*

'Bored?' he said. 'Why?'

It had been brewing since my days on the Piwi. 'I want to race other people, Dad.'

He sighed. 'Look, Jense, you need to get used to the kart first. Don't run before you can walk, eh?'

'But I need a track, Dad,' I said.

Dad frowned but understood. 'Come on,' he said, and we loaded the kart into the boot and went in search of the nearest phone box (yes, a phone box). He knew of a track near Dorchester called the Clay Pigeon Raceway and was wondering whether it would be open on Boxing Day. Surely not. Everybody would be spending time with their families playing Monopoly and watching James Bond…

It was open. We wasted no time and bowled over there straight away. It turned out that the reason Dad knew Clay Pigeon was because he himself had raced there. The track was built on the site of an abandoned military hospital, and the first race held on 5 May 1963. There to compete was my dad (along with a guy called Jonathan Buncombe, father of Chris, more of whom later). Nowadays, Clay Pigeon have a corner named after us, which is really touching. You'll find it after The Horseshoe and before Top Bend. A right-hander called Button's.

That day was cold and wet but Dad didn't have wet tyres, only slicks, so I had to go out on those, slipping and sliding all over the place. On the sidelines watching, Dad had decided that giving me slicks was inadvertently a stroke of training genius.

The difference between slicks and dry-weather tyres is, of course, the tread. Slicks don't have any, which makes them no good in the wet because there's no run-off like there is on a treaded tyre. On a treaded tyre the water goes through the grooves, allowing the tyre to grip the road and give you a more stable ride, whereas on a slick the water has nowhere to go. It just sits there on the flat surface and you either spin or you're forced to go at a snail's pace because you've got no grip and don't want to spin. It's why slicks are banned on road cars.

So using slicks slowed me down, which was very much in Dad's thinking at the time; it gave me a grounding in controlling skids and spins and helped me feel the tyres in a more intuitive way, since being on slicks in the wet is all about catching the slides. You find the front grip of the tyre, make your turn and feel the snappiness in the back. Doing that, you can find the limit and work out what the kart will do in that situation. That experience began a long and lasting relationship with tyres of all kinds, which is something all racing drivers need.

Dad kept me on the slicks for the next couple of visits before I nagged him into buying some wet-weather tyres. Even so, I learned a lot from that period of being on slicks. I was learning other stuff, too.

7

'The racing line', we call it. The fastest way around a corner. So, say if the corner is a right-hander, you'll start as far to the left as possible, you judge the turning-in point, hit the apex, and then let the kart run all the way out to the exit kerb. It's not necessarily the shortest distance around a corner, but it's the route that lets you keep your speed as high as possible, and that compensates for any extra distance.

If the track is empty or if the cars are in procession then the racing line is the same for every car. The difficult bit comes when there are lots of other cars around, that's the trick. In karting, it's complete madness.

To teach me the basics, Dad would stand on the side of the circuit at the very point he thought I should brake for the corner. He'd position himself about 150 metres from the corner apex, wait for me to pass – thumbs up or thumbs down depending on how I'd done – and then move closer to the apex of the corner for the next lap, the idea being that I'd carry more speed into the corner and brake later. He'd go so far up to the apex that I'd end up coming off, but I learnt from that, too.

They were great sessions. Thanks to the old man's tuition, Clay Pigeon was where I learned my racecraft, by which I mean how to overtake, how to position your kart when you're fighting for position, how to understand racing lines, the quickest way around a circuit, how to deal with the curveballs that catch you off balance, how to adapt to them – just a few of the tools you need in your toolbox as a racing driver.

It was also where my driving style was forged. In many ways I suppose you could say that I looked back to my time admiring Alain Prost. As a rule I try to be as precise as possible. I try to carry speed through a corner. I try to *feel* the car. In karting, for example, I'd always listen to the revs of the engine and make sure to keep the cornering revs as high as possible, and that's how I'd judge which racing line to take. I'd listen to the engine note and if the engine note died too much in a corner, I'd know it wasn't the best line. So next time around, I'd try a different line. Same in F1. Every corner I get to, I don't just see it, I feel it through my bum, through the car itself.

It's why I always get the maximum out of the car in the wet. Because of the way that I drive by feel, I can adapt to the unusual conditions and think on my feet.

A lot of drivers, they look at the circuit and they'll go, *Well, it's a bit wet in that corner, so I'll slow down*, whereas you need to arrive and you need to feel everything through the car and through the tyres.

That's how I always gain the time in those tricky conditions when it gets wet through a race or if it dries out and you're on the wrong tyre. So I could be in the wet on a dry tyre but I can always find the grip, whereas a lot of people can't. In Formula One, I've won fifteen Grands Prix and I think seven of them were in the wet.

Another thing I learned back then is that I love being in control of the rear of the car. If it has too much front grip the rear slides throughout, and I hate that feeling. A tiny bit of front sliding is fine, because I know where to put the car at the corner. But if the rear is sliding, *ugh*. I need the rear stable to carry that speed through a corner.

My style has stayed the same since those early days of karting. I mean, obviously you adapt little things here and there but basically that's the way I drive; that was the way I did it in karting and I've carried that style through my entire racing career.

I'll even do it on the road. I'm not a fast driver on the road. Yes, I have, in the past, driven very quickly on roads, but I was younger then and stupid. These days I don't. But I do bring racing principles to it. For example, if I'm arriving at a roundabout, even in a Range Rover, I'll shift down manually always, just to use the engine brake and slow the car down so it doesn't damage the brakes too much and then (having checked it's safe, obviously) I'll always do the racing line around the roundabout, I'll cut every kerb as much as I can, so that I've lined the car up for a good exit, and if I see a kerb that's quite flat, I'll always take a little bit of that kerb, just like on the circuit.

Precision, see? It has its plus points but it does mean that if I get a car that doesn't handle the way I want then I won't be as quick as Lewis Hamilton. I won't be as quick as Fernando Alonso. I need to fine-tune my car so that it works with my style and if I do that, I'll be unbeatable.

And like I say, Clay Pigeon was where my racing style was first developed. I was putting the rudimentary knowledge I'd gained in those early sessions to good use, getting better and better, increasing in confidence and skill. Because most of the lads who used Clay Pigeon were older, ten or eleven, I'd been learning the ropes by following them. One particular guy was Matthew Davies, hotly tipped, the favourite to win the Cadet championship. We knew all about him from our well-thumbed copies of *Karting Magazine*. Following Matt one afternoon, I pretty much stayed on his bumper for several laps, which for a young kid and rank rookie like myself was pretty good going.

'Why don't you put him in for a race?' said Matt's dad to my dad. Obviously I had to be a hotshot if I'd managed to go bumper-to-bumper with his lad.

'Nah,' said Dad, 'it's just something we do at the weekends, bit of fun, you know? Some father–son time.'

Later, though, when it was just him and me, Dad asked the question to which he already knew my response. 'Do you fancy having a crack at racing, Jense?'

I hardly needed to answer, I was that full of confidence and fearlessness. Dad knew I wanted to race but I think even he was taken aback by my enthusiasm. In most other areas of my life I was shy and unsure of myself, the boy from Northcote Crescent tended not to travel. But I'd found him, outside of his usual comfort zones. I'd found him in the driving seat of my kart.

8

At least my first race was on home turf. The Clay Pigeon Raceway was to be my testing ground, the category, Cadets, which was a fairly undersubscribed section, meant there weren't many opponents. Three, to be precise.

None of this did much to calm my nerves, and I'd never been so grateful to have my dad with me. He was kneeling, fiddling with the kart as he often did. He'd had to fix black plates to show I was a novice, the karting equivalent of 'L' plates. It would have been nice if having them meant I was given a head start over the more experienced drivers. In fact, it meant I had to start from the back of the pack.

He stood. The kart was ready.

'Just enjoy yourself, Jense,' he told me. 'It doesn't matter if you win or lose, just relax and enjoy it. All right?' Looking down at me, he fixed me with kindly eyes, gave me a reassuring smile.

I nodded in reply, not feeling especially relaxed. Not scared either. The right kind of nerves. More hyped up. Determined to do well.

And what do you know? It was wet – wet enough that when we got started I could barely see through the spray thrown up by the karts ahead of me. I could hardly see Dad on the trackside, but I knew he was there. I set my teeth and powered on, hoping I could at least pass the guy in front of me.

I did, and by now I was in some 'other' place, totally focused, utterly in the moment. I looked for Dad and saw him. I glanced behind and saw that I'd built up a good lead on the guy behind. Corners came and went, and by now I was gaining on the guy in second place. Next corner I chose my line well and passed him, and then the one after that until, incredibly, I was in first place. No longer was I suffering the spray from the karts in front. I was leading – and increasing my lead with every passing second.

I spun at a corner. Through a curtain of grey drizzle I could see Dad on the trackside, waving me back on and could tell he was yelling, 'Get going! Get going!' even though I couldn't hear him over the noise of the engines.

I regained the track but then, at the next corner, spun again, once more having to get back on track. This time I'd been overtaken but retook the lead before sailing over the finish line, savouring the sight of the chequered flag, thinking, a *chequered flag*. As I shuddered to a halt there was Dad, wet from the rain, leaping up and down with the biggest grin plastered all over his face.

I can't say I'd given any thought to what would happen if I won. Funnily enough, what struck was a feeling of embarrassment. I was first to cross the finish line and that was nice, but after that I was left feeling a bit like a startled rabbit, receiving congratulations and (what felt like) dozens of hearty claps on the back in a kind of daze.

Before I knew it, I was mounting the podium, where on the top step I was given the trophy and suddenly, like sunshine breaking through dark clouds, it all made sense. I looked at my trophy and then at the – smaller – trophies awarded to the runners-up and I found myself grinning and holding the trophy aloft, just like I'd seen on TV F1 coverage. *Oh yes*, I thought. *Oh yes, I like this a lot.*

*

You never overtake on straights, that's the thing. Unless you get a good exit from a corner or your opponent gets a bad one then you all have the same power on the straight so you're not going to get past anybody at that point. It's on the corners where you find the advantage, and what I was able to do in that first race was take my line. Most of the time the other guys weren't on the right racing line anyway, but what I did was find a line that worked for me, taking into account the weather, the fact that we were all slipping and sliding about, and managed to pass them that way. On the inside or the outside, it didn't matter. The fact was that I had the good line, and they didn't, or did and lost it, either by pushing too hard or making some other mistake.

And that's the reason so many drivers will tell you that their best races were in karting. It's because the kart is so simple. It's just a kart. You don't have five hundred people building it. You don't jump in it with your fingers crossed that it's good enough, only to find out that it's not. You can tweak it a bit, but not enough to affect the real battle, which isn't between engine manufacturers and technical directors, it's between the drivers.

Even if, say, all Formula One cars had the same chassis and engine, it would still be difficult to overtake. Firstly, because you're racing against the best guys in the world who don't slip up and understand exactly where to put the car, and secondly because you have downforce. And the problem with downforce is that it produces a lot of dirty air, which causes the car behind to lose grip in a corner.

In karting you don't have any of that. It's pure racing in a way that Formula One is not. And while Formula One remains the very pinnacle of racing and, whatever its flaws, has an allure you just don't get elsewhere, there are always those times when you miss the old days, when it was just about you and the driver in front. You're always going to look back on those early wins with special fondness, because back then it was all about proving your mettle behind the wheel.

That night, having shown off my trophy to Mum and my sisters, I took it to bed with me, grinning in the darkness.

9

My second-ever kart race. Dad entered me into the British Championship at Little Rissington in Gloucestershire. Why not?

By now it was a few weeks later but we were still surfing the thrill of that first win and maybe feeling over-confident. Little Rissington wasn't a circuit I knew, but I made it to the final and was doing well, mid-pack through turn four, when I got hit from behind.

It might have been just a nudge on my rear wheels but it was enough to upset the kart, and I spun. Not the end of the world as long as…

Another kart went into me. Again I spun, only this time I was facing in the wrong direction and the next thing I saw was a kart bearing down on me, the driver's eyes wide like, *what the fuck?*, and then impact.

It was a bad knock, enough to send my helmet flying, give me a nasty bash on the arm and end my race. It was also my first proper accident. Before when I'd spun off, I'd stayed on the circuit, got back on the track and ploughed on, but this time I was out of the race and actually hurt. By the time I reached Dad I was cradling my arm and in a bit of a state, feeling like a little boy lost in a department store. It's funny. When I drove the kart it was as though I matured as soon as my bum hit the driving seat. But outside of it I was still just an eight-year-old kid, fearless one minute, fearful the next, prone to tears, seeking the comfort of my dad.

'Listen, don't worry,' he said afterwards. 'It was silly of me to put you in for that race. You did so well in the last one, I just thought… Look, let's take it easy in future, shall we? Make sure we don't lose sight of the fact that we're here to enjoy it?'

That sounded good, and so for a while we stuck to local club races. I recovered my confidence and kept improving, kept winning. Pretty soon what had started as a hobby, just a weekend pastime, became something of an obsession as any other interests I had were sidelined. For the next nine years, the answer to the question, 'What were you doing at the weekend, Jenson?' was 'Karting.'

Not that anybody asked. Those few friends I'd made at school knew nothing of my double life. To them, I disappeared off the face of the earth every Friday, materialising again on Monday. Meantime, I was making new friends in my weekend world. There was Richie Williams, who'd taken up karting about a year after me. He and his dad had turned up to Clay Pigeon Raceway looking lost, not sure what to do with Richie's new kart, an eleventh birthday present. Oh, the indignity as I, a mere nine-year-old, showed him the ropes. Still, he didn't hold it against me and we became mates.

Then there was Chrissy Buncombe, another driver who'd followed in his father's footsteps. His dad, Jonathan, had raced my dad, at Clay Pigeon no less. By the time me and Chrissy met in 1989, Dad had become fed up with the constant slumps of the motor industry, sold his dealership and opened a kart shop in Frome instead. It became Rocket Motorsports, and he gained a name as a master of tuning engines.

In turn, this brought him a bit of heat in the form of paddock gossip. What started out as four or five dads wondering aloud if my success had anything to do with Dad's engines being somehow 'fixed' soon became a major ball-ache when the RAC, which was the governing body at the time, began insisting on stripping down his engines at the end of each race to check for 'irregularities'.

They never found anything because there was nothing to find. What they and the other lads' fathers couldn't quite grasp was that Dad was an expert at putting everything on the limit; he had the eagle eye of an F1 designer, looking for a loophole in the regulations and exploiting it. After a while of being the RAC's favourite port-of-call, he got so seriously pissed off that he'd get the engines checked over and then sealed so that there was no way he could fiddle with them after that, and thus, hopefully, stop the cheating gossip once and for all.

It did. The dads stopped gossiping that Dad was cheating and started saying that he had the RAC in his pocket. Again, they just couldn't accept that he was making good engines and tuning them brilliantly, winning championships with them. In all he won eleven karting championship with his engines. Lewis Hamilton won a championship with one of Dad's engines. Dad and Lewis's dad, Anthony, ended up reconnecting in the F1 paddock, where the joke was that Anthony still owed Dad £300.

Anyway, Dad had the shop and it was there that Chrissy Buncombe and Jonathan came one day. Chris and I hit it off, and bingo, the beginning of a beautiful friendship.

Meanwhile, Dad had bought a Transit van that he painted in Rocket Motorsport colours and converted so that I could sleep in the back on journeys home. One time he locked himself in overnight and was forced to have a wee in a water bottle. Waking the next morning he forgot about the wee, took a swig out of the water bottle and got a nasty surprise. He was prone to doing things like that.

Next he bought a caravan from travellers and we used to tow that to circuits, turning races into mini-holidays. We had a huge octagonal tent that was the envy of other karters and often became a bit of a social hub. My dad's vest and mop of unruly blond hair were soon a familiar fixture on the scene. As with his old Colorado Beetle, he just couldn't help but stand out.

I won the Clay Pigeon Club Championship in 1988, which was pretty cool, and set me up to make the leap to bigger races. Come the following year I was competing in the Clay Pigeon TVS Super Prix, which was the first televised event for that category, top prize, 'hi-fi goods to the value of £350'. As you can imagine: great excitement all round. Johnny Herbert, who had just made his debut in Formula One, was commentator and pundit; kids and dads were interviewed, including me and the old man. I was wearing a treasured Alley Cats T-shirt, but even so, it wasn't exactly a slick appearance. My dad, meanwhile, was asked about the commitment it took. 'It's my hobby,' he grinned, 'he's just the pilot.

'What he wants to do in the future, I don't know,' he added. 'They all say they want to go into Formula One, but as long as he's enjoying himself, that's the main thing.'

'We could well be looking at a future Johnny Herbert...' prompted the interviewer.

'Well, he seems to have that something extra,' beamed Dad. 'We'll have to see.'

The TV people were another lot who couldn't get my name right. Listen to the commentary and you'll hear Jenson pronounced the Scandinavian way, so it sounded like 'Yenson', and on several occasions even managed to turn it into 'Jesper'. Oh well. At least they didn't call me Jason.

My competitors were top names: Marc Hynes, Justin Wilson, Anthony Davidson, Claire Bogan, Craig Murray, Dan Wheldon. At twelve years old, Claire Bogan was something of a veteran. She'd won the Cadets British Championship in its inaugural year, 1987. Dan Wheldon, however, was the reigning champ, having first won the title in 1988. This was big competition, maybe my toughest yet.

I did well in the heats. In heat three I had laboured in fourth, and then, with the end of the race in sight, I slipped past Anthony Davidson and made up a place, now sitting in third behind Justin Wilson and Dan Wheldon, his kart bearing the coveted number one, befitting his status.

We came burning down the straight. I quickly choked the engine, which is something you see karters do with their right hand, when they cover the airbox. The reason is because karts are run lean, which means they're run on low fuel, which in turn gives you more power because the leaner the engine the hotter it runs, thus the more power it produces.

However, the kart's two-stroke engine relies on fuel for lubrication, and so when you reach the end of a straight – i.e., when the engine is at its leanest – and you lift off the throttle and brake, you choke the engine to keep it cool and lubricated and thus stable in the corner.

So I did that. And then, as we came into the corner, I saw my chance, an unprotected line. I glanced behind to check my rear, saw that the coast was clear and then swung out behind Justin Wilson, finding the line and slipping past him on the inside as we came through the first part of the S-bends. Before he could do anything to stop me I'd nipped past Dan, too, going from third to first in the space of about three seconds, and going on to win.

Now for the finals – soon everybody would know the name of Jesper Button – and I was on pole, out in front as we came around on the warm-up lap, the combined noise of our 60cc karts like Second World War bombers taking off. The pitch rose as we were flagged to start and I used my pole position well, drawing away from the pack right away.

And there I stayed, increasing my lead lap by lap. There was an accident behind that took out Dan and a couple of others, but even so, nobody had a chance of catching me that day: Clay Pigeon was about 900 yards long in total, and by the end of the race I had a 150-yard lead.

The biggest race of my year, the toughest competition, a televised event, and I walked it. In heat three I'd used tactics, but for that final race I used my other great racing strength, which was smoothness, something always insisted upon by my rough diamond of a father: be smooth, precise, find the line. Once again, these were principles that I took with me throughout my entire career.

That year I was also runner-up in the Cadet championships and won a Super Prix at Silverstone.

Winning, that was the thing. I was angry with myself when it didn't go well. I worried what people would think of me. I had to prove to my dad that I really did have that something extra.

10

Mum remarried. His name was Chris and he had something to do with bouncy castles, which was pretty much his only saving grace. He'd get angry. Well, probably not *angry*, but way more cross than I was used to. I hated being told off so much it was almost a phobia. I just wasn't used to it. The hint of a raised voice and I was wounded to the point of tears.

Still, they got married and left Northcote Crescent. So – get this – my dad and Pippa moved in to care for me and my two sisters, like a game of parental musical chairs.

I got on better with Pippa than I did with Chris, although we weren't massively close. She liked animals, which automatically made her more of a goodie than a baddie. When we eventually moved out of Northcote – that was a wrench – to a little village called Lower Vobster, we had an acre of land bordered on two sides by a river, and she made the most of it by filling it with animals. Five cats, three goats and a Boxer dog.

Mind you, she needed the company. Dad was never there. Weekdays he was working in the karting shop, while every weekend he took me, the kart, the Transit, the caravan, the swanky tent and his vest to tracks all over the country: Kimbolton, Shenington, Rye House, Fulbeck, Wombwell, Brands Hatch, Rockingham, Snetterton, Silverstone, Donington. We went all over.

In 1990, the British Cadet Championship was retained by my (friendly) rival Dan Wheldon. His reign, however, was about to come to an end. The following year, I entered, won all but one of the thirty-four races and took the title that he'd held for the previous three years. The only championship race I didn't win that year was Hull, where they created a circuit around the city centre (just like Monaco, except slightly less beautiful) and I couldn't get past the guy on pole (just like Monaco).

And that was it. I was the country's Cadet champion. I stood on the podium with my trophy in my hand, my wreath around my neck and a grin on my face so wide that my cheeks began to hurt, loving the feeling, drinking in the attention.

Came down to earth with a bump afterwards, though. By now I was at Selwood Middle School, a sort of halfway house between primary and secondary, where they'd somehow got wind of my win, probably from the local paper, and asked me to take part in a strange ceremony they put together.

I was horrified, proper vampires-and-crosses reaction. 'Come on, Jense,' urged Dad, 'It'll be good for you.' From his grin I could tell he thought it was a great wheeze. He had several species of smiles, from the reassuring, tight-lipped smile he'd give me just before a race, to the wide beam of delight he wore if I won and a mischievous East End twinkle he was wearing at that moment. But I'm not sure he ever realised quite how retiring I really was. Him, Mum and my sisters would all have been surprised to learn that I disappeared inside myself the moment I left home for school every morning, that every second of my school life was spent in an attempt to not stand out.

But Dad was persuasive and so was the head, and so reluctantly I agreed. On the day I found myself sitting in my kart, full kit, helmet on. Except instead of being on a track I was on the school stage, the curtains drawn across in front of me, hiding me from the school who were at that moment being treated to the kind of inspiring monologue that would put Mel Gibson in *Braveheart* to shame. The head was talking about what you could achieve if you put your mind to it, and I was thinking, *Yeah, and if your dad buys you a go-kart.*

And then the curtain went back and hey presto, it's whatshisname Jason Button, sitting in some kind of little car on the stage.

Dying inside, I was asked to remove my helmet and then walk along the ranks of seated kids in order to best show off my natty racing duds. It was hideously embarrassing, but in the end also quite illuminating, because afterwards everybody was pretty cool about it. There was none of the scornful, mocking reaction I'd expected for standing out and being a bit different. You might even call it a grudging respect.

Before we get carried away, it wasn't as though I was suddenly the most popular kid at school. They didn't hoist me aloft and bear me through the hallways, chanting my name. But I did notice a shift in the way I was treated. Before, they all assumed I was a geeky loner because I never hung out. I wasn't present at the usual birthday parties, fetes and carnivals, all the stuff that make up a normal kid's life. I was off karting. Only they didn't know that. They'd just assumed I was weird. That revelation alone was enough to make them look at me differently. The fact that I'd won something and been on the TV made me interesting, maybe even a little bit exotic. Every cloud and all that.

Not long afterwards, of course, came the move to upper school: Frome Community College, and that's another story altogether. In the meantime, Dad and I were formulating grand plans. And we were karting. Always karting.

Aww, who's that little angel in the front seat? Don't let him near the handbrake...

Here I am on my 50cc motorbike, a Christmas present from Dad. I soon tired of the limiter and wanted to go even faster.

My dad used to race rallycross in his day. Here he is in 1976 with his Beetle outside the front of his car dealership. *(© Bath in Time)*

1987 – first time in a kart, I loved it straight away.

Above left: 1989 – winning the Super Prix, a televised event with Johnny Herbert commentating.

Above right: After my dad and mum split he married Pippa. Here we are all spruced up at the wedding in 1994.

1990 – me and dad (who seems to have gone full John Rambo) at Rye House karting track.

Above: 1995 – racing and winning in Italy. *(© Sutton)*

Right: 1997 – becoming European Super A karting champ was a massive deal and set me up for taking the next step. *(© Sutton)*

Below: My 18th birthday down at the track.

1998 – I won the Championship in my only season in Formula Ford, without ever really enjoying the racing. Here I am with my trophies and close competitor, and friend, Dan Wheldon.

(All © Sutton)

My one season in
Formula Three in
1999 was my first
experience of racing
with downforce. I finished
a slightly disappointing
third, but by now I was
desperate to make that
next step into the big
leagues. *(All © Sutton)*

Meeting my hero Alain Prost, while testing for one of his F1 cars in 1999. After a few laps I was delighted to hear my times were quicker than Jean Alesi's. *(All © Sutton)*

Following a dramatic testing shoot-out with Bruno Junqueira, I landed
a spot on Frank Williams's F1 team. Little did I know that making the team
was just the beginning. *(All © Getty)*

11

Starting out, we'd never really thought about Formula One, beyond wild flights of fancy. The same way you wouldn't go picking out your Oscars outfit if you'd just landed a walk-on part in *EastEnders*. Even with the links we had to the racing world, Formula One seemed so far away and unattainable. So we just did what we did, one race at a time, and if I carried on as well as I'd started then who knows what might happen?

But now I was a British champion. And that changed things.

'People keep telling me you'd be good enough to race seriously,' said the old man one evening in the kitchen of our Vobster house. 'What do you think of that?'

I went to answer but he stopped me. 'It's fine if you don't fancy it. If you just want to stick to club racing for fun, that's absolutely fine, but you're British national champion now, and...'

'Dad, I want to do Formula One,' I told him firmly.

He nodded. He knew all along I was going to say that. Next thing you know he was sitting me down and drawing what he called a 'karting pyramid'. At the bottom were the thousands of weekend karters, but I wasn't one of those any more because I'd won the title. By virtue of my age I was maybe *here*. He pointed to a position about halfway up the pyramid. But I was due to move from Cadets to Juniors the following year, and that would push me a little higher, and if I could keep winning and get *here* – he indicated the top of the pyramid – then maybe, just maybe, I could do what the likes of Ayrton Senna, Johnny Herbert and plenty of other drivers had done, and use karting as a springboard to F1.

At the same time we made another decision, basically that we were getting on each other's wick. Again, it came back to that family thing. Dad had been a patient and creative teacher when we first started out. He was the one who said, 'This one's the throttle, this one's the brake, this is how you use them,' who showed me the racing line, and taught me about braking and throttle control, always emphasising, 'Smooth, Jense, keep it smooth.' He'd grounded me in the basics of karting, which in turn was the fundamentals of all racing. He was my number one mentor and always will be.

There was one problem. He was my dad. He'd never really stopped watching me like a hawk, and in truth never would, and I was beginning to feel claustrophobic, as well as finding it difficult to hear him tell me I was doing something wrong. For whatever reason, I found myself not wanting to listen to him when he was giving me advice. We spent a lot of time together. *A lot.* Just him and me. Five a.m. starts, late nights, up and down motorways. All that and shared DNA. It was a recipe for disaster.

For his part, Dad felt that he'd imparted what racing knowledge he could. He knew all about engines but maybe we needed a little help fine-tuning the set-up. In short, what we needed was a knowledgeable third party, coach and referee. That man turned out be Dave Spence.

A familiar face to karters, a mechanical and engineering genius, Dave had two sons, Jamie and Danny. I'd raced with Jamie when I first started out, but by 1992 he'd made his way out of karting and into Formula Ford, the category above, where drivers have engineers, mechanics and all the benefits that being in a team brings. Like many karting dads before him, Dave suddenly found his services were no longer required, and for the time being, at least until young Danny stated Cadets, he was kicking his heels and casting around for something to do.

'Would you mind helping our Jenson?' Dad asked him one day. 'He's moving up to juniors and, to be honest, I've gone as far as I can with him. We need a bit of outside help. What do you say?'

'There's a big difference between Cadets and Juniors,' said Dave.

'Exactly,' said Dad.

I was introduced to Dave, the big man. Well over six foot, he was thin on top and softly spoken. I'd soon learn that he was capable of surprising displays of temper and emotion, especially, no, *only*, where racing was concerned. But mostly he was a gentle, considered guy, just the sort you want showing you the ropes. Which is what he did.

We watched videos of my driving. Grainy, scratchy old VHS tapes. 'Very smooth, Jenson,' he told me.

'Thanks, Dave.'

'But you won't get away with that in Juniors.'

The difference was that while Cadets used a 60cc engine with six horsepower and a top speed of 50mph; in Juniors I'd be driving a kart with a 100cc engine, 25 horsepower and a top speed of 75mph. It was a major step up in terms of power that meant I'd have to rethink my racecraft. Smooth and precise would no longer be sufficient to win the day. I'd need to be a bit more aggressive in my driving, use my bodyweight to turn; I'd need to know how to use the tyres.

Up until then I'd never paid too much attention to tyres. They were just tyres. But all that was about to change because it turned out they're just as big a deal in karting as they are in Formula One. For a start, there was huge competition between tyre manufactures. Vega, Bridgestone and Dunlop were the three big ones in karting and they were always producing softer and softer tyres in a bid to claim that they had the tyres with the best grip.

As you probably know, when a tyre's hard, it's a just a rock. You can't generate grip. But when it's all soft and gooey it'll grip the road a lot more effectively. Too effectively, sometimes. At one point they were supplying us with tyres so soft you'd go into a corner and the kart would pick up on two wheels, there was that much grip. We had to change the kart to make it wider. Drivers got in the habit of shifting around in the kart so it wouldn't tip up on two wheels. It was amazing how much we had to work around these stupidly soft tyres they gave us.

Thanks to Dave I was about to add yet another tool to my driver's kit – knowledge that would once again form the bedrock of my later career. See, the thing with tyres is that they're the only four things that touch the ground, so you need a close relationship with them; you need to be able to read them.

In a kart you can see the tyres to monitor their condition, the most common complaint being that they start to grain, which gives you terrible understeer and makes you start slipping and sliding all over the place. On a kart tyre you can actually see the graining begin to form; you can also see when the rubber starts to come off, when it begins to pull away from the canvas, and that's a bad sign, too, you need to watch out for that.

So you have to be gentle with the tyres to avoid any of the adverse effects. Same way you are with the engine when you choke it to lubricate it and give it a rest. Part of your job as a racing driver is to feel the car and know when it needs a bit of TLC.

The weirdest difference is that the tyres in F1 are way worse than those we used in karting. Or perhaps I should say that *in my opinion* the Pirellis they use in Formula One aren't as good as the tyres we used in karting – or indeed what we used to have in Formula One, when we used Bridgestones and Michelins.

Every driver in F1 complains about them. Every team struggles to make them work. In karting, they were our trusty rubber friends. You'd drive out of the pits and *boom*, you had tyre grip straight away. In a Formula One car, it's different. Sometimes you just can't get them working at all. And by 'working' I don't mean rolling along the ground, I mean getting the right temperature in them, because a cold tyre is a hard tyre; a warm tyre is soft and grippy.

So say if you put two identical F1 cars next to each other, one with cold tyres, one with warm, the cold one's lap time would be about twenty seconds slower. A lifetime in Formula One. And that's if you made it past the first corner without spinning out.

That's the problem when they put amateurs in an F1 car, celebrities, sponsors or whatever. The guy jumps in, the mechanics take off the tyre warmers and off he goes. But as soon as he's got to Turn One, the tyres have cooled down, because he's gone into the corner too slowly, and he spins.

A Formula One driver, on the other hand, will exit the pits and go flat out straight away because he knows you have to keep the tyre temperature up. As soon as you drop out the window, the car's a bundle.

So tyres was something Dave taught me, and to be honest, I've been learning about them ever since. It's one of the things I love about motorsports – you're always learning, always having to adapt and develop. It's not like tennis, where the rackets might change a bit but everything else stays the same. If you're in motorsport, the formulas are always changing. The regulations, the tyres, the power, the type of engine. It keeps you excited.

12

The step up to Juniors meant I'd be racing against hardened veterans. The class spanned an age range from eleven to sixteen, so at one end you had innocent little kids like me, still wiping Mummy's lipstick off their cheeks, while at the other end were grizzled lads on the brink of adulthood. Kids who were shaving, who were old enough to have sex and smoke – all three at the same time if the mood took them.

'You'll have to be tough,' said Dad, echoing Dave's words.

We got to the first competition of the season, the O Plate at Clay Pigeon, me in my new powerful kart. The sights and sounds of karting that I loved washed over me, only now the noises of our kart engines were different. This time I had a lot more power to play with. Dad had purposely restricted my practice time because he didn't want my core driving style to change based on the new kart. Just as long as I took into account what Dave had been telling me, I'd be okay.

Starting it up, I thought, *This is something a bit new. A bit different.* It was wet, my favourite conditions. Sure enough, I qualified second for the final and then won the O Plate.

This isn't too bad, I thought. *Dunno what Dave and Dad's on about. I can handle this.*

A week later it was the first round of the British Championships, the 'Super One National Championships', to give them their full and formal title. The championships were decided over seven rounds at different tracks around the UK, and the first round that year was again at Clay Pigeon.

The old man was excited. After my O Plate win he had high hopes for this one, and wasn't doing a lot to keep his hopes in check. Zipped into my suit, I eyed the competition and caught one or two of them glaring back.

First heat, the lights went to green and we roared off the start line, twenty-four of us, two-by-two in a rolling start.

There was a left-hander just off the start. I was on the outside, trying to move into the pandemonium of the pack, checking my rear, always mindful of other drivers, especially early when the bunch is so concentrated and everybody's vying for position, making sudden alterations to their line, coming at you from unexpected angles, front-runners swinging across to protect their lead.

But that was okay. Defensive driving is much more a part of karting than it is in other classes, especially Formula One. Dave had prepared me for what was to be a sharp increase in aggressive driving in the Juniors, and this was it.

Or so I thought. Having checked my rear and found it clear I suddenly felt a bump from behind. Not a nudge either, a little dink the driver quickly corrects. This was a full-on fuck-you, a Dodgem-car wallop that took me off the line of the corner and sent me spinning out in the tyre barriers.

And that was the first time I ever had a petrol tank hit me in the balls. When you think about it, it's daft place to put a petrol tank in such close proximity to the driver's testicles. But there you have it. What the crossbar is to the cyclist, the petrol tank is to the karter. And it was just as eye-wateringly, nausea-inducingly painful.

Out of the race for good, I was bruised and dazed. Returning to Dad (who raged and threatened to go and beat the kid up) I found myself feeling confused. I hadn't really expected hostility, not proper rivalry. But it seemed that not only was I reigning Cadet champion and so needed to be brought down a peg or two, but I'd put a few backs up by winning at Clay Pigeon in my first Juniors race. Evidently, I needed to be taught a lesson. Welcome to the big leagues.

13

Around this time my dad was offered a rallycross drive in a 6R4, which was *the* car to have at the time. It was a Metro, which doesn't sound like much, but it had a tubular frame made by Williams, big wings, 800 horsepower. I'm sure he'd have loved driving it.

He turned it down in order to concentrate on my karting. What's more he had the kart shop to keep up. My wins were bringing customers through the door.

Meanwhile, I went to my first-ever Grand Prix, the European Grand Prix at Donington Park, which turned out to be a special race because I got to see Ayrton overtake several cars on lap one in the wet. Awesome.

The following year, we took the caravan to Silverstone for the British Grand Prix and camped. I remember the toilets – holes in the ground, basically – but more than that I can recall the noise of it all.

This was when Formula One was really noisy, of course. Even for a kid accustomed to the constant clamour of kart racing it seemed loud. The other thing I remember was that the cars seemed able to turn on a dime, which I guess was my introduction to the phenomenon of down-force, that mysterious marriage of air, ground and racing car that will give the car more aerodynamic grip. Seeing it was a revelation; the idea that you could carry *more* speed through a corner, that you'd have the grip to do it, and that's what produces G-force. *Whoa.*

I'd always been in love with Formula One, but sitting on the bank at Silverstone I fell even deeper.

At home, meanwhile, I used to wind up my sisters. They'd bring boyfriends back and lock themselves in their bedrooms for hanky-panky, but I was the annoying kid brother always on hand to break up the party.

Honestly, I should have had 'passion killer' printed on my T-shirt. I used to drag the boyfriends away for video-gaming sessions. We had most of the early systems: Atari with *Pong*, followed by a Nintendo, and then a Super Nintendo, and then a SNES, which is where shit got real, thanks mainly to the game *Super Mario Kart*.

As you can imagine, *Mario Kart* was right up my street, and nobody could beat me on it. If you've ever played you'll know that players get to select from a variety of karts, each with its own strengths and weaknesses. Most gamers tended to plump for either Mario or Luigi, because they were good all-rounders. Princess was quick off the line. Yoshi was no slouch.

Me, I chose Bowser. A big burly turtle-type creature, Bowser's selling point was his top speed. The drawback was that he was more difficult to manoeuvre and his acceleration was terrible. What I knew from karting, of course, was that the trick was to maintain his top speed. You'd drift him, make sure he didn't spin out and keep the minimum speed up as high as possible, keep him consistent around the track. You had to know how to drive Bowser, but once you had the hang of that consistency and you were keeping the minimum speed high, he was unbeatable, and that's exactly the same principle for all racing.

We used to pull all-nighters on *Super Mario Kart*. I loved it. Even so, it came a distant second to the real thing, because while I loved *Super Mario Kart*, I *loved* karting, to the point of obsession.

And just as I loved karting, I hated school. I remember so many Sunday nights driving home from a race and the high of karting fading into a sense of dread that I had to go to school the next day. There was such a chasm between the two lives. I'd end the weekend standing on a podium, golden boy grinning from ear to ear, trophy held aloft. 'Eat my dust.' At school I was the shuffling little dork who gets picked last for football. The guy nobody wanted on his team because I had all the ball skills of a three-legged yak.

You've heard the expression 'going from hero to zero'? Well that was me every Monday morning, suffering massive kart comedown. Gritted teeth, clock-watching until Friday, when at last, like a caged tiger, I could escape into the other world.

I'd be dead excited before a race. Confident? Sometimes. It would depend on the circuit and weather conditions, and if things weren't going my way in that area then maybe my excitement would have nerves for a companion. But mainly I was just gagging to get out there and race.

At the same time, I'd suffer occasional lapses in confidence. Doubt would creep in. As a racing driver you can learn about the racing line, tactics, braking, throttle control, engine care and tyre maintenance. And if you're serious about your craft then you'll need to master those things.

But you need something else as well. An extra something. A talent that, because you can't quite define what it is, makes it easy to fear you've lost it.

However, my obsession was beginning to crowd out my enjoyment. I was doing well on the track, but I was starting to lose sight of what it was I loved about racing. That joy was becoming overwhelmed by a sense of expectation – most of it my own. After all, I knew that if I wanted to keep racing then I had to perform. Money was becoming an issue. After a race in Larkhall in Scotland, Dad had to borrow cash to get us home. It was costing him something like six grand a season to keep me running and he couldn't afford to keep doing that just to watch me make up the numbers. I had to do well.

That's all right then. No pressure.

14

The cracks began to show in 1992. Even though I won a championship that year, it was the Junior TKM, not the Junior 100B, which was the more prestigious and hotly contested of the two. And while I had some great races, I had some really bad ones too – ones where I finished right at the back.

'Are you okay?' asked the old man after one particularly poor performance. We were in the Transit, driving back from Scotland to Somerset so he'd had plenty of time to mull it over before he popped the question.

'Yeah, Dad,' I said quietly, even though I was feeling dejected and doubting my abilities and wondering what was wrong – the usual mix of toxic emotions that are a bigger and more dangerous opponent than any rival driver.

'Well, you know, I just thought I'd ask, because the last couple of races have been bloody awful, haven't they, Jense?'

Didn't mince his words.

'Yes, Dad.'

'Listen,' he said, after a pause, 'if you want to give it all up, that's up to you. I'm all right with that. If you want to take a couple of months off then that's okay too. We can do that.'

At the mention of having two months off I perked up a little.

'But you've got to remember,' he added, 'that if you take time off then you'll probably never come back again, not at the level you are. If you take time off, that's it…'

I knew what he meant. If I relaxed at all then I could kiss goodbye to any dreams I had of making it into the big time.

'I want to carry on, Dad,' I told him. But somehow the issue of my form was left hanging, and the conversation ended, eaten up by the M74.

I felt wretched. Whenever I did badly I always felt I was letting people down, but the feeling was never as specific as it was at that moment. Right then I knew I was letting my dad down. That he was hurting.

The rest of our journey was silent. Three hours during which we were both lost in our own thoughts, both wondering where the love of racing had gone; asking ourselves if it was worth it, all these early starts and endless hours on the motorway. Maybe Dad was wondering what was wrong with me. Being astute as he was, he probably already knew the answer.

And the answer was that somewhere along the way I'd lost the will to win and that, along with racecraft, and the indefinable 'something' we'll call talent, is an essential part of the make-up of any racing driver.

It's not optional. You have to have it. You have to have that will to win, that burning desire for competitive edge. In Formula One the most prevalent example of that competition is between teammates, because the best test of your skill as a driver is when it's pitted against a driver in exactly the same car. That's why the rest of us line up on the grid behind Mercedes and Ferrari. Not because we want to make up the numbers. Not because we want to look pretty. Because we want to beat our teammate.

But you need it at all levels. And you certainly can't do what I'd been doing, which was cruise around, not overtaking, not fighting for position, almost as though I assumed I didn't have to go hunting for the win. That it would come and find me. I just didn't have that fire in my belly.

So that's what I'd lost, or temporarily misplaced, meaning the next question was why, swiftly followed by how was I going to get it back.

As to the first, I was growing up, and I was tired of the weekend-hero-weekday-zero cycle. My teenage years had arrived, made a searching audit of my social life and found it severely lacking.

Mainly, I wanted friends: male friends, girl friends, girlfriends. I wanted to fit in and be part of the in-crowd. It's not like I was bullied. But I got the piss taken out of me a lot. Just stupid things, nothing specific. Nor was I ostracised. I ended up making a good group of friends who helped me through. But I always got the impression that I wasn't well liked by the general school population. And that was a situation I wanted to change.

So I started making more of an effort to socialise. I got into booze. Once I even bought a pack of cigarettes. All in an effort to fit in that didn't do me any harm at school but definitely shifted my focus away from karting.

It was a difficult phase. Somehow I wasn't able to reconcile those two aspects of my life, the weekend and weekday bits. At races I was in my comfort zone, but I wanted that guy to come to school with me. In the meantime, the whole shitshow was endangering what I'd built up at the weekend.

One night we were driving back from a race, and Dad was in the front with Pippa while I was asleep in the back. Except that I wasn't really asleep, and I could hear their conversation. And what I heard him say, very softly, in a whisper, was, 'I don't think he's got it. I really don't think he's got it.'

I decided then that things would change.

15

What to do? How to get that fire in my belly back?

We called Dave.

Before, Dave had offered me advice. Now – indeed, for the next two years – he was going to run me. He and Dad built the kart, so there's a lot of maintenance needed, but as far as racing and set-up went, I'd be dealing with Dave, whose job it was to take me to the next level, help me improve as a driver and most importantly, recover my competitive edge.

He did it. And the secret turned out to be getting off my arse and working at something that I've never had to work at before.

The thing was that in 1991 I was used to sitting in my kart and being the fastest, job done. It came naturally to me. But the karts we were using now were so much more powerful and complex that I couldn't do that any more. I'd have to work at mastering that. Secretly, I decided that I'd also have to work harder at reconciling my two lives. After all, I still wanted to do 'normal' teenager stuff. But I was determined to get things back on track. The words *I really don't think he's got it* had cut deep.

Dave began by instilling in me some discipline. He asked my headmaster if I could use the school gym instead of playing football. I wasn't allowed fizzy drinks either.

Now, I'm not saying that I followed his new rules religiously, because that would make me a big fat liar. I'd go to the gym, work out for ten minutes and then watch *Neighbours* for the rest of the session. Neither did I completely forego fizzy drinks. Come on, Coke was practically a religion at that age.

But as with so many of the principles laid down during that period of my career, fitness would become central to my life in F1. Being fit as a racing driver isn't just a case of looking good in a flame-retardant suit, that's just a pleasant benefit. For a start, there's the G-force to consider. When you go through a high-speed corner, you're pulling 5G, which means that your head is five times heavier than normal. Your head normally weighs, say, 5kg, so that's 25kg. You're also wearing a helmet and a HANS device, which is the U-shaped restraint we wear that sits on the shoulders and stops the head from whipping around in an accident.

Together the helmet and HANS device weigh about 2.5kg so multiply that by five for the G and that's 12.5kg. Add them together and you're trying to support almost 40kg with your neck. That's like attempting to carry four one-year-old children on your head. Cornering's the worst of it, but it's there all the time. The G-force in a racing car is absolutely phenomenal throughout the race. The constant pressure of it physically drains you.

So to deal with that you have to have a good base, in other words a mixture of strength and overall fitness. Drivers tend not to do massive strength work, but you do need to make sure your body is in decent enough shape that it can cope for the period of a race.

You also need to keep an eye on your weight. The weight limit for a car used to be 600kg, including driver. Obviously, we try to make cars as light as possible, but if it's a heavy car, which just happens sometimes, you've really got to watch your weight. McLaren's car was always a great weight at the beginning of the season, only for them to start adding components, extra wings here and there, which are heavy. The weight of the car went up, and to compensate my weight had to come down.

At one point they wanted me to weigh under 74kg, which is just over eleven stone, including helmet, HANS device, suit, gloves and boots – and the kit weighs a combined total of 4kg.

It got to the point where I couldn't lose any more weight. I just couldn't get any lighter. I can't remember which race, but I definitely lost seconds because I was overweight so I took myself off to a specialist in Monaco who told me I was eating too many carbohydrates.

Prior to that I'd been wolfing down the carbs, to be honest. Pasta for breakfast, lunch and dinner with pasta for dessert and a light snack of pasta. I thought that's what you were supposed to do if you were exercising. But no. Apparently not. According to this guy, my body fat was 12 per cent, which he said was too high for the amount of training I was doing.

His advice was to limit carbs, and then only eat the good carbs – complex carbs – like brown rice and sweet potato, rather than pasta, potatoes and bread. I did all that and dropped to 6 per cent body fat. It was too light for me at the time, but I needed to be there in order to drive the car.

And that was my diet for the rest of my time in Formula One. I basically had to give up carbs all year round; I'd often fast before a race. And I'm about average for a driver. Sebastian Vettel and Nico Rosberg are lighter – they don't struggle so much. Me and Lewis are roughly the same, around eleven stone, no carbs for us. The likes of Nico Hülkenberg and Mark Webber, being bigger – a whopping eleven stone nine in the case of Mark – used to really struggle.

It was tough. In the last four or five years of my career, one of the main things that drivers would complain about, besides the tyres, was the weight limit. Plenty are like me, over six foot, and we felt we were being penalised for being tall. Go to a gig and it's a benefit. Not if you're a jockey or a racing driver. When the weight limit went up all the drivers were overjoyed, apart from Felipe Massa who wanted it left as it was. Why? Because he's a short-arse.

But anyway, it went up, the drivers were happier, but then the team started making the cars heavier again, so we still had to lose weight.

Of course, I'm not a racing driver any more. But I'm a keen triathlete. The Jenson Button Trust runs a triathlon each year and I can't let the side down; I have to stay in shape, so it's lucky that I love it. Racing drivers tend to sleep in. They don't have to get up early, but training for a triathlon I'll be up at 6.30 every morning when I'll go for either a five-mile bike ride, an hour run or an hour-and-a-half swim. And I still don't drink fizzy drinks – apart from something they have in the US called Zevia.

Something else Dave taught me – and by now you know what I'm going to say, but yes, something else that's proved an essential part of my driver's toolkit – was the ability to watch, really watch, the racing.

I'd always had a good eye for predicting what might be about to happen in a race, and that dated back to watching F1 with the old man when I was younger. Even so, I was still watching it like you might a movie, one step removed. I wasn't concentrating on what other drivers were doing, not really thinking about how they were driving and how they were reacting to one another.

'Right,' said Dave one day at the track. 'We're going to stand at turn one and watch every single kart that comes through, every single lap of the race. Got it?'

'Yes, Dave.'

We'd become good friends. Dad and I often stayed with the Spence family, and though Jamie was usually away we'd got to know Dave and Danny well, the four of us forming something of a crew at the races, like four travelling gypsies. I trailed after him as we went to stand near turn one.

'Look at the drivers,' he instructed me. 'Have a good look at what they're doing, how they're interacting with the kart. Watch how they work with other drivers on the circuit.'

All race we stood there and I did what he said. It was the beginning of a time when I started to learn from the more experienced heads. To adapt to Juniors, I needed to learn to read the race. In my F1 career that ability became one of my core strengths. Standing at turn one with the big man by my side was when I first started flexing that muscle.

So Dave helped me no end. My next real mentor after Dad. He coached me through a 1993 season where in truth I was still learning to reconcile my normal-teen life with my racing-teen alter ego, and didn't do as well as I should, and then helped me with an even bigger step: just before I was due to turn fourteen I was invited to test for an Italian team called Team Rambo (I kid you not) in Sicily. The circuit was just below Mount Etna and I impressed the team and got the drive.

By the time I started Team Rambo had changed their name to the much more boring Team Astra. They were owned by a Serb who was also a customer of Dad's, hence the connection. And that was it. I began racing abroad. Once every three weeks or so I spent the weekend in Europe – man of the world – combining that with racing in the UK. It was an exhausting schedule, but thanks to Dave I'd located my love of racing and my will to win once more.

And then something terrible happened.

16

It was the end of 1994 and I was competing in the winter series in Italy when I got the news. Dad had been told but he let me race and then broke it to me on the flight home.

'Danny Spence was in an accident, Jense,' he said. There was a crack in his voice. 'He's dead, son.'

We were so close back then, the Buttons and the Spences. We had the caravan and our octagonal tent; they had a big motorhome, and we always used to park them together, creating a little community within a community. We'd get up early, have breakfast and then convene in the big tent to prepare the kart for the day's racing.

Jamie wasn't there much, but when he did come we were all in awe. All us younger karters looked up to the guys who had already started in car racing, mainly because that's what we wanted to do, including Danny. No doubt he would have done it, too, coming from such a racing-mad family. Like his brother, he had the talent.

Danny was with us all the time, a permanent fixture whether he was racing or not, helping his dad on the karts, causing trouble, just like Jamie. I think it must have run in the family. They loved racing, those guys. Dad and I were into it *way* more than any sane person should be. But the Spences lived and breathed it. Danny and his dad had a bond you don't often see in a father and son. My dad and I were close but those two were like best mates. They had great fun together. Dave must have had high hopes for him as a racer. It was about the same time as I started racing in Europe that he began to be competitive.

Danny was just nine when he died. He was racing at Kimbolton in Cambridgeshire, a track we all knew like the backs of our hands, when another kart flipped on top of his, and though it wasn't a terrible accident, he didn't walk away from it. Apparently, he stood up afterwards but then collapsed and died, the cause of death was injuries to the head and chest.

Dad was right to tell me after my own race, of course. Danny was the first person I'd ever known who had died, and for him to die racing was devastating, not only because I'd lost a friend — we all had — but because I'd lost him to racing. After all, racing was the thing we did for fun; it brought us together. It was the agent of good times. It wasn't supposed to kill us.

I couldn't make sense of why the accident had killed him if it wasn't that bad. I remember that very clearly, being unable to process the fact that it wasn't a fireball, a huge multi-car pile-up, it was a fairly minor prang in a 60cc Cadets kart. You're not supposed to die doing that.

The next weekend, I was back in the kart. It's the best thing to do. You fall off your bike and your dad insists you get straight back on, and that's exactly what the old man did with me. It's especially true of motorsports. You've just got to crack on in the sure knowledge that injuries are rare and fatalities even rarer. You've got to trust that it won't happen to you. Besides, I always had a feeling of invulnerability when I put the helmet on.

The following week the whole of British karting turned out for the funeral. I later learned that Lewis Hamilton was there, too, having witnessed the accident at Kimbolton. Hopefully he had a better journey to the funeral than me and the old man.

Dad was driving a BMW Seven Series at the time, a nice car in principle but this one was really old and its one saving grace was that he'd apparently got a good deal on it. The bumpers were hanging off it when we got it, but he'd put it all back together again and it seemed to run all right. Well, until that day of the funeral, when it chose to conk out on the way, meaning that we had to wait for an AA man and were eventually towed to the funeral, arriving late.

I wish I could find the humour in that, but there isn't any. One thing you can say about the funeral of a nine-year-old boy, there's no humour in it. You're not celebrating a life, you're just wondering why it's been taken so soon.

Sure enough, the funeral itself was a wrenching experience. The place was full of kids my age and younger, other karters come to pay their respects alongside shell-shocked mums and dads. The constant sobbing that accompanied the service told its own story.

And nobody knew what to say to Dave. Me most of all. What do you, a fourteen-year-old boy, say to a man who will never see his son grow up to be even your tender age? The wake was held at the Spences' house, a place Dad and I knew as well as our own home, having stayed there so many times, each room still fresh with memories of Danny. There Dave took me to one side, sat me down and, in what I now see as an extraordinary display of courage, explained to me how Danny had died, made sure I understood what was going on, and talked me through it. He told me that I wouldn't get to see Danny again, and although I already understood that, I also knew that these were things Dave needed to say, to help himself through, and they helped him as much as they did me.

*

Dave changed after that. It was hardly surprising that he would, but he'd lost a son, a best friend, a protégé, and I don't want to speak for him but I'm sure it changed him at a really profound, almost cellular level.

For a start, he simply dropped out of karting. No farewells or reasons given, not that we needed any, he simply stopped coming. Jamie was still racing in high formulas but I don't think Dave was even going, he was beside himself with grief. In the end his wife decided that the only thing they could do was get out of the house in which they'd lived with Danny; go and live in Spain, leave the UK altogether.

It was for the best, and for years they stayed out of sight. And then one day in the mid-2000s, I was testing at Barcelona. My dad was there, too, so he got in touch with Dave and invited him down.

It was good to see him again. He was maybe not quite the man he used to be, *reduced*, you might say, by his loss, but he absolutely loved coming down to the track that day. I think it was his first visit to the races since Danny had died.

After that we'd invite him down whenever we were in Spain and he loved the races, but it was testing he liked best. We'd introduced him to all the mechanics and engineers and they were happy to let him stand to one side and watch them work. He'd do that for hours, just watching the mechanics at work. If he had the headphones on and he heard me comment about the car then he'd come to talk to me. 'I think you could change this. You could do it that way.' He's a very special man.

And as for Dan, he was very special, too. When we all got back to karting after the funeral, Danny was a bond we all shared, all us karters, and we knew that we'd always remember him.

17

And in the meantime, I was still trying to be a normal kid and mostly succeeding. I got into music. Prodigy were my favourite. *Music for the Jilted Generation* was my soundtrack to those years, real angry, adrenalin-pumping stuff. I was into movies like *Pulp Fiction* and *Reservoir Dogs*. Clotheswise, I was rocking my Reebok pumps and – don't laugh – a shell suit or Joe Bloggs clothes, which were really big at the time – literally, they were really baggy and swamped you. I got a girlfriend, too, Kimberley, who was in the year below me at school. From the outside, I started to look just like any other normal kid, which of course was exactly where I wanted to be in life.

I took canal holidays with my dad. We used to throw a Safeway bag full of beer overboard to keep the cans cool. In karting I was away competing in the European and World Championships, my nose pointing towards Formula A, which was the next karting category, after which came Formula Super A, after which was cars. I was going all around Europe, America, Japan.

I didn't take GCSEs. No, I tell a lie, I took one: a French SEG modular course that you did as coursework throughout the year. So I got a B in that. But as for sitting down and taking a written exam, I never did.

The reason, of course, was karting, and that was all down to having a really tolerant headmaster who let me have time off to attend races. His thinking was that if I'd shown promise at any other sport, athletics, football, balance-beam whatever, then the school would have been right behind me, giving me leave of absence to develop my talent. 'Why shouldn't we give you the chance to go and drive?' was what he said, and so off I went, with barely a backward glance.

His backing helped enormously. These days, of course, you can't simply gallivant around the world while your schoolmates are sweating it out in an exam hall. You have to take your GCSEs, which makes it a lot trickier for people who want to go into karting.

Even so, it was a massive risk, and not a decision we took lightly, painfully aware that I was putting all my eggs in one basket. That said, I know a lot of guys who didn't finish their education and did very well. Chris – Chrissy Buncombe – was a top student but didn't stay on and study A levels, preferring to concentrate on driving instead – and he's won Le Mans. My PR guy, James Williamson, didn't go to university, either, and he's as bright as they come – you should see him do the numbers round on *Countdown*, he's a demon. It's not like I'd recommend anyone to drop out, but maybe exams don't set us up for adult life as well as we think. After all, my B in French didn't help me. I ended up living in France for seventeen years and the best I could manage was a bit of Franglais. *C'est le truth, guv'nor.*

I understood why Dave had to leave the sport after Danny's death, but I missed him terribly, both as a friend and as a teacher. I'd have to wait to reconnect with him on the first score, but as far as coaching went I was lucky to find another good tutor in the form of a Belgian guy called

Paul Lemmens. I'd joined Paul's team, GKS, in 1995 when I moved into Formula A. It was a great team, where I found myself temporary teammates with Sophie Kumpen, who was dating Jos Verstappen and two years later had a baby with him. In other words, I raced with Max Verstappen's mum, which is one of those things, like policemen getting younger, that you try not to think about. Later I got to race with Jos and Max, so I've got the full house there.

But anyway, Paul took me under his wing. He was a tough guy, hard on his drivers but fair with it, and for the last year of my karting career was even paying me, which was a first. He brought me into the family, and I spent a lot of time in Belgium, Genk to be exact, where me and another driver, Jan Heylen, were almost permanent houseguests. To pay for our upkeep we were put to work, working on karts and running them in.

Meantime I was making a name for myself in Formula A, and that year went to the World Championships, winning the semi-final on soft tyres that I absolutely loved.

Into the final we went and I built up a good head of steam; only the two behind had any hope of catching me. I was gripping the wheel, teeth set, thinking, *This is it, I'm about to win the World Championship*, when suddenly the tyres just went and the next thing I knew, I was slipping and sliding all over the place. I'd forgotten Dave's lesson about tyre use and pushed them too hard in the semi. I was overtaken, knocked down into third. I managed to claw back a place but in the end I finished second, absolutely gutted, because although I'd still come second in the World Championship I knew I could have won.

What I should have done, of course, was settle for a third or fourth in the semi and conserve the tyres for the final, but it's easy to be wise in retrospect.

In 1996, I did enough to win an invite into the following year's Formula Super A, which was the last karting category prior to car racing and easily the most prestigious. There I found myself in the last round of the Formula Super A European Championship, a tournament formed of eight races at four locations all over Europe, which meant that every weekend you had two races, one on Saturday and one on Sunday.

The final weekend was at my local track in Genk. I knew it so well. I'd probably done more laps on it than anyone else there. What's more, it was raining. I fancied my chances for the European Championship. Bring it on.

18

The track at Genk was tight and twisty, which in theory isn't good for me as a tall driver, because there's grip down below and weight up high, and the kart jumps on those tight corners, which in turn bangs your ribs against the side, which in turn is like *Ow*.

But I loved it anyway. Even with bruised ribs. All those fast-flowing corners, lots of little chicanes you can throw the kart over. It was perfect racing.

The stands were crowded that day, I remember. I'd never seen them that busy before. This was the European Championship, after all, and we'd drawn a big crowd, mainly families, probably the biggest attendance I'd had at a race up to then. Assembled were the best drivers from all over the world. Each kart was stickered with its national flag and looking around I saw the flags of Japan, Australia, America, Italy, Norway, Sweden… There were lots of Italians – they love their racing. Lots of Scandinavians – ditto. *Oh my God*, I was thinking. *All these spectators, all these drivers, here at what is basically my home circuit.*

Saturday, I qualified second for the final; Sunday, the hour of the race, and we lined up and began inching forward for a rolling start, two by two, waiting for the lights to go green and set us free.

By this stage I knew that all I had to do was finish third. It literally didn't matter where anyone else placed. As long as I came third or higher then I'd be European Champion.

At the same time, I was concerned about three other guys on the grid who were also in contention, one of them being the Italian Giorgio Pantano, who went on to race in Formula One and Formula 3000, a karter that other drivers like Nico Rosberg and Fernando Alonso revered. All through my international karting career, from fourteen to seventeen, Pantano was my main rival, and one of the things I remember most about him was that in Italy, where kids were allowed to drink, he'd always go into the bar before a race and down a grappa.

Also on the grid were Alessandro Manetti, who still had a title shout, as well as Johnny Mislijevic. Those two I'd have to watch. They would want to see to it that I didn't come third. Talking beforehand, Dad and I knew full well that given half a chance they'd try to spin me off.

The lights went to green and I floored it, jumping the kart, willing it to pick up speed quickly and terrified that Mislijevic was going to come at me from behind. We thundered along to turn one, a corner I must have taken a thousand times.

Disaster. I was so worried about Mislijevic that I overshot, braked too late, locked the rear tyres and slid off the circuit in a sideways spray of gravel and rainwater. I glanced up and saw the old man. He'd been standing at the turn to watch out for argy bargy but right now he was yelling, urging me back on track, just like he did that first-ever race. By now the whole field had shot by, putting me in last place. I was still moving, though, no need to get out of the kart, lift the rear, run and then jump in, which was the usual way of starting a stalled kart. So there was that at least.

Fortune shot me another smile. At turn two a pile-up had put four or five karts out of the game and I sailed through the carnage, no longer last and back in the chase.

And now I started picking off some of the back markers, Prodigy playing in my head. Choosing my lines, totally focused but – and this was something new to me – angry. Furious with myself for having made such a mess of turn one and determined to repay the faith shown in me by Paul, my dad, Dave, everyone. My moves were aggressive. I was shooting up the inside, taking out kart after kart. There were thirty-four racers that day, and I managed to make it up to fourth with about eight laps to go when at last I had sight of Pantano in the lead.

I needed to be third.

And then Pantano hit the kerb. He hit it so hard that he broke the chain, and on a chain-driven go-kart that's terminal. Game over for him.

I was in third. The championship was mine.

As long as I stayed in third.

In first place was Mislijevic with Manetti behind (it might have been the other way around, but it was definitely those two) and they were teammates, so Manetti started to slow down and impede my progress in the hope that I'd be overtaken, lose my third-place spot and thus the championship.

I glanced behind and saw another kart, Max Orsini, closing fast. The laps came and went and we tussled, Manetti slowing me down and backing me up as Orsini threatened to pass, but I held him off, repelling attack after attack, until by the last lap he was right on my bumper, a hair's breadth away, close enough to try an overtaking move and with nothing to lose, no reason not to at least try.

The final corner loomed. That's where he'd do it.

If I could just hold him off on the corner.

We screamed into it. My line was good but his would be, too, and the next split-second was crucial; the timing of the brakes would decide who won the corner. I held my nerve, banishing visions of my turn-one lock-up, time slowing down and daring to brake late – later at least than Orsini who stayed on my tail, weaving in frustration but without the momentum to get past.

I came out of the corner still in third and that was how it ended – Mislijevic, with Manetti, Button and Orsini nose to tail across the finish line. And I was European Champion, easily the biggest win of my career to date.

All this on the team's home track as well. Paul Lemmens was crying. I'd never seen a grown man cry before, and certainly not someone like Paul, who's really tough. The whole team was jumping up and down with joy, the old man was leaping, capering. The celebrations would go on for days.

Before the race I'd said to the guys that if I won we'd all shave our heads, the whole team, and we all did apart from Paul and my dad.

A shaved head is not the look for me, I soon realised. I've got a really lumpy back to my head. Kim said, 'Oh my God, I'm glad this is for a good reason, because it looks awful.'

I didn't care. I was European champion.

Next stop, the big leagues.

19

Somewhere around this time I took my driving test. During the test I had one of those situations with cars parked on your side of the road, which in theory means you should give way to oncoming traffic. In this particular instance I had heaps of time to get past a row of parked cars before I met the approaching car so I pressed on and it would have been fine, except the lady coming in the opposite direction panicked and went up the kerb, which she had absolutely no need to do. God's honour. But the examiner said it was dangerous driving. That was actually what she said. Not 'careless' or 'reckless', but 'dangerous', like I was Mad Max or something.

'Have I passed?'

'No, Mr Button, you have not.'

It was all a bit embarrassing, to be honest.

Still, I passed second time round. But the real kicker is that now I live in the States I've got to take my driving test *again*, and assuming I can keep my Mel Gibson tendencies in check and pass, my insurance will be through the roof, even though I've been driving for something like twenty years. I have to take my motorbike test again. The things you do for love, eh?

Back to the late nineties, and having passed my test I'd used prize money – *prize money* – from my wins to kit myself out with a second-hand Cavalier. My dad had said, 'All right, Jense, here's a bit of an incentive. If you win the European Championship I'll get you a new set of wheels for your car,' and of course I won, so as well as an off-putting haircut, a fancy carbon-fibre trophy and the attention of the motorsport world, I also got some new wheels for my Cavalier. They were seventeen-inch twin five-spoke jobbies that perfectly complemented my other modifications. Remember *Max Power* magazine? That was me. Archetypal reader. I got the suspension lowered so it handled like a kart, installed big speakers in the back and de-badged it. The bumpers were black plastic so I got them colour coded (i.e., I sprayed them the same colour as the rest of the car). By the time I'd finished it looked so cool that I got stopped by the police once, and this is no word of a lie, the guy didn't know what make of car it was.

He said, 'What are you driving there?'

I was thinking, *Are you serious? It's the most common car on the road.*

'It's a Cavalier,' I deadpanned.

'Well you've got a light out,' he said, with a just a hint of colour in his cheeks.

I think I may have said that I don't drive fast on the roads, and that's true now I'm thirty-seven. But when I had that car I was seventeen and being a right pain-in-the-arse boy racer I drove it fast all the time, like. There was one particular occasion when me, Kim and a bunch of friends took a trip to Newquay, the idea being that we'd do a bit of surfing, have a McDonald's, normal stuff; me and Kim in the Cavalier, a couple of mates in other cars.

Half-past seven in the morning and we arrived at a little spot to park up before taking steps down to the beach. It would have been idyllic but for the fact that there were already a couple of guys in Metros doing doughnuts on the grass, round and round, baseball caps on, grinning like gibbons, high on life.

At that age you're eager to take up any challenge, even when no challenge has been made, and deciding to show them what I was made of, I put my foot down, piled on to the grass, wrenched the wheel and pulled on the handbrake at the same time.

It should have been a showstopping handbrake turn and probably would have been, but for two things: one, I was in a big Cavalier, not a nimble little Metro, and two, the grass was still dewy and I had no traction and thus, as instantly became apparent, no control. Kim in the passenger seat began screaming. In slow motion we watched the two Metros part, and with all the beauty and choreography of a synchronised swimmer we slid perfectly between them, the back end of the Cavalier swinging lazily around. As we circled I saw their faces in the rear-view mirror, mouths dropping open in surprise before the view was replaced by one of the cliff edge as we slid inexorably towards it, the sea glittering beyond.

This is it, I thought. *We're going to go over the cliff and we're going to die and they're going to write 'Here Lies Jesper Button' on my gravestone.*

Immediately before the sheer drop to the beach below was a gravel path and it's that path that I have to thank for the fact that I'm alive to tell this story. Traction was at last achieved and we came to a queasy halt inches (oh, all right then, a couple of metres) from the cliff edge.

Kim was angry at first but then thought it was hilarious. I thanked my lucky stars that we were alive (and I wasn't in the doghouse). We spent the rest of the day surfing and messing around until suddenly she looked at her watch and gave a start. 'I'm going to be late for work.'

My confidence was fully restored after the near-death experience. 'I'll get you there,' I said, and to be fair, that's exactly what I did. It was just that after reaching 134mph on the motorway, sliding sideways through an amber light on the handbrake, skidding into the car park of the Red Lion, turning to her and saying, 'See? We made it!', she was in no fit state to work.

20

Not long ago a crate arrived from the UK with about twenty-five of my crash helmets in it.

Brittny took one look at them. 'What are we going to do with all these?'

'These can go in the boy's room,' I beamed.

'Boy's room? What boy's room?'

That particular showdown would have to wait for another day.

I've got another seventy-five or so helmets in a storage facility in Essex, along with my trophies, one of the most treasured of which is that one for the European Super A Championship, which at that point was by far the most awesome trophy I'd ever seen in the flesh, let alone been a recipient of.

It turned out that one of the great things about winning the champs was that it's an FIA-run series, which meant that I got to attend the FIA Awards, gawp at drivers from other categories and collect my carbon-fibre trophy with 'FIA' written on it.

I hadn't won the World Championship of karting that year. I was running second when my engine failed. Later on that year I was fighting for the lead in Japan for the World Cup when my chain broke and like I say, that's terminal. I did, however, win the Ayrton Senna Memorial

Cup, awarded for the most combative driver during the weekend. I'd overtaken fourteen karts to get to the front, and if it hadn't been for that chain … well, let's say it was bit of a disappointment. I certainly knew how Giorgio Pantano had felt at the Euros.

So now I was officially a big noise in the world of karting I was faced with a decision. Although I could have stayed there, in my mind I already knew that I wanted to race cars, which meant finding a drive. Formula Ford was the next logical step, but despite Dad and I hunting around for seats and a couple of opportunities arising, things didn't quite pan out for one reason or another.

Doubts began to creep in. Lurking in the back of my mind was the thought that I'd left school for this. Driving was supposed to be my career. In my last year of karting I'd been paid – an actual wage for driving – but for now I was earning a bit of extra cash working in Dad's karting shop.

It felt like a bit of a comedown. On the one hand it was something of a draw for the shop to have the European karting champion stripping engines out the back. But at the same time the expected interest from agents and managers hadn't quite materialised. This was supposed to be my Alice-through-the-looking-glass moment. So far it felt like I'd just walked into a mirror and bumped my head.

Then came a stroke of good fortune. A Norwegian guy called Harald Huysman, a former racing driver now based in Belgium, got talking to Paul Lemmens. Chewing the fat, Harald asked Paul who were the three best karters he'd ever seen. Ever.

'Not three, two,' replied Paul. 'Just two: Ayrton Senna and Jenson Button.'

'Who?' said Harald. And he wasn't asking about Ayrton.

Paul told him all about me – a glowing report, obviously, because Harald was interested enough to tell a British guy called Dave Robertson, who was keen to manage a driver and steer him into Formula One.

Shortly after that the phone in Vobster was ringing and Dave was on the line. He wanted me to test a Formula Three car at Pembrey in Wales. Did I fancy doing that? He was bit cagey about it. Stingy with the details, you might say. But off we went anyway.

We arrived to find reps in attendance from Carlin Motorsport, who were major players. What's more, the car was a 220bhp carbon-fibre composite Dallara Mugen-Honda, not the nail we'd been expecting. This was a proper shot.

I did all right, considering the car was different from anything I'd raced before. It had gears, for a start, although I'm pleased to say I got the hang of them fairly quickly. The other major difference was, of course, downforce.

A wing on a Formula One car operates like the wing on an aeroplane except in reverse. So whereas the aircraft wing generates lift, the wing on a car does the opposite, pushing the car down to the surface of the track and creating aerodynamic grip or downforce.

Broadly speaking, the faster you go the more of that aerodynamic grip you generate, so in a low-speed corner your downforce is minimal and therefore your traction is mechanical, but as you pick up speed, the car moves from using mechanical to aerodynamic grip.

This means you can achieve shitloads of traction in high-speed corners, which in turn allows you to carry a lot of speed into them. If you're coming from a form of racing that doesn't use downforce then dealing with that fact messes with your head. You have to recalibrate your racing brain to accept the fact that – up to a certain point at least – your grip will increase with speed.

It's totally counter-intuitive, like eating fat to get thin. You're thinking, Are you sure about this? Are you sure this is right? because it goes against everything you've learned up to that point; it seems to contradict the very laws of physics.

As with so much racecraft, using downforce correctly is all about timing and working the numbers, listening and reacting to the car. You may need to take a corner at a certain perfect-downforce-generating speed. Dip below that speed and you will have less grip which may cause you to run off track or spin. On the other hand, if you push it too far you'll be going too fast to make the corner.

I'm not sure you ever stop learning about downforce, but that day in Pembrey was the beginning of my education, and I managed to get the basics on that first test, which was good because a lot of drivers can't make the leap. I know plenty who are bloody good in a normal car, but put them in a downforce-generating car and they're just not as competitive.

Meanwhile, if you asked me which I prefer, mechanical grip or aerodynamic grip, I couldn't give you a definite answer, apart from saying that if you could get as much mechanical grip as we do from downforce, I'd rather do it with mechanical grip. The reason for that is the racing's better, because you don't lose that mechanical grip when you're following another car, whereas with downforce, you do. That's why in Formula One we have all these systems now, like DRS – Drag Reduction System – to make it possible to overtake.

Still, I got a good enough handle on downforce and looked confident enough in the car that Dave and Harald offered me a management contract. The percentage they wanted was eye-watering but otherwise they seemed like a good option.

'We want you to race in Formula Three,' they said. It wasn't unknown to make the jump straight from karting. Jarno Trulli had done it, for one. But…

'I can't race in Formula Three,' I told them. 'I've got no experience of car racing and I don't want to make the mistake of jumping in a Formula Three car and not being competitive straight away.'

It was decided I should do Formula Ford for a year. So I did that for a year and won the British and World Championship, as it was called. That was very satisfying, of course, but I didn't especially enjoy it as a formula. The racing was action-packed but the cars weren't fun to drive; they were lazy, slow and unresponsive, and because they were low-powered and had no downforce you'd just drift through corners.

Still, I did my bit, and although I didn't really enjoy the racing I did well, which was the main thing at that stage of the game. After which came another break. I won the McLaren Autosport Young Driver Award, previously won by the likes of David Coulthard (DC) and Dario Franchitti. The format was that you had to take a series of different tests in different cars, a Formula Three, a 300 horsepower British Touring car – which was amazing – and a couple of others. From that I won a huge amount, £50,000, plus a Tag Heuer watch that I still own.

Now there was a bit of heat beneath me. The good kind of heat, where you know that people are talking about you, and what they're saying is complimentary.

That year I went to the Spanish GP in Barcelona with Harald, who wanted me to schmooze, network and glad-hand as many people as possible. This was only my third-ever GP, and here I was in the paddock, behind the velvet curtain in the presence of the gods I'd admired growing up. I was introduced to a dozen or so big names in the sport, including Patrick Head, Frank Williams and even Keke Rosberg, who used to be my dad's favourite driver back in the day.

Keke had his son Nico with him, who's five years younger than me but was acting even younger that day. He was pulling at his dad's arm as we were talking, trying to pull him away.

I remember looking down at him, silently cursing him for messing up my introduction to Keke, thinking, 'God, just leave us alone.'

21

It took me a while to get a seat in Formula Three. Nobody really wanted to take a punt on an inexperienced driver. The age-old problem: how do you get experience if nobody will give you the chance to gain it?

Still, Dave and Harald pushed hard to find a drive, and got in touch with Serge Saulnier who was running Promatecme, a team based in France that used Renault engines.

'We can't take Jenson,' Serge told them. 'All of our drivers need to come through the Renault programme and Jenson isn't a Renault driver.'

Undeterred, they kept pestering him. And then the guys from Mygale, my Formula Ford team, started hounding him, too, saying, 'You have to just test him, you have to test him,' and then Paul Lemmens, from Belgium joined the chorus, until at last Serge finally caved.

'All right, I'll test him.'

Off we went to Magny-Cours in France, a beautiful circuit I'd never previously visited. I was the only non-Renault driver there and determined to prove myself.

I did a run of ten laps. As I came in, Serge smiled at me. I was looking back at him thinking, *I don't really know what that smile means.*

Then he shook his head, and I was like, *oh God, I really don't understand now* and then he came over and said, 'You can get out now.'

A short while later he called us into his truck. 'If you want it, you've got the drive,' he said.

Just like that. Eighteen years old and I had a drive in Formula Three. In short order – and full credit to Dave and Harald here – I had a sponsorship deal with Marlboro and Fina too.

Brilliant. Serge took over the mantle of coach, doing what my dad and Dave and Paul had done before him. He gave me part two of the downforce lesson, which boiled down to the fact that it's all very well using downforce on a test in Pembrey, but there's a lot more to consider when it comes to a race situation.

For a start, you have to be aware of the fact that downforce can easily be disrupted. You hit a bump, the seal is broken and suddenly you lose it. The other thing to watch out for is a sudden change in wind direction, which can completely change the way the car feels. Same as if you're following a car closely: that dirty air we've mentioned means you lose downforce. The floor is producing downforce and that's not affected when you're following a car but the wings are. Get close enough to the car in front and it feels like the pit crew have taken the wings off. You literally have to change the whole way you drive at a split-second's notice. Suddenly you're driving a mechanical car, rather than an aerodynamic one.

This is why it's so difficult to overtake in Formula One and Formula Three, because as soon as you get in position, you go through a corner and while the guy ahead has got full grip you've lost 30 per cent of yours, which means that when you turn in, you've got more front slide and more rear slide and the gap opens again. That's why, when you get a chance, you have to make a move instantly, because as soon as he's gathered himself he's got more grip than you.

It was Serge who gave me the grounding in that, though like I say, you're always learning. I've never stopped.

The only fly in the ointment of that time was that while Promatecme were great at set-up they were let down by the engines, which weren't quite fast enough. That season I won three races, qualified on pole four or five times, finished third in the championship and I was top rookie. Even so it was disappointing. To be honest, I felt I should have won.

So at the end of the year I had a decision to make. Where next? I had itchy feet and I didn't really want another year in Formula Three so I tested a Formula 3000, which was the next natural step up, but it was a monstrosity. It used a sequential gearbox and you had to be really aggressive with it. I just didn't like the way it drove. The test went okay, but I didn't enjoy it at all.

Then, at the end of 1999, I tested a McLaren F1 car at Silverstone as part of my Young Driver of the Year award prize. It was only thirty laps, not much, but I invested a lot into it. I told myself it was either going to help me get into F1, or it was going to be the end of my career. This or that. No in-between.

22

Arriving, what struck me first was the sheer size of the McLaren operation. In Formula Three, we had two mechanics and an engineer and that was it. Here there were what felt like hordes of mechanics and engineers working on a single car, not to mention the truckies, whose job it is to look after the tyres and keep them warm, catering, PR, marketing. The whole shebang.

Zipped into my suit, clutching my helmet, I fought down a feeling that I didn't belong here; that I was an imposter and would soon be found out, kicked out on my arse.

I was to be driving the car that had won the championship the year before. Mika Häkkinen's car. The conditions were tricky that day. It had been wet, so it was drying but not quite dry enough for slicks, so we had to run wets.

I came out of the pits on my installation lap, which is a warm-up lap you do to run the car in and get a feel for it before you return to the pits so the crew can check it over, give you the all-clear and send you back out again.

God, the difference in this car. Going from 240 horsepower to 800 horsepower was a quantum leap. The car felt crouched beneath me, ready to spring forward and fly, yet at the same time obedient, awaiting my command. It had a smooth feel, flowing like water in the direction of my thoughts. I wasn't wrestling with it as you are with so many cars. I was guiding it.

I was still tentative, of course, braking early, not full on the throttle, getting to grips with the car, but with an increasing sense that I could really push this thing. Like, give me a bit more time in this and I'll be taking it to the limit. Cheesy, I know, but I felt at one with it.

Along the back straight a voice came over the radio. 'How's the car?'

The radio had a blue flashing light and I switched it on to reply. 'This is amazing,' I screamed at them, busting eardrums. When I drew in, everybody in the pits was wearing big smiles, feeding off my enthusiasm. Dad was there, as nervous as I was, maybe more so, the way you are when matters are outside of your control. But he was smiling, too, and I knew why, and it was because he could vividly remember the kid in his pyjamas who sat in his first kart on Christmas Day. And here was that same kid, in the cockpit of an F1 car, making the pit crew grin.

'Try not to stall it on the way out of the garage,' I was told, and that would have been even more embarrassing than failing my driving test, so I took it easy, eased it back out on to the track with pride intact and began my laps.

Oh, the buzz. The feeling like, *Mama, I'm home*. It felt so natural, was the thing. For so long I'd dreamed of being in Formula One. It had never really occurred to me that I simply might not be suited to it. Here I was, though: absolutely loving it.

By the end of the run, the tyres were starting to be eaten up because the track was too dry. They didn't want to put me on dry tyres for some reason, but were happy for me to go out again.

'No,' I said, 'that's enough', which was a wrench. I could have driven that car all day. But on the other hand I knew that if I went out again it would be a pointless run. I didn't want to leave them with visions of me slipping and sliding all over the place. I wanted them to remember my last run.

I had a chat with the engineers. As much as the driving they were interested in seeing how I debriefed the run, which is basically feeding back information on how it drove, the balance of it and so on. I got changed in the McLaren truck and stepped back out. The team were looking my way. Waves. Winks. 'Well done, lad.' I was in no danger of feeling like an imposter now. Nineteen years old and I strode through the paddock feeling like a Formula One driver. It was a surreal but utterly brilliant feeling.

Again, though, it wasn't quite the Alice moment I'd hoped for. I had a lot of fun and done well, but I pretty soon clocked that it didn't really mean a great deal to the team. It wasn't like putting a sponsor in the car for a jolly, but neither was it what you'd call a proper test. Belatedly, the penny dropped. That's why they didn't want to put me on dry tyres.

Coming down to earth – *bump, ouch* – Kim and I took a holiday to Cancun in Mexico. We were supposed to be there for two weeks. That was the plan anyway.

23

To be honest, I'm a bit of a nightmare on holidays. Unless I'm doing something, I get bored. So it was in Cancun. Sitting on a beach was dull, so I managed to persuade Kim out on the speedboats – anything to do with speed – but there's only so much speed-boating you can do, and by the beginning of the second week boredom was beginning to creep in.

And then one morning we were in the room when the phone rang. It was Dave. 'Jenson,' he said, 'you need to go to Barcelona.'

'But Dave, I'm on holiday,' I replied, 'I can't just leave—'

'Trust me,' he said. 'You want to come back. Alain Prost wants you to test.'

'You what?'

'Yup. Full day of testing, mate, from nine a.m. to five p.m.'

I was sitting on the edge of the bed in Cancun trying to process this latest bit of information. Alain Prost was my hero. He wanted me to test. And not a competition-winner test either. A proper one.

'Why?' I said. 'Why does he want to test me?'

Dave chuckled. This was a coup for him. Big for us all. 'He wants to see if you're as good as everybody keeps telling him you are.'

*

Kim was cool about it. Throughout our relationship she never really *got* motor racing, and I don't suppose she could really comprehend how deep my passion went, but she certainly understood how much it meant to me.

They sorted us tickets from Cancun to Madrid and then on to Barcelona. Dad was there at the airport with my helmet, my old Formula Ford overalls and a tear in his eye. A taxi took us to a hotel up in the hills, which looked down upon the Circuit de Catalunya, the sight of it bringing things home to me. We went to our room, showered and changed. December and of course it had been boiling in Cancun but it was a lot cooler in Barcelona so I wasn't dressed for the weather – not quite Bermuda shorts but near enough as we took another taxi down to the track, where I was introduced to Alain Prost.

I'd met him before, but it was during the whirlwind whistle-stop schmoozefest of the Spanish GP in 1998, so was all a bit of blur and I hadn't been in the right frame of mind to savour the meeting. Talking to him now, he really was 'the professor' in person. Calm, very relaxed and cerebral – everything you want Alain Prost to be.

'Just enjoy the test,' he purred, and I couldn't help but hear an echo of Dad in those words. 'Enjoy the test, give as much feedback as you can.'

I spent the rest of the afternoon being fitted for my seat, nervous excitement growing. This was a different feeling from the McLaren Silverstone test, which I'd built into something make-or-break, thinking I had to show them what I was made of. But here I felt they'd invited *me*, not because I'd won a prize and they fancied a bit of extra feedback on the car, but because I'd stood on podiums clutching trophies. Because I'd impressed people that Alain trusted. They wanted to see if I was good enough to drive for Prost.

To put it another way: these guys weren't going to stint on the tyres.

Back to the hotel. Beddy-byes. Then rise and shine and taxi to the circuit, where because all the prep had been done the day before it was just a quick pep talk and then straight in the car.

Jean Alesi had been testing for the last two days. His best was 1m 24.9s in fine conditions. The day of my test the weather was fine too, and I went out with a similar fuel load and the same tyres. 'If you do a 1m 28s lap at the end of the day, that's very, very good,' they told me. 'If you do a 1m 27.9s that's fantastic. But don't worry about lap times. Just learn the car and learn the track.'

They started it up and oh, the sound of that V10, a rich growl that reached right into my soul, and off I went on my installation lap.

'Everything okay?' they said, when I came back in the pits.

Thinking: *Just hurry up and check the bloody car so I can get back out there.*

But saying: 'Yes, thank you. Everything's brilliant, thank you.'

Got back out and I was just loving this. More than the McLaren? I don't know. You never forget your first. But definitely *as much*. And this in Barcelona too.

The last two corners of the Circuit de Catalunya are really fast right-handers. You take the second-to-last pretty much flat-out and the last corner just off full power. I came round there the first lap and I nailed the kerb on the exit. In other words, I used the full width of the track, going to the very edge of the kerb. An inch wider and I would have been off. But I nailed it. I trusted the car. It felt like I had so much grip I could do whatever I wanted.

There were other guys testing that day. Apparently, Humphrey Corbett, a Prost race engineer, had been in the garage and heard a car come round. 'It was using all the road and all the revs,' he said later.

'I went to the pit wall and asked when Jenson was due round, and somebody said, "That was him going round then."

'And I thought, *That couldn't have been, because the guy was on it. Using the kerbs.* People on their first run usually take it easy, but he was inch-perfect on his exit of the corner and his speed on the straight was within 10kmh of Jean's the previous day. He really was on it.'

Pretty cool. They were like, *The kid learns quick.* But the fact is I was having a blast out there. I was doing what my dad had always said I should. I was taking Alain Prost's advice. I was just enjoying myself.

Every lap of that test was so enjoyable, the team so great to work with. The only problem, and I've since learnt this is true of most tests (the McLaren one being an exception), is that the team remain inscrutable. I'm telling you, they've got the composure of Russian chess grandmasters. They don't give anything away. You're looking for a reaction. 'Well? Well?' And you get zero. Blankface. Not even a little wink to let you know you're doing okay.

Anyway, on the thirty-third lap, I went round turn three which is a really fast right-hander and the engine seized. When that happens the wheels go solid and suddenly the car's a skateboard, except a weird kind of skateboard that slides sideways off the track, leaving fat rubber marks on the track. That was the end of my session

Turned out my best lap was 1m 24.4s, which was 3.5 seconds faster than they expected but, even more thrilling, half a second faster than Jean Alesi the previous day.

There are two problems with a test at this level. Firstly, 'test' can mean a multitude of things depending on what the team want it to mean, including but not limited to: 'We'd like to test the car and want your feedback.' 'We want to test you.' 'We want to audition you for a possible drive.' 'We want to get the measure of you before the competition does.' And, 'Oh, why the hell not.'

And the second problem is that they don't tell you which of those things they mean by the test. More than likely they're not quite sure or haven't yet decided themselves but either way, it can result in a period of 'so, what now?' on the part of the driver, which is exactly where I was left after my thirty-two-and-a-bit laps. I'd loved driving the car, everyone was great – Alain, Humphrey, the rest of the team – but they were playing their cards close to their chest.

'The times were good,' we said as we left the track that day, feeling none the wiser, knowing only that we'd 'hear' – about what, we didn't quite know – in the next fortnight.

'The times were good but it's about more than that, Jense,' said the old man. 'They need to know how you integrate with the team, how you feed back, all of that.'

We were waiting for our lift back to the hotel. I'd gone from the exhilaration of the test to feeling a bit confused and disconsolate.

'I thought I did that all right.'

'They've already got two drivers.'

'Yeah. So what now, then?'

'Dunno.'

Just then I noticed how cold it was in Barcelona compared to Cancun. I was thinking, *What do I have to do? What more can I do to prove myself?*

It was about a week later, maybe even less, that they invited us out to Prost in Paris, where we sat down with Alain hopeful that he'd end our uncertainty, preferably with an offer.

What's the expression? 'Be careful what you wish for, you might just get it.' Alain made an offer. He wanted me to join the team as their Formula 3000 driver for two years, then one year as a test driver and then into Formula One.

It wasn't appealing. Not because I'd expected to leap straight on to the frontline of their F1 operation; I was happy to pay my dues, and spending a couple more years honing my racecraft was a good idea if – and here was where more doubt crept in – *if* they definitely offered me an F1 drive at the end of it.

The problem was that they weren't prepared to commit to that bit of the contract. Effectively I could be throwing away three years of my career on what was little more than a promise.

But we didn't say no, and off we went home to celebrate Christmas in Frome, where on Christmas Eve I found myself with a few mates having a lunchtime drink in the Vine Tree. It was a proper old-school, sticky-floor pub, notorious among me and my friends for its all-you-can-eat lunches. Me and my mate Brad took advantage of the offer to stage gargantuan eating competitions, which was a bit daft, but considering this was the period I was driving my Cavalier off cliffs and going at warp speed down the motorway, very much in the spirit of the times.

So anyway, that was the Vine Tree. Things would likely get a bit lairy later, but it was only lunchtime, we hadn't got stuck in just yet, maybe like half a pint down, when the phone rang.

'Hello, is that Jenson?'

Posh voice. Alarm bells.

'Yeah,' I said. 'Who's that?'

'It's Frank Williams.'

24

What do you say when a legend of motor racing calls you out of the blue? My advice is you don't say what I did.

'Who?'

'Frank Williams.'

'Oh, come on, who is it really? Dad, is that you?'

Suspecting it might be a wind-up, somebody doing an impression, I tapped Brad on the shoulder, gave him googly eyes – *is this your work?* – and he looked at me like, *What? What's the matter?* clearly not a scooby what was going on.

'No, Jenson, it's Frank Williams.'

Fucking hell. Hardly able to believe it, I scooted outdoors to escape the noise.

'Uh, hello. Hello, Frank.'

It was cold in the car park, but quiet. My dragon breath bloomed.

'Can you hear me all right, Jenson?' It was him all right. There was no mistaking that distinctive voice. Well spoken, but with an almost frail quality.

'Yes. I can now, thanks…'

Do I call him 'Frank'? 'Mr Williams'?

'…Frank.'

'Good. I hope you don't mind me calling on Christmas Eve, but I wanted to make sure you don't think I'm not interested in your career, just because I haven't phoned you yet,' he said.

'No, of course not,' I said.

Frank Williams' failure to contact me had never been an issue, I must admit. I'd met him during the schmoozefest and, like everyone who encounters Frank for the first time, I'd been in awe of him. After all, he's part of racing folklore, a team owner of the old school. As I'm sure you know, he had a serious car accident in 1986 that left him a tetraplegic, confined to a wheelchair for the rest of his life. His life-goes-on fortitude in the face of that alone is an absolute inspiration. And that's before you consider his track record in the sport. Running the Williams team with Patrick Head, he was the man behind championships won by Nigel Mansell, Damon Hill and Alain Prost, to name a few. He's genuinely one of the blokes about whom you can honestly say that they broke the mould when they made him. And here he was apologising for not having been in touch.

'Your test seemed to go very well – your test with Prost,' he said.

I wasn't sure how he knew about my test with Prost; it's not like teams are in the habit of merrily exchanging information. But there you go. It remains a mystery.

'Thanks,' I said.

'Do you think you're ready for a season in Formula One?' he asked.

And of course I said…

'No, Frank. Truthfully, no. I don't think I'm ready.'

There was a pause. 'I see. Well that's a shame. Perhaps we'll talk in the future, then. Merry Christmas, Jenson.'

'Merry Christmas, Frank.'

The call ended.

Oh God.

Why did I say that?

It wasn't just the cold that made my fingers shake as I dialled my dad's number.

'Dad, I've just told Frank Williams I'm not ready for Formula One.'

Sharp intake of breath. Silence. And then, 'For fuck's sake, Jense, what did you say that for?'

'Because it's the truth.'

'It's not.'

'It is.'

'It's not. Bit more testing and you'd be on it. Look – look how you did at Prost, for fuck's sake. But anyway, anyway, that's not the point. The point is that you don't go telling somebody you're not ready for it. You don't go telling Frank bloody Williams you're not ready for it. You got his number?'

I did. Frank bloody Williams's number was now inside my fancy flip-up Sony Ericsson.

'Yeah.'

'Then ring him back right away. Quick.'

I did. I hit the callback button. Got through straight away.

'Oh, hello, Jenson.'

'Uh, hello, Frank,' I said. 'Um, I think I am ready. I mean, I *am* ready. What I said a moment was just a reaction. I think I was a bit shocked by you calling.'

'Well, that's excellent,' he said, as though he'd known I'd be ringing back. 'We'll schedule a meeting.'

And that was it. That was how I spoke to Frank Williams in the car park of the Vine Tree pub in Frome on Christmas Eve.

Why did I tell him I wasn't ready? Good question, and I'm not altogether sure of the answer if I'm honest. After all, I'd been tooling around Silverstone and the Circuit de Catalunya in F1 cars and loving it, gagging to get out there and do it again in race conditions. Dad was right, a bit more testing and I would have been fine.

Perhaps it was the setting. Perhaps a little doubt crept into that cold pub car park in Frome on Christmas Eve. Or maybe it was Frank. *The* Frank Williams. Calling me up. Catching me on the hop. Perhaps my nerve temporarily failed me. Maybe I wanted Frank to say what my dad had said. I wanted *him* to tell *me* I was ready.

Or maybe just a brain fart.

Either way, as I stood there in the car park with my phone in my hand I began to feel my initial excitement ebb away a little. Another meeting. No doubt another test. If things ran true to form it'd all come to nothing.

Still, I thought. Might as well celebrate. I ducked back into the pub.

25

After a Christmas where, true to form, Mum spoiled me rotten, Dave Robertson and I visited the Williams Factory at Grove in Oxfordshire. There I was given a tour of the works – didn't see any F1 cars, funnily enough – before being ushered into Frank's office, which was the sort with windows all around so Frank could keep an eye on the staff.

In the office was me, Dave, Frank, and his assistant, Hamish. You don't shake Frank's hand, we discovered. He hasn't quite got the movement. We took our seats, we got down to brass tacks.

'Hello, Jenson, thank you so much for coming,' he said. It was always 'thank you for coming' from him. He was a tough character but unfailingly polite.

Meanwhile I was practically levitating with excitement. Phoned on Christmas Eve. Given a tour of the factory. Now summoned to the inner sanctum. I was allowing myself to believe that they were going to offer me the position of test driver. Maybe even race driver.

Frank said, 'I have a list of drivers that I'm thinking of for race driver and test driver next year,' said Frank.

He paused. I swallowed, ready.

'And you're not on either of them.'

Oh. I looked at my manager.

'But I would like to test you,' added Frank. 'I'd like to test you in our car.'

Nodding. Okay, Okay. Thinking, *What now?*

'The test is at Jerez,' said Hamish, pronouncing it 'hereth', which is how most people tend to pronounce it – being as that's how it's pronounced.

'No, it's not. It's in Jerez,' corrected Frank, pronouncing it the Brits-on-holiday way. 'We're not bloody Spanish, we're English and we pronounce our letters like we're English. So Jerez is where we're testing.'

So off we went to Jerez in January, a private test for Williams and two drivers, myself and a guy called Bruno Junqueira, who had just won the Formula 3000 Championship and had been a test driver at Williams in 1999. These days there are lots of restrictions on testing – when you can, when you can't, what you've got to wear – but back then it was relatively easy-going and you could do things like that, just book a track, drive, boom.

The car we were testing was a 1999 model with a BMW engine shoved in the back, which was great in theory but turned out to be terrible in practice when I reached turn four of my first run and ground to a halt, smoke billowing out of the engine.

We came back to the garage, where they put the car up on stands, bolted in a new engine and cranked it up – only for it blow up there and then, still in the garage.

That was day one of testing over. Day two, I got to turn six of my first run and the engine did the same. Meanwhile, Bruno was having similar problems. Out he went. Engine blew up.

One thing you have to say for all the engines going *poof* was that at least it took our minds off the sticky business of what we were actually doing there. As ever, the Williams staff were inscrutable. Me and Dad were cooking up theories: was it some kind of 'shootout'? Ralf Schumacher was safe in one seat but as far as we knew Williams had nobody to replace the departing Alessandro Zanardi. Perhaps it was down to me and Bruno to prove ourselves.

Either way, we didn't do much driving in Jerez, however you pronounced it, and so a week later the whole Williams caravan decamped to Barcelona, where they got some reliability into the car and we did some running at last.

By now we were almost certain: this was a shootout test. The launch of the 2000 season car was imminent, still no second driver had been announced. This was about more than just a test driver, surely? This was for the second seat.

Not a lot of running, I'd say about thirty or forty laps each in wet/ dry conditions. I went quicker than Bruno. Not by a lot, two-tenths, a tiny amount, but faster – and that's what counts.

'Right,' they said, 'the driving's over, now you do your debrief with the engineers.'

I told them how the car felt and where I think I could have gone quicker.

'Okay,' they said, 'and now we're going to give you a test' and I was just thinking *But that's why we're here, isn't it? To test the car?* when no word of a lie they handed me a pencil and a four-page-long test and told me to find a quiet spot.

I took the test to the car that Dad and I had rented, wanting to get away from any distractions, thinking that I hadn't even taken an exam at school, and here I was having to do one at the Circuit de Catalunya. Weird.

The questions were mainly theoretical. 'If you had this problem what would you do?' 'If you change this, how will it affect the balance of the car?' Stuff like that.

I did my best, but don't think I did that well. Okay, I know for a fact I didn't do that well, because they told me later. But if it proved one thing (other than that the written test will never be a field in which I will excel), then it was that Bruno and I were shooting it out for the second seat.

All doubts were gone now. As the thought came upon me, my pencil hand literally began to shake, each new question feeling like a fresh mountain to climb. I was filling in the test while thinking, *These answers are for a drive in Formula One.*

I handed in my test, left the circuit and returned to the hotel where I went to bed that night thinking that I'd torn it. *Bloody written test. No chance am I going to get this drive.*

The next day was the official launch of the car and still we were none the wiser as to who was going to be driving alongside Ralf Schumacher. Nobody knew apart from Frank Williams and Patrick Head, not even Ralf.

As I looked around I saw people shaking their heads, exchanging quizzical looks. The poor PR guy, Nav Sidhu, was tearing his hair out, fretting, 'I don't know what they're doing. This is the weirdest thing.'

Uh oh. Bruno was called forward to have his picture taken with Ralf. *The decision's been made*, I thought, and was just about to skulk off with my tail between my legs when I was called forward and it was my turn to have my picture taken with Ralf, as though it was me who'd been chosen.

As Nav said, the whole thing was just weird. Building up to the announcement I was whisked from one place to another, seemingly for no apparent reason, and I kept passing Bruno, who was also being whisked from one place to another, seemingly for no apparent reason. We'd exchange odd apologetic looks, both wondering what the hell was going on, not quite knowing how to deal with the situation or each other. You know that bit in reality shows where they drag out the result of the public vote? 'Tonight's winner is…' pause, pause, pause, '… Tanya!' This was like that only with the pause stretched out to fill an entire day.

'Jenson, do you want to come with me?'

It was like being called forward for the dentist. I looked at Dad and he looked at me with an encouraging smile I knew so well from karting. For a moment I hesitated, almost as though I didn't want to leave him. 'Go on,' he said, with a tilt of his head. I left with Nav.

Steps led to a level above the garages. A media room was beginning to fill with F1 journalists, telly crews setting up cameras, people waving laminates. The idea was to announce the drivers in there before everybody would troop down to the garage and they'd reveal the car.

Next door to the media room was an office with its own reception area. This was where Frank had based himself for the weekend, where he could exchange notes with Patrick and hold private meetings. It was there I was taken by Nav and asked to take a seat in the reception.

Nav disappeared. I sat alone, foot jogging with nerves. From next door came the muted hum of journalists awaiting the press conference.

The door opened and out came Bruno. But if I was hoping for a clue then I was disappointed. Bruno just looked at me with an enigmatic Mona Lisa smile, didn't even say anything as he left.

In his wake I was even more confused. Was that a victor's smile? Surely he'd be wearing a bigger smile if he'd just been given the drive?

On the other hand, he didn't look that upset. If Frank had asked Bruno not to give anything away then he did his job perfectly at that moment.

Now I was waved in by Nav, who left, and I took a seat across from Frank who looked at me, unreadable smile on his face, knowing full well that for me time was standing still.

And then he said, 'We've decided to go with you.'

PART TWO

'The race was tough, I'm disappointed with the result, my dog has died, my wife has left me, and my pick-up truck won't start.'

26

I'd been a Formula One driver for all of ten seconds, stammering, 'Thank you, Frank, thank you,' holding back tears and thinking, *I've got to tell Mum and Dad, I've GOT to tell Mum and Dad,* like it was an actual physical necessity, when suddenly Ralf Schumacher bustled into the room, took up position opposite Frank and pulled his best diva face. 'I'm not coming in tomorrow if the car isn't waiting for me,' he pouted.

I was thinking, *Bloody hell, you can't speak to Frank like that,* but Frank's equilibrium was undisturbed as Ralf continued, giving it the full Mariah Carey. 'I mean it. I mean it, Frank. If the car's not waiting outside the hotel for me, or if it's late, I'm not coming in. I'm not going to test.'

'We'll make sure it's there for you tomorrow,' said Frank, unruffled, and Ralf was about to flounce out, toys successfully jettisoned, when Frank added, 'More importantly, Ralf, I've chosen Jenson as the second driver.'

Ralf looked at Frank and then at me. 'Yeah, I know,' he said imperiously.

Whether Ralf really did know or was just being a cocky bastard, who can say? Either way it was a strange way to start a relationship with a teammate. Still, as I was soon to discover first hand, in Formula One the word 'teammate' is used in the very loosest sense.

Anyway, I had all that to come. For the time being I was savouring my first moments as a Williams driver. Frank had more stuff to say to Ralf, so I was excused for the time being and floated out of the office. There waiting in the little reception area was Dad, no doubt fetched by Nav. He stood up from his seat, looking at me expectantly, like, *Well?*

'Dad, your son is a Formula One driver,' I said, and in the next instant we were in each other's arms.

'Bloody hell, Jense,' he said, eyes gleaming with tears, 'bloody hell. Bloody hell, mate.'

'I've got to ring Mum,' I said. And I tried her, but for the first time in living memory, she didn't answer her phone. It went to answer machine. If I could change one thing about that moment it would be that I'd spoken to Mum before it was announced to the world, but it was not to be. I had to be satisfied with leaving a tearful message on her answer machine. Turns out she'd just popped to the shops and she cried her eyes out when she heard me blubbing on the message.

Next we all piled into a press conference: me, Frank, Ralf and Bruno, the whole thing passing in a bit of a dream as I was introduced as a Williams driver – one of the youngest-ever in Formula One – and the press began firing questions. I told them I was delighted, that I wasn't going to let Frank down. They asked Ralf how he felt about having me aboard and he said he was going to have to get used to no longer being 'the young driver', but that's pretty much all I can remember about the press conference, mainly because I was unable to concentrate over a voice in my head screaming, 'You're a Formula One driver! Bloody hell, you're a Formula One driver,' over and over.

Just to add to the blur we were due to go straight to testing, where among other things I would try to accrue the miles I needed in order to gain my super licence, the piece of paper you need if you want to race Formula One professionally.

Trouble was, the engines kept breaking and Barcelona was covered in a blanket of snow. I had a birthday in the meantime, too, my twentieth, marked by cake and pictures of me and Dad both wearing awful turtlenecks and cheesy grins.

Fact was, I still hadn't come down to earth, and what with snow and engine explosions and dodgy knitwear I arrived for my debut race in Australia, having managed to only notch up 15 per cent of the miles I need for my super licence.

Meetings were held and after a bit of deliberation and FIA arm-twisting it was decided that I should be able to race anyway, which of course provoked howls of outrage. This was something else I was soon to discover. Anything one team does provokes howls of outrage from other teams. My lack of a super licence, combined with my age and the fact that I was perceived as gate-crashing Formula One with little or no experience, was getting old-timers hot under their collar. Chief among them Jackie Stewart: 'I don't believe you can go straight from kindergarten to university,' he fumed.

Meanwhile, the papers were calling me 'the most hyped driver since Senna'. 'I hope Jenson can handle it,' chimed in Mika Salo, then racing for Sauber. 'If he can't, he will hurt himself or somebody else.'

Thanks for the support, guys.

27

My first race was the Australian Grand Prix at Melbourne. My mum and sisters watched at home but Dad was there. After I'd been announced for Williams the phone at his kart shop had rung off the hook. People kept calling to say their son was the new Jenson Button, which was weird because I'd only just started being the new Jenson Button myself. But there you go.

What became apparent right away was that Dad couldn't manage the business and keep an eye on me, and I'd already decided that I wanted him around – not with me day and night like a chaperone – just *there*, keeping an eye on things, helping manage my affairs. So, with a bit of urging from me, he decided to sell the business and keep up his position as the founder member of Team Button. Like I say, he was there for that debut race and would be for every race after that.

Obviously, I was aware of more interest in me since the announcement had been made; I was getting used to seeing my name with the words 'golden boy' and 'Ayrton Senna' not far away. But in Australia it felt like a hot blast of attention came my way, and things got hectic. Nav and his team were rushed off their feet dealing with enquiries while Frank and Patrick did their best to keep me focused on the racing. However, as I eased into the car for first practice on Friday, looked out to see the garage door fringed by photographers, flashes blasting away, I felt my mind's field of vision narrow to the job at hand. And when I reached to my visor and flicked it down, it was as though I clicked a mute button. The roar of the V10 filled the garage, the pit crew shooed away the photographers and I drew into the pit lane, revs building as I headed to the track. And I found my peace.

Ahead of me was Michael Schumacher. I stayed behind him for the installation lap. Because of the way it is designed, the floor of an F1 car sucks everything up and then spits it all out behind. There were a lot of leaves on the track that day and as we came on to the straight I saw that Michael's Ferrari was spouting a rooster tail of leaves ahead of me.

That's what I remember. The inner sanctum of the cockpit. The rooster tail. The smell of the leaves. Thinking, *You're doing this. You're really doing this.* That feeling alone was the best of the weekend – one of the best of my entire F1 career.

I almost came off the track on the second to last corner. I'd walked the circuit but I don't think I realised just how tight that corner was. Otherwise practice went well.

Saturday morning we had an hour of practice before qualifying, and this time I wasn't so lucky. I hit a wall out by turn seven, just trying to push the car and going too hard. No doubt Mika Salo and Jackie Stewart were having a laugh about that (although in the interests of fairness, I should point out that Mika later apologised for his comments), but I was gutted that it would have to happen then, one of my first times out, running tenth fastest at the time.

They got the car ready for qualifying, but it was all a bit of a rush and the upshot was that I qualified twenty-first, which was pretty poor compared to Ralf in eleventh. Even so, I had a fun race. 'Just enjoy it,' they told me, and I did. I remember coming off the start line, looking around, and thinking, *Oh, this is so cool. I'm in Formula One*. And although the McLarens and the Ferraris were a long way up the road, in front of me in a Jaguar was Johnny Herbert – the same Johnny Herbert who had once presented the prizes at Clay Pigeon. Now here we were sharing the same track.

Ahead of me, Pedro Diniz and Nick Heidfeld collided, so I put them behind me and then overtook Marc Gene's Minardi on turn two. Johnny Herbert's clutch broke, which awarded me another place. Damn. I slipped behind Alex Wurz on lap three, a mistake that took me on to the dirt, but then went past Eddie Irvine and Pedro de la Rosa who had tangled.

All of which meant I was eleventh, lapping at a similar speed to Ralf in eighth. Pit stops took me to seventh, and then Heinz-Harald Frentzen retired, taking me up to sixth and into the points. For a glorious moment, I thought I was going to score points first time out, but then as I came down to turn three, the engine broke, the rear wheels locked up, I went off into the gravel and that was it, game over. Ralf finished third.

It was a good start. Retired through no fault of my own. So close to being in the points. If nothing else I'd proved that I wasn't just this lucky amateur who had happened to fluke his way into Formula One; I'd repaid the faith shown in me by Frank and Patrick and earned my place on the grid.

In Brazil, I outqualified Ralf, ninth to his eleventh, but he beat me in the race, finishing sixth to my seventh. I'd been running in eighth before I dived down the inside of Jos Verstappen in the Arrows at the hairpin and got past him, but it wasn't enough, meaning I finished just outside the points, which was a shame.

Ah, but then… I'd returned to the hotel, showered and was on the bus cracking open a beer on our way back to the airport when someone from the team said, 'You finished sixth. DC's been disqualified for something illegal on the car.'

So we had a few more drinks and it was a lovely flight home, knowing I was on the scoreboard – at twenty years old, the youngest ever driver to register a championship point. At Imola for the San Marino Grand Prix, I made a bit of a balls-up in qualifying. The kerbs were troubling me and I only managed eighteenth on the grid to Ralf's fifth. I thought I could fix it in the race but after five laps my engine broke. DNF. Did not finish.

Next stop, Silverstone. I was adjusting my tie and shooting my cuffs, metaphorically speaking. I wanted to make a good impression in front of my home crowd.

28

Qualifying at Silverstone went well. I was sixth on the grid beside Michael Schumacher – pinch me – with Ralf keeping Jos Verstappen company behind. I took Michael at turn one, which was pretty cool, and then ran fifth behind Rubens Barrichello, Frentzen, Coulthard and Häkkinen, which again was huge for me.

We had a problem with the engine halfway through the race, so I was running on nine cylinders, not ten, and I still finished fifth. So that, for me, was a special race. DC won so the crowd went wild, and afterwards I got to reflect on the fact that in the four races so far – my first four Formula One races ever – I'd outqualified my experienced teammate twice, scored points twice, and had briefly run in front of Michael Schumacher.

Some old schoolfriends had come to see me. A small group, obviously, but the friends I'd made had stuck by me and it was great to see then. Straight after the race, I took them to the Williams motorhome, where we colonised Patrick Head's office and asked catering to bring us up a load of beers. Sure enough, we ended up getting pretty hammered.

Right after that, DC had a party at the circuit where I found myself on stage with DC, Jacques Villeneuve and Norbert Haug – who was the main man at McLaren-Mercedes, DC's team at the time – all of us on stage wearing black wigs in front of four hundred people, absolutely obliterated, singing karaoke. What a night.

That was the first time I'd spent any proper time with DC, but we became close after that, partly because we both spoke the same language, literally. Most Formula One drivers aren't British, so it was great to compare notes with someone who spoke the lingo. After that he took me under his wing; we'd spend time together, go on holiday together with our girlfriends and so on. There was one particular boat trip that we took from Monaco to Sicily and then Sardinia. I remember me and him sitting on the front of the boat drinking Bloody Marys all the way down to Sicily. Got there, both red as lobsters. Undeterred we went out on land and kept drinking, no doubt attracting attention, because when we arrived back at the boat there must have been fifteen paparazzi hanging around on the quay waiting. We made our way on to the boat and continued the party, things getting a bit messy, until DC announced, 'Right, I'm going to give them a show, these photographers,' took all his clothes off and dived towards the curtains, planning to fling them back and, 'Give the paps a proper show in me birthday suit.' Only my rugby tackle saved his blushes.

The fact that he was about to do it? So DC. The fact that he remembered and thanked me afterwards and then told the world how I'd saved him from making a dick of himself? That's him all over.

It was thanks to the guidance of experienced hands like DC (when not on his boat), Frank and Patrick that I settled into F1 so quickly. I felt at home, even though I was never actually *at home*.

In those days, it was busier between races than it is now. Back then you'd finish a race and go straight to three days of testing starting

Tuesday or Wednesday and then either travel home or to a sponsor event, which was usually one of the European circuits: Paul Ricard, Barcelona, Jerez, Valencia, Silverstone. Then you'd have two days to turn yourself around and get to the next race.

That's if the race was in Europe. If they were abroad, you'd go direct from one to the other. So, if you were racing in Australia, and the next race was Brazil, you'd go straight there to acclimatise.

Accommodation was in hotels. It's always been in my contract that I can choose the hotel I want and I pay for my own. Being a creature of habit (when it comes to hotels at least), I've got a handful that I like.

Ask me my favourite hotel. Go on. Okay then, it's the Grand Hyatt in Tokyo. A lot of that is just because I've had such good times in Tokyo, whether I'm racing in Japan or whether I've simply gone and spent time there.

Other hotels that I like on the F1 calendar are the Crowne in Melbourne, who always upgrade my room to a huge suite, which is just stunning – I ended up getting quite superstitious about that room – the Cyber View Lodge in Malaysia, where they have a butler who walks you to the restaurant, walks you back to your bedroom and so on. Weird but cool.

Having said all that, I did splash out on a motorhome, a forty-five-foot Newell and I stayed in that for European races. I'd park it either at the circuit itself or just outside. When I retired from racing I sold it to Chrissy Buncombe who reckons it's like a boat with wheels, and he's right, it's an absolute beast of a thing. It's massive – it's so big you're not allowed to register it in the UK so we had to do it in Ireland – and it's got something like 500 horsepower under the hood; it'll do 100mph if you're brave or foolish enough.

Still, it wasn't all fancy hotels and plush motorhomes. Turns out there are downsides. Not the racing. I loved that. The other bit. The fame bit.

At first I enjoyed being recognised, and the reason for that can be boiled down to the simple fact that I was twenty years old, and you show me a twenty-year-old kid who doesn't want to be famous, and doesn't think it's just about the coolest thing you can be, and I'll show you a twenty-year-old who's lying through his teeth.

But the thrill of being recognised wears off pretty quick, and of course while it's more than welcome when you're signing for Williams and being hyped as the best driver since Ayrton Senna, it's not so great when you're behaving like an idiot and you'd prefer to keep a low profile.

Take the speeding incident, for example. I'd been testing a Formula One car in France and needed to get down from Le Mans to Monaco for the Grand Prix. Luckily, our engine supplier, BMW, had lent me a 330 turbo-charged diesel BMW that was just as fast as it sounds. Despite it being a diesel, I hit 227kmh. In other words, about 143mph.

A stupid way to drive. Older and wiser now, I restrict my road-racing impulses to the correct racing line for a roundabout, but I can't lie and tell you I was a sensible young Formula One driver tootling along in my 330 turbo-charged diesel BMW, because that would be dishonest. The truth is I drove like Joe Stink.

So the police were pretty angry when they caught me at a *péage*. This one guy took it really personally, started having a go, telling me they'd taken my picture so I was bang to rights, but if I paid a fine I could be on my way.

At this I couldn't believe my luck. But then his colleague came over, and to my dismay he overruled the first guy and said, 'No, you're coming to the police station.'

So now I was like, *Erk. Shit just got real.* We went to the police station where they pointed at a cell. 'You'll be in that cell unless you can pay up in the next hour,' they said, and then they made coffee and asked my name.

I told them.

'Oui, and what is it that you do for a living, Chanson Bur-turn?'

I told them.

'Pardon. Formula Un, you say? *Mais oui, bien sur! C'est Chanson Bur-turn. Il est dans le Williams team!'*

(There you go. Knew that French GCSE would come in handy.)

And at that, of course, the whole atmosphere changed, and we sat talking about Formula One for a bit, while I mustered up the courage to phone my dad.

'All right, Jense?'

'Yeah, Dad, thanks. Um, you know the credit card you gave me, in case I had a problem? Well, I've got a problem. I could do with the PIN for it, if that's okay? I got caught speeding.'

'Fucksake, Jense, how much you need?'

'Four thousand francs.'

Pause.

'That's a lot for speeding. What were you doing?'

I told him.

'Fucksake, Jense. Right, pay up, get it done and move on. But the problem is, the press will probably find out about this.'

Oh no, I thought. I hadn't considered that. Anyway, so I paid up, carried on to Monaco and then two days later it was in the papers that

I got caught speeding, which was a bit embarrassing. But I spoke to BMW: 'I'm so sorry for this and it's such bad publicity for you, but I was caught speeding in France…'

Don't worry, they said. In fact, I should have called them and they would have paid my fine. Nobody thought diesels were quick back then so for one to be clocked at 143mph, probably the quickest a diesel had ever been on the road, was just about the best advertising ever.

So that's a story that ended well, even if it did mark the beginning of what you might call a certain type of publicity – the minting of a reputation, not always deserved – that's dogged me ever since.

29

Monaco was crap. Beautiful place. The jewel in the F1 calendar. My dad was in love with it and, like me, he ended up moving there. But as a race in 2000? It was crap. I qualified fourteenth and should have done better. After one false start we reached the Grand Hotel hairpin where I nudged Pedro de la Rosa who was in the process of trying to cut across me, sending him into a spin that caught Pedro Diniz and Nick Heidfeld and clagged up the road.

The race was red-flagged, but back then you could use your spare car if you had one, so those drivers with a spare in the garage ran down the hill to begin again – our third start, this time from the pits.

Trouble was, my car was set up for Ralf, and besides I was called in after seventeen laps because the telemetry said I was losing oil. That was it for me. I was out of my first Monaco.

Canada, I was eleventh. France, eighth. Austria, I managed fifth after tussling with Villeneuve and Mika Salo. Back in the points at last.

At Hockenheim I crashed on pit entry, which is never a good look.

The thing was that, since hitting the wall in Melbourne, I'd been very careful with the car, and was probably being a bit tentative on pit entry.

'Push it more, Jenson, push it,' urged Frank. 'You're losing a second and a half to Ralf on a pit entry, not even on the circuit, the pit entry. Push harder. If you crash, you crash.'

Drivers love to hear 'push harder', so I didn't need telling twice. But then during practice on the Friday I did crash. I crashed on the entry to the pit lane and broke the front end of the car on the pit wall. Had to walk back to the pits with my helmet tucked under my arm, feeling a bit sorry for myself. Practically the first Williams boss I saw was Patrick, who was furious and typically forthright when it came to expressing it. 'What were you bloody doing, Jenson? You were in the pit entry and you crashed. I know you're a beginner, but you've just crashed on the pit entrance.' He was shaking his head. 'This isn't good enough.'

It was a proper bollocking and, as you know, I hate those.

'Patrick, Frank told me to push,' I said in my defence, and thank God Frank overheard and put his arm up to indicate that we should go over to him.

'Jenson, you did the right thing,' said Frank. 'I told you to push and you did. You made a mistake, but you'll learn.'

Patrick was very posh. If he was talking to you in front of the crew, you always got a little smile from the mechanics because he was so old-school in the way that he would talk about a car. He also had that posh-person habit of not mincing his words. He didn't suffer fools gladly, called a spade a spade, that sort of thing. I remember midway through 2000, he said, 'Jenson, I think you could lose some weight.'

'Okay, Patrick.'

'Yes, you could lose some of that puppy fat, Jenson. Yes, absolutely.'

And that was it. Off he went. Having delivered a stinging comment that I'd be recounting in my memoirs, he probably never even gave the matter another thought.

But I liked that about him. Frank too. You knew where you stood with them. They didn't play games. And what's more they were both great listeners; they loved to hear what drivers had to say. Of the two, Patrick tended to get worked up more than Frank. But Frank had that ultimate authority, and Patrick listened to him. I'm sure they had issues between them, but I never saw that. There was always a really good atmosphere in the team.

Come the race, and although I'd qualified sixteenth, I thought I could make up the places. But then, on the parade lap, disaster struck.

You probably know all this, but I'm going to say it anyway: F1 cars don't have an ignition. They don't even have a starter motor on board. There's an external starter motor, which is first used when the car is in the pit garage, after the engine has been warmed.

Cars then leave the pits for the installation lap, which is when we test various functions, brake, throttle, steering, and get a feel for the circuit, ending up at the grid, where we form up. At this point, engines go off and crews get ready to start the engine again for the formation lap, sometimes called the parade or warm-up lap. The formation lap is when you see drivers weaving to try and get the heat up in their tyres.

Now, what you really don't want to do is stall the car at the beginning of the formation lap, because if you do that, if you – in the words of the regulations – 'fail to leave the grid before the last qualifier' – then you'll have to start the race from the back of the grid.

And that's exactly what I did at Hockenheim. Stalled it. Sitting there like a lemon with pit crew swarming around me to try and get me started again.

Still. You put me at the back and there's everything to play for, and when the lights went out I got my head down.

Lady Luck had flicked me the V-sign for the formation lap but now she gave me the sweetest smile in the form of a disgruntled ex-Mercedes employee in a plastic raincoat. This guy had made his way on to the track in order to disrupt the race, presumably to protest his sacking, or perhaps because he just fancied getting run over. Either way, out came the safety car followed by a procession of drivers making use of the lull by coming into the pits. But not me. I used the opportunity to make up some places and pitted late, making up time by avoiding the traffic jam.

The guy in the raincoat was a nutcase but he was right about the weather. It started to piddle down and I was the first to go on wet-weather tyres. Another decent decision – thank you, god of tactics. Belatedly, others started filing in for the right tyres, too, which gave me the chance to move up the field, and by now I was flying. Pretty good feeling to sail past Mika Salo, who was struggling on his slicks, and make into fourth, which was where I finished. My best result yet.

A little dampener came in the form of a quote from Niki Lauda. 'I don't understand why Williams want to replace him,' he said, meaning me. 'He's done a good job this year; they have invested in him and to me it's probably a bigger gamble to run Montoya.'

Which leads me on to what we'll call The Juan Pablo Montoya Situation.

30

In 1999, Frank had arranged a driver swap with a guy called Chip Ganassi, who ran a CART team in the States. Frank gave Chip Juan Pablo Montoya, and in return he got Alessandro Zanardi.

Zanardi had a torrid year in F1 while Montoya was a sensation in CART. Unsurprisingly, Frank wanted Montoya back at the end of it, but Montoya wasn't done with CART and wanted to stay for another year, promising to return after that. Needing rid of Zanardi, Frank held the shootout that got me the job.

To be fair to Frank, he'd always been upfront about wanting Montoya back, right from the beginning of the season. 'Juan Pablo Montoya has great ability,' he told the press. 'With [him] wanting to come back, and Jenson and Ralf Schumacher in the car this year, our long-term future is rich with options. Jenson will need to show us what he can do to keep Juan Pablo out. That's quite a position for us.'

So I always knew it was a possibility. Maybe even a likelihood. After all, I was only contracted for a year. I was pretty relaxed about the whole thing, to be honest. It was an issue but not a major one.

Still, you can't really say all that to the press, or at least I didn't at the time. They decided to pursue a narrative of their own, convinced that the Juan Pablo Montoya situation had unsettled me and was responsible for my run of, well, not poor, but maybe not-quite-as-glorious-as-we-might-have-hoped results. Nothing to do with reliability, of course, or me finding my feet in F1 or Pedro de la Rosa trying to overtake on a hairpin. All to do with Juan Pablo Montoya.

It wasn't accurate, like I say. But at the same time it increased the noise around me, a sense of things unravelling – which again was a perception, not the reality – a situation not helped by a press story that had emerged earlier in the season. No, not the speeding story, although that probably wasn't helpful either. This one had to do with Kimberley.

She and I had split up, our lives no longer compatible. She was my first girlfriend, my first love; I'd lost my virginity to her. But I was now a Formula One driver, never in one place for very long, and she was still in Frome, and it was as though we now lived on different planets. Right from the beginning of our relationship, she'd never had much appreciation or understanding of my world, and it wasn't like things had changed in that regard. So I finished it. It was very sad. Not done lightly. But you move on.

Next thing I knew, one of the papers: 'I Gave Up Everything for the Golden Boy of F1. Even Our Unborn Baby.'

It was during my time in Formula Three that Kim had become pregnant. I was away when she broke the news by phone. We talked it over. She was eighteen, I was nineteen; we were too young to have a baby, and so we made the joint decision that she should have a termination. I was still away when she and her mum went to the clinic. Our relationship continued into the following year before I finished it.

To see all this in the paper was one of those big wake-up-call moments. After all, the speeding business was self-inflicted and the stories surrounding it had at least been accurate and factual. This, though – this was something different, where the salient facts were *kind of true*, but the *actual truth* was twisted to serve an inaccurate interpretation of events – in this case to make me out to be the heartless, career-minded bastard that I really wasn't.

The worst thing was that I knew Kim wouldn't have chosen to word it like that. Her mistake was to sell the story: twenty-six grand, she got. But I spoke to her afterwards and she was very tearful, very sorry. She'd intended it to be a nice story about our time together, the baby issue an incidental, bittersweet detail. She certainly hadn't expected it to be the main focus.

But that, as I was now discovering, is the press for you. Their excuse is that you're a role model, so it's fair play that your adoring public should know what a terrible person lies underneath the smiling exterior. But I remember thinking that, firstly, I hadn't done anything terrible in that instance, and, secondly, I'm not a pop star who needs your approval. I'm not courting popularity in that way. I'm a sportsman. People don't follow me because they think I'm an awesome role model, they do so because they like what I do in a car. But it makes no difference.

Another thing I soon discovered is that while the article itself is often balanced, the headline will always, without fail, be something lurid and misrepresentative.

You contact the journalist: 'Thanks for the interview, but what's all this in the headline? That's not really what I said, is it?'

'Oh, I don't do the headlines. And if you read the actual text of the piece, it's all very clear.'

'I did read the piece. The piece is good. Thanks.'

'That's okay.'

'But the trouble is half the people who see this article won't read the whole thing. I mean, that's no reflection on you, it's a very good piece, but a lot of people will just see the headline and assume they've got the whole story. It's the headline I'm bothered about.'

'Ah, I don't write the headlines.'

'Well, who does?'

'Uh, I'm not sure who wrote that one. Someone on the subs desk, I think. Let me see if I can find out and get back to you.'

And that's it. That's the extent of any accountability you'll get from the press.

The net effect of all this, of course, is that you get scarred and end up doing what I eventually did, which was to close down, and from that is bred a situation where the fans get nothing but a procession of robot racing drivers who are afraid to say anything. Which is rubbish for the sport. People bemoan a 'lack of characters' in the sports, well, they're there, they just keep it hidden from the press.

Nowadays we have Twitter. People in my position can have their say direct to fans without the filter of the newspapers and magazines adding the wrong emphasis, taking things out of the context and every other trick in the book to make you look bad. Twitter probably came along too late to benefit me personally. I was no longer such a target by then; I'd thrown up enough barriers and developed strategies to ward off the worst of the press intrusion anyway. But it's good to know it's there.

What hasn't changed, of course – and in fact has got worse – is the pictures. On the one hand, selfies, which I don't mind at all, because it's fans and you've got to love the fans, they're an awesome bunch. The trouble is, you can have a hundred people wanting a selfie, pose for ninety-nine of them and the one person to whom you say, 'I'm sorry,

I'm so busy, I've got to scoot,' is the one who goes on Twitter to tell the world that you've got too big for your boots and so on.

That aside, I love the British fans. They adore their motorsport and aren't as flag-loyal as other countries, which makes them a more interesting bunch in my eyes.

The Japanese fans are great, too. Japan is the only country where they replay the race again on the screens, so they watch the race and stay there until eight or nine at night, watching it again and again on the big screens. It's great for us drivers. After a win you do all your media interviews, which takes a couple of hours, then you do your debriefing for an hour or so, after which it's dark, and you're wandering around in the paddock, deflating a bit, wanting the love to continue, thinking, *I'd really like to celebrate with the fans.*

Well, at Suzuka you walk outside and *they're still there* watching the replay on big screens. It's mad. You go out there with your trophy and they greet you like you're the second coming. You're standing on the pit wall with your trophy hold aloft, flashes blasting away. It's a brilliant feeling.

Frank and Patrick were great that first year. 'You're a rookie, you're going to make mistakes' was their mantra, whatever the circumstances. I began to pick up a few interview tricks as well. Here's one: however downbeat your comments, as long as you end on a positive, it makes a big difference. 'The race was tough, I'm disappointed with the result, my dog has died, my wife has left me and my pick-up truck won't start. But I'm *really* excited about the next race and *really* looking forward to it.' It works.

The worst thing, though, is the paps. I can't remember the first time I was papped but it was definitely in that first year and it's amazing how quickly they become a fact of life, like wasps or verrucas. Now living in LA, I get papped a lot. Not coming out of restaurants, funnily enough, because the paps who hang around outside restaurants don't know much about Formula One, so I'm safe there. But there are a lot of South American paps in LA, and they always recognise me. I'm running in Brentwood, of all places. You think, *There's never going to be paps in Brentwood.* And there they are, taking pictures of me running. It's the strangest thing. It never ceases to amaze me how they know where you're going to be.

In London it's even worse. Not so much now. They don't give a shit about me any more. But my first few seasons in F1, they were everywhere, and they always knew exactly where I was going to be. I got paranoid. I was inventing theories that they were somehow able to patch into the CCTV and track my movements. How else could they know?

London paps are different from LA paps. In LA if you stop and give them a picture – thumbs up, cheesy grin, 'All right, lads?' – they'll bugger off. British paps are more tricky. They say, 'Come on, Jenson, give us a picture and we'll leave you alone. Just a quick picture, mate, can't say fairer than that.'

So you give them a quick picture, thumbs aloft, cheesy grin, 'All right, lads?' only for them to go back on their word. What they want, of course, is a shot of you looking harried, because that's the one they can use to illustrate a story about you being a bastard, or how you're cracking up under the pressure, or whatever else it is they've decided to say about you this week.

You get in your car and they follow you in theirs. I've had them tail me home and take pictures of me going into my house. You feel trapped. You're being chased and that's not a nice feeling.

What people forget is that the picture they get is dictated entirely by them. You're not looking pissed off in the photo because the F1 pressure is getting to you, or you're having love-life problems, or whatever bullshit reason they attach to it; you look that way because there's a pap standing in your way taking your picture. One time we were in the car and a friend put his hand in front of my face to shield me from them. The story was that Jenson's driving dangerously, larking about with his friend's hand in front of his face, when of course I wasn't driving, because there were paparazzi in the way, and the reason my friend's hand was in front of my face was to stop the paparazzi getting a picture of me.

All of which brings me back to the Juan Pablo Montoya situation. I wasn't unsettled as the media said. Yes, I hoped to somehow show Frank that I was worth keeping, but how that would work with Ralf and Juan Pablo I didn't know. I was just enjoying the driving, enjoying F1, having a ball. Besides, it wasn't real to me. I was the guy at Williams, Juan Pablo was in the States.

And then about halfway through the year, Frank called me: 'Juan Pablo's going to come back, Jenson, and he's going to take your seat. Thank you very much for everything you've done.'

It became real then.

But even so, I took a pragmatic approach. I wasn't upset. I wasn't angry. I knew I had a one-year contract. Frank can do what he wants. Like I say, it was his name above the door. He obviously wanted a guy who was more experienced than me to come in and start winning immediately and he evidently didn't think I was in that position. Or maybe he had this handshake deal with Juan Pablo and didn't want to go back on it.

I don't know. Obviously I wanted to stay at Williams, but it's just the way it is. You get your managers to find you another job while you concentrate on trying to be as impressive as you can for the following season.

31

Hungary was a crock. A cracked exhaust saw me finish ninth, trailing Ralf, who was in sixth. Any concern I had over the future was then laid to rest just before the Belgian Grand Prix at Spa, when it was agreed that I'd be joining Benetton to partner Giancarlo Fisichella, a two-year contract.

Suitably fired up, I notched up my best qualification of the season, third behind Mika Häkkinen's McLaren and Jarno Trulli's Jordan-Mugen Honda.

'Not bad for a schoolboy,' grinned Frank in the garage, ushering me off to attend my first-ever top-three qualifying press conference. Maybe he was wondering if he'd made the right decision. I hope so. But Frank was Frank. I understood why he'd done it.

We began the race in single file behind the safety car because it was wet, which was a blow because I'd noted the weather and hoped to use it to my advantage. Right away, Trulli was holding me up, giving Michael Schumacher a chance behind me. Sure enough, Schumacher made use of the opportunity, slipping past me in the Bus Stop chicane on lap three. I tried a move on Trulli, but we touched and he spun, giving DC and Ralf the opening to overtake. I knew I could have scored a podium on that race. As it was, I had to be satisfied with finishing fifth.

For the Italian Grand Prix in Monza, Ralf qualified seventh, me twelfth. We should have been much quicker than that.

The first chicane at Monza is a tough one. Having got off to a good start you have to get on the brakes hard and cars tend to bunch up. Sure enough, the Saubers tangled with Eddie Irvine's Jaguar. Things were even worse at the second chicane when Frentzen and Trulli, both in Jordans, got in a pickle that also involved DC in the McLaren and Barrichello's Ferrari. Worse still, Pedro de la Rosa rolled his Arrows after clipping Zonta's BAR and rear-ending Herbert's Jaguar.

By the time the track was clear, I was running sixth place behind Schumacher, Häkkinen, Villeneuve, Ralf and Fisichella. As race leader Schumacher was pacing us behind the safety car. Emerging from the Ascari corner he slowed down as expected, but instead of then accelerating he braked, which caught us all out behind him. I swerved to avoid hitting Villeneuve, ended up on the grass and hit the guardrail, damaging my left rear wheel. Race over.

To add insult to injury, I was accused of overtaking under the safety car, which just wasn't true. I had to swerve or hit Jacques. I had nowhere to go but the grass.

All of which paled into insignificance when I heard a marshal, Paolo Gislimberti, had been killed by debris from the pile-up at the start of the race, a devastating shock, which I hadn't known about at the time.

Indianapolis was a blast. I qualified sixth on the grid and was due to come in eighth when an electrical fault ended the race for me.

Then came Japan, the second-to-last race of the season and my penultimate race with Williams. With the eyes of the world on the title battle between Schumacher and Häkkinen, I was pleased that the spotlight had moved away from me, and excited about racing at Suzuka.

Not only are the fans great, but also the track is a real challenge – one that can take years to become accustomed to, let alone master.

I was fifth in qualifying, behind the McLarens and Ferraris and ahead of Ralf. Added to that I was fastest through Suzuka's legendary S-bends – the esses – which are like threading a needle.

My start wasn't great. I overheated the clutch and watched others sail by, including Ralf, putting me in seventh. Still, I was in the groove, feeding off the atmosphere and enjoying the comparative lack of pressure, making my way into sixth and staying on Ralf's tail. Lap thirty and I was grinning in my helmet when I passed him and moved into fifth, which is where I finished. Ahead of me Michael Schumacher had claimed his world title, but I was overjoyed with my fifth.

Malaysia, last race. Bah. My engine broke, which was no way to say goodbye to my first-ever season in F1. But there you go.

Looking back at that first momentous season with Williams, I had mixed feelings. On the one hand I was eighth in the Drivers' Championship (Ralf was fifth) and I was named Rookie of the Year.

But on the other hand, I realised that I hadn't really learned enough. I saw that I was spoiled with the car, the team, the support, everything.

Which is a roundabout way of saying that I was in no way prepared for what would happen at Benetton.

32

Things started badly. The new Benetton line-up was to be unveiled at the Cipriani hotel in Venice, prior to unveiling the new car, the B201, in St Mark's Square. I was ill. Poisoned by a dodgy shrimp salad. I'd get up, do some interviews and then escape back to bed or the toilet – mainly the toilet. I should have known then that it would be a year to forget.

The problem, well, the *main* problem, was the car, which at the risk of getting all technical on you, was an absolutely shitbox, a total dog to drive.

It didn't have power steering, there were brake and gearbox issues, it was beset by electrical problems and oil leaks. Its two biggest flaws, though, were that it was slow – really slow – and that my teammate Giancarlo Fisichella, 'Fisi', drove it better than me.

No getting around the fact. Not only was he well established at Benetton and a big favourite at the team, but Fisi is also something of a specialist at getting the best out of a bad car. So it proved that year.

And then there was Flavio Briatore, the managing director of the Benetton racing team. Flavio was the guy responsible for turning Benetton into a viable F1 outfit, steering Michael Schumacher to successive Drivers' titles in 1994 and 1995 and winning the Constructors' Championship in 1995. Like Frank he was a legend in the sport. He had a shock of white

A smiley start to a nightmare time at Benetton where I clashed with team boss Flavio Briatore and was outraced by Giancarlo Fisichella, who had the knack of getting speed out of a dog of a car. *(© PA Images)*

Monza 2001 – a shunt with Jarno Trulli rather summed up a torrid two years with the team. *(© Getty)*

Above: A bright new dawn at BAR in 2003, where all was sunny (apart from my team mate Jacques Villeneuve, who seemed determined to knock me back). *(© Sutton)*

Right: A fantastic 2004 saw me score my first pole at Imola... *(© Getty)*

Below: ...and 10 podiums on my way to third in the Championship! Here I celebrate with legend Michael Schumacher and rival (and future team-mate) Fernando Alonso at Hockenheim. *(© Getty)*

Hungary 2006 – my first win. In the rain (of course). *(All © Getty)*

In 2009, out of the ashes of Honda's departure came Brawn GP, and a car in which I could finally challenge for the Championship. *(© Getty)*

Hugging Ross Brawn, our Team Principal, after winning
the opening race in Australia. *(© Darren Heath)*

Reign in Spain – 1-2 with teammate Rubens Barrichello. *(© Darren Heath)*

Nothing beats winning in Monaco – my fifth win of six that year
(© Darren Heath)

Number one – securing the Championship in 2009. *(All © Darren Heath)*

hair and was usually wearing shades, the collar of his team shirt turned up – he was what you might call a 'colourful' character. He and I had met before, when I was in Formula Ford, and there was talk of him managing me and steering me into F1. It all sounded promising until he named his price: 50 per cent of everything. I didn't take him up on it.

At first, Flavio was good fun and great company. However, it soon became apparent that he expected me to win races, which in that car was an impossibility. And when I didn't win races was when he started being no fun and shitty company. Frank and Patrick had been outspoken; they weren't given to sugar-coating the truth. But with them it had always come from a place of wanting the best for their rookie, wanting to nurture me. Not so with Flavio. He was particularly forthright with the media, especially when you'd had a poor race, which was pretty much every race that season. Never mind ending the interview on a positive; that tip would have been wasted on him. His policy was to start with unfavourable, continue with pessimistic and end on damaging.

So the season started badly – DNF with an electrical fault at Canada – and didn't improve much from there. Eleventh in Malaysia, tenth in Brazil, twelfth at San Marino. These were not great places for a team that could still remember being world champs. Plus Fisi, while hardly troubling the podium, was producing better results than me.

In Spain, we were both lapped by rookie Fernando Alonso in a Minardi. That was humiliating. Austria was more blah: I spun off with engine problems, having been trounced by Fisi in qualifying. Never the most welcoming bunch, the Benetton team were beginning to glower at me in the garage, as though I was letting the side down.

Could I look to Flavio for support? Answer, no: just before Monaco he told the press he thought I was 'a lazy playboy'.

33

The dictionary I'm looking at defines 'playboy' as 'a wealthy man who spends his time enjoying himself, especially one who behaves irresponsibly or is sexually promiscuous'.

That's what Flavio said I was. A lazy one of those.

Okay, so 'wealthy', yes. Guilty. I had, somewhat foolishly in retrospect, listened to my manager who told me that my continued prosperity in Formula One was assured and that I should rent an apartment in Monaco, which I did. I also bought a yacht, that I called *Missie*. And I had, also somewhat foolishly in retrospect, parked that yacht in Monaco harbour. A bit flash, I grant you.

But I wasn't lazy and I didn't spend my time enjoying myself, certainly not at Benetton, because it was a miserable year by anyone's standards. And as for being sexually promiscuous, well that's just not true either.

The situation there was that I'd had girlfriends after Kimberley and I split up. Nothing serious, but on the other hand, not one-night stands either.

Then, at some point in 2000, I was at a film premiere and I wandered down to get some popcorn. They were giving it away free at the entrance and I wanted some – you can't say fairer than free popcorn

– when I passed a girl on the stairs. I looked at her. She looked back. At the party later we swapped numbers.

Her name was Louise, a singer in a band called Orchid. I was living near Oxford at the time but looking for that apartment in Monaco so I invited her out there for a couple of days. She declined, but even so, we got together.

In 2003 she took part in *Fame Academy*, and you know how on those shows they cut to the contestants' friends and the family in the audience? Well there I was: 'boyfriend'. That same year we got engaged in Barbados, planning on marrying in 2005. Then, three months before the wedding, we separated.

Me again. My fault. I told her I wasn't ready. She was all for calling off the wedding but staying together as a couple. But I felt I'd had those marital doubts for a reason, and that I should probably call it off for good.

I was with Louise the entire time I was driving for Benetton, which by my calculation makes it two serious girlfriends and a handful of less-serious girlfriends in ten years. Hardly makes me Warren Beatty. Quite the reverse: I'm one of those people who likes to be in a relationship, a serial monogamist. It's true I've dated a fair few models, but one of the reasons the old cliché about racing drivers going out with models is true, is because if my girlfriend had a nine-to-five job then I'd never see her. As a racing driver you're on the road *all the time*, because that's what the job demands. I'm not saying it's hard, working-in-a-coalmine-hard, but it's certainly not a suitable job for a homebody. When I retired and went back to LA it was the first time in fifteen years that I'd spent more than three weeks at home.

The person you date has to understand that. The flexible hours of a model are handy, yes, but the fact that a woman makes her living as a model doesn't make her a prop for a playboy lifestyle, and it's insulting to say otherwise. Not just to them but to me as well.

And while we're here, let's not forget the great irony of Flavio's statement. Put it this way, the dictionary I'm looking at defines 'pot calling the kettle black' as 'Flavio Briatore labels Jenson Button a playboy'.

Mind you, I didn't suppose Flavio was sweating the details of that particular dig. He just wanted to be rude. Tough love, maybe. But I read his comments and thought they were petulant, childish and unnecessary. And worse than that – they really, really got to me.

After that came the race in Monaco, where I finished seventh, which in the context of that season wasn't bad at all. Afterwards Flavio did his speciality, which was to say nothing to me, letting a lingering dirty look do all the talking before storming off to a press conference.

'Jenson looked as though he was driving around Monaco looking for an apartment to buy,' he scoffed, among other things I've since blocked from my memory.

And this was me driving an underpowered car with no power steering and still finishing seventh, almost in the points. Power steering in an F1 car isn't a nice optional extra. It's essential. My hands were a mass of blisters after that race.

Flavio's hostility shook me up, I don't mind admitting, especially since I was the sole focus. Giancarlo was a DNF at Monaco, but he always escaped Flavio's wrath for three crucial reasons: he was Italian, he was doing a better job than me, and Flavio managed both him and Mark Webber, who was our test driver at the time.

Nothing on the track scared me, but Flavio gave me the screaming heebie-jeebies. I'd never had anyone speak to me like that before. I'd never had anyone speak *about* me like that before. My inability to get to grips with it – at least at first – put me in a pretty dark place.

Sure enough, from Monaco onwards I was scared of not performing, which meant that I didn't perform, which made me even more scared of not performing, and…

You get the picture. I still had another year on my contract. I was thinking that I'd never pull out of the slump. Thinking that maybe I shouldn't have bought that bloody yacht.

34

I was in Enstone, the Benetton base in Oxfordshire, having a tense conversation with Flavio about my future. I'd finished the season in seventeenth, Giancarlo eleventh, but that was the last year of Benetton as a Formula One team, their worst-ever results. Renault bought the team outright, though Flavio remained in charge.

'Well, it's up to you,' he shrugged, palms up. 'You either work harder or you retire – and you definitely don't have enough money to retire. What do you think about that?'

Oh. That was what I thought about that. *Oh.* But to be fair to Flavio, he didn't leave the ball entirely in my court. It was his suggestion that I should use the winter break to spend time with the designer, Mike Gascoyne. 'Right,' echoed Mike, 'you need to learn about the car for next year.'

So I did, and what I learned was that you can't just get into a car and expect to be able to drive it fast, however good you are. I've talked about *feeling* a car, and I definitely had that feel, but what I needed was the tools to understand it. Mainly I needed a better grasp of the set-up parameters.

Basically, the set-up parameters are adjustments that tailor a car to its driver. So when we talk about, say, the two Mercedes being the same car, they are, in the sense that they share the same chassis and engine, but they can be quite different in terms of set-up.

Tweaks you can make are to the front and rear spring rates, which is the stiffness of suspension and tends to be adjusted to take into account the surface at different circuits. Then there's rollbar stiffness, which controls the balance of the car and determines how much the car will 'roll' over bumps; if it's stiff that's good for the aerodynamics, but the car will struggle on the kerbs, and vice versa. It's really up to the individual driver and how they feel the car will perform on a given circuit. Personally, I like to use the kerbs. I'm all about pushing that track to its limit, so that's an important setting for me.

There are the damper settings, which control oscillation of the springs – in simple terms how 'bouncy' do you want the car to be. Then there are the wing settings, which are crucial to get right for downforce, as well as the ride height, which is basically the distance between the car and the road and again is essential because it's so intrinsically linked to downforce. Next there's the camber, castor, toe-in or toe-out of the wheels, which are all the angles of the wheels and can be adapted to the steering preference of the driver.

I learned what the different settings could offer me as a driver, how I could tailor them to suit my style and ensure they were right for the circuit. Doing that helped me find a way of communicating with the engineers so they could understand what I wanted from the car, and I could understand from them what the car was capable of giving me. The short version is that over the winter the engineers and I finally got on the same page.

I also spent time with Flavio in Kenya, his favourite bolthole, which was a good opportunity for us to sit down and talk things through.

From then on, we were much closer – although I still couldn't understand a word he said.

I told him, 'I know where you're coming from. I probably haven't focused as much as I should have done, and I'm going to change that.'

And I did. Where before I was pure instinct as a driver, expecting to succeed on natural talent alone, now I focused on the engineering side of racing. It all became clear to me. The penny had dropped: Fisi had been better because he understood the car and he had fine-tuned its set-up, and what's more he was used to driving bad cars well.

For 2002, I'd be paired with Jarno Trulli, while the new test driver was Fernando Alonso. Jarno was one of my karting idols, and I'd loved racing with him, so being his teammate was a bit extra-special.

I got on with Fernando too. He'd come with us to Flavio's place in Kenya, and we had great fun together. We used to go cycling and running and one night he took an anti-malaria pill that affected him in a really weird way. He just couldn't stop laughing. It was like he was drugged, laughing his tits off all night long while we laughed at him. He's a very different character when he's not on malaria pills, of course, but we had some cool times together.

And things improved at the team. They really did. Not only had I raised my game in the break, but the car was much better too. It was faster. It handled better. It had power steering. Plus it featured a great 'launch control system', a bit of software that helped with standing starts by avoiding spin (that was eventually outlawed in 2004).

In other words: game on. I was in third in Malaysia with two laps to go and I thought, *oh my God, this is it, this is my first podium*. Michael Schumacher was six or seven seconds behind in fourth and no way was he going to catch me, and then, just as I started my last lap, the rear suspension failed on one side, and you can't drive fast with the car in that condition so while I was able to limp on, I was forced to watch helplessly as Michael passed me. I can still remember it now, that feeling, as fresh as this morning's coffee, a feeling like, *No, give me back my podium. Give it back*, as I crossed the line in fourth.

But if you could encapsulate the difference between that year and the one before in a single race it would be that, because there I was disappointed with fourth, *disappointed*, when the year before I could only dream of being fourth. I would have been turning cartwheels at fourth.

That's racing for you. It recalibrates your attitude to competition. When you're really flying nothing but a win will do; you're disappointed with second or third, inconsolable if you're not on the podium. But when the team isn't doing so well you're happy with an eighth. You're overjoyed that you've beaten your teammate.

It's different from practically any other sport I can think of in that way. It changes your perception of what it is to 'win'. We all line up on the grid, but the reality is that most of us know there's no chance of getting on the podium unless something untoward happens to Ferrari, Mercedes and Red Bull. So lining up behind those guys we've got our own personal targets and objectives – this guy wants to improve on ninth, this guy wants to be in the points for the first time, this guy wants to beat his teammate…

And all of that takes second place to the primary objective of scoring points, and thus making money for the team.

Profit in F1 comes from a variety of sources – media rights, sponsorship and so on – and in 2016, for example, totalled £1.8bn. Of that, half goes to the Formula One Group and its shareholders, and the other half is distributed amongst the teams. The way it's distributed is one of those mysteries known and understood by very few, and is often dictated by individual agreements between the teams. In 2016, for example, Ferrari earned more (£209.4m) than Mercedes (£202.7m), even though Mercedes had beaten them in the championship. That's because Ferrari get a special 'Ferrari Payment', while Mercedes and Williams have to make do with a lesser 'Historic Payment'. I guess it's a kind of loyalty card scheme.

What's crystal clear, however, is that the better you do in the championship, the more of the pot you will get.

Firstly, you have to be in the top ten to win anything significant. In 2016, Marussia were eleventh and they got £10m for their trouble, but that was it. In the top ten, meanwhile, each team received an equal-share prize of £42.7m just for turning up. However, it's up to them to improve on that by finishing races, scoring points and thus boosting the 'performance' payment, or if you're really flying, getting a share of the 'Constructors' Championship Bonus Fund'. So as a driver you're always fighting for something.

So that season, 2002, I was being a good earner for the team. Getting in the points. Challenging for podium places. Flavio noticed. The team noticed. I was feeling pretty buoyant, looking forward to building on that success for the next season. It's like that bit at the beginning of a superhero movie where the guy learns to use his newly acquired powers. Next he goes out and starts kicking supervillain ass. I felt like that – like I was just making that transition from one phase to the other.

And then one night I arrived home, well, the house where I was staying in Weybridge, the White House it was called – very presidential – when the phone rang.

It was Flavio.

'Jenson,' he mumbled, 'we won't be continuing our relationship with you in 2003. We have a contract with Jarno Trulli and also with Fernando Alonso, our test driver.'

It came as a shock. People ask if losing my Williams seat was a shock, but it wasn't. It was a bit of a bummer, especially in the light of the crappy season that followed, but it wasn't a shock.

This, though, this was a shock because I didn't know that Jarno and Fernando had contracts. I knew that mine was due to run out, of course, but I thought I'd done enough in that second season to earn my place; indeed, I objectively *had* done enough to earn my place when you consider that the announcement was made just prior to the French Grand Prix, by which time I was well ahead of Jarno.

By the end of the season, I'd been in the points seven times to Jarno's four – fourteen points to his nine. I had done what Flavio had advised me to do, which was to 'work harder'; I'd done what Mike asked me to do, which was to learn about the car. No doubt about it, I was going to leave Renault a better driver in pretty much every respect, but I didn't think I should be leaving at all. They had made clear their intention to challenge for the title in 2005 and I wanted to be around for that.

None of it mattered, though. If the press expressed surprise at my removal, Flavio would shrug and say, 'Time will tell if I am wrong.' What went mostly unremarked upon was that both Jarno and Fernando were managed by him.

Okay, I thought. Well, on the plus side, I never really fitted in at Benetton-then-Renault. I always felt like someone visiting rather than a permanent fixture. At least I wouldn't have to put up with Flavio any more.

But I was sweating. Thinking my career in F1 might be over. Cursing Flavio and his team, pledging never to buy another Benetton sweater and spitting on the name Renault. What was Flavio playing at? Putting me in a dark place and helping me clamber out, only to shove me back in again.

And then, a stroke of good fortune. BAR – British American Racing – came in for me. Partnered with Honda, they were a team that had grown out of the old Tyrrell set-up after legendary driver-turned-team-owner Ken Tyrrell retired from the sport. Among those who had taken over was Jacques Villeneuve's manager Craig Pollock. Jacques was installed as driver, and though they'd been a bit inconsistent, Jacques had scored a few podiums. The years 2001 and 2002, however, were bad ones, and there'd been some major changes as a result. Out went Craig Pollock and Jacques' teammate Olivier Panis. In came a new team principal, Dave Richards. And me.

Walking in through the doors of their offices in Brackley was like taking a breath of fresh air: welcoming, friendly a good atmosphere, which, I can't stress enough, is essential for a driver. It gives you confidence and focus. I'd be working with Dave and the designer Geoff Willis, both of whom I really got on with.

The only person who didn't want me there was Jacques Villeneuve.

35

The first I knew of any animosity was at the press conference.

There we were, doing our bit on stage with the car, smiley, smiley for the photos after which we were put into groups. Dave Richards was answering questions with one group, me with another, Jacques with another. During his session, Jacques was asked what he thought of his new teammate.

'Well,' he said, 'he's inexperienced, he looks like he should be in a boy band.'

I was next in with this particular group of journalists, who, like annoying younger brothers, couldn't wait to snitch on Jacques and tell me what he'd just said. What did I think of that? they asked.

'Uh…' I started, trying to process this new development. After all, I'd always enjoyed healthy competitive relationships with my team-mates. Friendly rivals. So this kind of open hostility floored me. I pulled it together enough to say that I hadn't joined the team to win praise from Jacques, I'd joined the team to win races, and afterwards the team were really apologetic and quick to assure me that Jacques spoke only for himself, not for the team. That was certainly the feeling I got from them, so everything was cool in that area.

But Jacques. God. He didn't speak to me. He wouldn't even look at me. If we passed each other in the paddock he'd find something interesting to look at in the opposite direction. Maybe I should have approached him: 'What did you say that for, Jacques, about the boy band? Which boy band exactly?' but I didn't, mainly because he gave every indication that any approach I made would be rebuffed.

Then came the season opener. Back to Melbourne. I qualified in front of him, but during the race he overtook me at the start.

It came to the first pit stop and he was supposed to pit first. Back then cars were fuelled for qualifying and you carried whatever you didn't use over to the race, which meant that you'd need to pit for refuelling during the race. Engineers would work out how much fuel you had and when you'd need to come in for more. 'Jacques, you pit for fuel on lap blah. Jenson on lap blah blah.'

At Melbourne, Jacques was supposed to pit on lap thirty and me on thirty-one. However, Jacques had saved a bit of fuel through the first stint of the race and didn't pit, even though they were calling him in. Instead, he deliberately came in on lap thirty-one, knowing I wouldn't be able to go any longer than thirty-one and that I'd have no choice but to pit behind him.

So it proved. I lost ten to twelve seconds in the pits, aeons of time. I stayed behind him. Whereas if he'd pitted when he was supposed to, I might well have overtaken him.

Why did he do it? Partly mind games, partly because he wanted to beat me – all's fair in love and F1, you might say. But it was a dick move, and for a driver of his quality, a fairly incomprehensible one. He might have felt that he didn't want whatshisname from Westlife coming in to beat him, but as a former World Champion he would have known the importance of keeping the team onside, and with that one act of petulance he turned them against him.

What's more he ended up looking worse in the end, because although I lost that twelve seconds I still finished the race on his bumper.

It was a situation that cast light on that age-old F1 conundrum: is your teammate a buddy or a rival?

The answer is that it depends on the teammate and it depends on the team. If you're racing for Mercedes or Ferrari, for example, you have to be aware that you might be asked to give up your leading position in order for your teammate to get championship points, and to me that's something rotten in the state of F1 right there, because in any sport it's wrong to ask a competitor to deliberately 'not win'.

Doing that in F1 is called 'team orders', and for about ten years it was banned, after Rubens Barrichello slowed down in Austria in 2003 to let Michael Schumacher pass. But the ban was lifted and now you can swap drivers around, do whatever you want, which is real shame in my opinion. You look on the podium and see the face of the guy who finished second. He's still up there but he's gutted because he knows he should have won, while the undeserving guy in first is there celebrating like he's had the best race of his life.

It happens everywhere, not just in F1. The other day I saw Porsche racing in the Le Mans Series and they held the lead car in the pits for an extra twenty seconds so that the other car could win and get more points for the championship. It's so sad to see: drivers give everything for their team and suddenly it's taken away from them.

Back to Jacques, and in Malaysia I beat him in qualifying and finished seventh. He retired early. In Brazil I outqualified him again, but that time I spun off. He retired in Imola. I came eighth. They'd changed the points system for that year, moving the cut-off to eighth, which meant that by the end of the season I'd been in the points four times but Jacques had only managed one.

And whaddaya know? He began to thaw. Suddenly Jacques was a nice guy. He started by looking at me, progressed to conversation, and then moved to the next stage: joking around. I wouldn't say we became great mates but we'd have the odd beer together. We'd even occasionally chat over a glass of wine in his motorhome. It was very civilised all of a sudden.

The reason was because I'd won his respect. I'd proved myself as a driver, despite my apparent inexperience. As we became closer, he opened up about the reasons for his previous unfriendliness. He wasn't upset about *me*, as such. He was upset with the team because Dave had taken over from Craig, his manager, and brought me in as 'his' driver. Jacques felt that he and Craig had built the team and now they were being usurped. It was nothing personal, he told me.

You might say that this statement rather contradicts what Jacques said to the press, given that comparing me to a member of a boy band is what most of us would consider 'personal', like telling someone they have bad breath or bogies hanging out of their nose. I'll let you draw your own conclusions about that. The point is that Jacques and I made up and he's been complimentary about me since, so we'll leave it there.

Besides, my teammate wasn't the only thing I had to worry about that season. There was the small matter of nearly killing myself.

36

Qualifying at Monaco was split into two sessions, one on Thursday afternoon and one Saturday. Thursday went well. Very well. I was third behind Michael Schumacher and Rubens Barrichello in the Ferraris, leaving in my wake the likes of DC and Kimi Räikkönen in the McLarens and Trulli and Alonso in the Renaults (spit).

You have to do well at qualifying in Monaco. The circuit's notoriously difficult to overtake, so I was especially pleased with my progress.

Saturday was a lovely day. They usually are in Monaco. It's a special place, which is one of the reasons I rented an apartment there, and why so many of us live there. (Friendly taxes, a lack of paparazzi, and the proximity of the motor-racing community are three more that spring to mind.)

That particular day was very sunny. The grandstands were heaving and the harbour was packed with boats, while up there on the road I was feeling full of beans, having the time of my life. Little less than a year before I'd been working my notice at Renault, chewing my nails as my managers worked to find me a new drive and wondering about my future in the sport. Now here I was, riding on the crest of a great Friday's qualifying. Boy from Frome metaphorically flicking the V-signs in Monaco. Keep it up in the afternoon and I could be looking at a podium.

With practice over, I set out for my first timed run. In the meantime, we'd changed the set-up. I had too much understeer, so we'd altered the balance of the car by adjusting the rollbar stiffness on the rear. Going stiffer on the rear mechanical grip means you get less rear grip but you have a stronger front end, and I should have compensated for that in the drive.

But I didn't. Or not enough. I came out of the tunnel, braked for the chicane and the rear wheels locked solid.

Which is bad.

What happens next takes place in a split-second: it's me feeling the brakes lock, releasing the brake, sensing the rear snap around, the lurching, floating, spacey feeling as my world spins and I know I'm no longer in control as its hurled at the left-hand barrier just outside the mouth of the tunnel and hits it with a horrendous screeching sound that they hear on the boats on the harbour, wiping out the two front wheels and ending what slim hope I have of controlling the skid, turning me from driver to passenger, skateboarding backwards with the G-force threatening to pull the skin from my body, everything, even my heart, feeling as though it's being gripped by an invisible giant hand that wants to separate my bones from the rest of me, as though I'm being sucked into a tube that's too small for me, expecting impact and thinking *this is going to hurt, this is really going to hurt* and then *bang* hitting the second barrier.

And being out cold.

The next face I saw was a marshal. He was mouthing something but I couldn't hear him. My vision had partly returned but my hearing was still shot. Other faces bobbed before me. My car, beached on the road and all twisted up around me, was surrounded by marshals.

'I don't understand what you're asking' I tried to say, but my helmet was on, and I was still trying to remember what had happened and wondering if everything was all right. If I was all right. If I was still in one piece.

Then I saw the face of Sid Watkins, the FIA chief medical officer. Now sadly departed, the late great Sid was a man who knew more about tending to drivers in crashes than anybody else in the world.

'Are you all right, lad? Where does it hurt?'

'Everywhere,' I told him, surprised and really quite pleased to hear the sound of my own voice, because at least that was concrete proof I wasn't dead.

'Just relax, Jenson,' he said.

They started cutting up my suit. *Why are you cutting up my suit?*

Needles went into me. Adrenalin, maybe, like in *Pulp Fiction*, although I can't say it had the same effect.

'Can you feel your legs?'

For some reason this struck me as funny and I started giggling.

'Where does it hurt?' he pressed.

Maybe ask me these questions before *you give me the shot of whatever it is you just gave me.*

It was Sid who developed the method of taking a driver out of a car without moving him and potentially aggravating any injuries. They used it then, taking the seat out in one piece with me still attached to it and then getting me on a gurney. The sun was in my eyes, I remember. Lovely Monaco day.

'Am I going to be okay?' I asked the nurse when at last they'd installed me in the ambulance. I still didn't know what if anything was wrong with me.

'I don't know,' she said.

Well, can't you just lie?

Next thing I knew we were at the hospital. They put me in a room. Louise was there. And my dad. And Dave Richards, the team principal.

Dave looked concerned but not too concerned. Louise and my dad, on the other hand, were ashen. Just seeing their stricken faces brought it home to me what had happened, but at the same time I was dazed and saying, 'I'll be okay. Whatever happens, I'll be fine. Just get me in the car, let me qualify.'

'No, Jense…' started Dad.

'Look, let me just finish qualifying and then I can come back here and we can do all the tests then.'

Not thinking straight. Not able to fully process events just yet. The fact that the session had been red-flagged and they'd winched my crippled car off the track, nose and rear crumpled, skewiff tyres giving it the appearance of an F1 pancake. Thinking only of the fact that during the previous day's qualifying I'd been third, and that would have meant a podium for sure.

'No, mate,' said Dad. His mouth was set. Eyes flecked with concern. 'You've been knocked out. They're not going to let you leave the hospital and even if they did you definitely can't drive.'

A French doctor had arrived, having caught the gist of what was going on. 'You're not going anywhere,' he said, 'we've seen your brain-waves and they're all over the place.'

'But they were like that before,' I said. Neither Louise, Dad or Dave Richards laughed at the joke, and the doctor just sighed. 'Even so, you're not allowed to go.'

There followed the usual battery of tests: CAT, CT, MRI, before I was allowed to leave the next morning, but of course unable to take any further part in the race, although I was press-ganged into doing various interviews, and I was allowed on to the grid, where I wished Jacques well.

It's like they say about falling. It's not the fall that kills you, it's the landing. Same with a crash like that. It's the stopping that hurts. That's why mine was a bad one. You can flip a car and walk away from it, but when a car that is braking from a speed of 180mph meets an immovable object like a barrier, the G is immense. *Immense*. It's why I had to have yet another battery of tests before I drove again for the next race in Canada.

But I did it. I raced again as soon as I could. And I did it without a second thought, because, believe it or not, having an accident like that has a beneficial effect when it comes to the fear (or not) you feel when you next clamber into a car.

The reason is simple: you've just survived a massive crash. I'd effectively driven into a wall at something north of 100mph. That's an impact that would instantly kill everybody travelling in a road car, but I'd walked away without a scratch on me. (I didn't literally walk away, but you know what I mean.)

You're protected in an F1 car. Or you *feel* protected, which is the main thing, even if it's an illusory feeling. Because while the carbon-fibre safety cell provides a barrier between you and whatever it is you hit, it doesn't fully address the main problem, the G, and the impact that can cause your brain to rebound off your skull.

All I can say is that I went into the next race, not daunted by my experience but emboldened by it. I went in feeling quite happy to have that same accident again in the knowledge that all the systems had been working the way they should.

Mind you, try telling that to my mum. She'd been watching qualifying on TV and had spent a tearful couple of hours trying to find out if I was okay. I really got it in the neck for that.

37

Funny thing about braking, though. You do really need to get it right. It's one of the main principles of racing.

But, of course, you need to do it carefully, otherwise you'll get what happened to me in Monaco, which is the brakes locking up. Locking up is when you've braked but you grab the brake disc too hard, so the tyre will stop moving momentarily. You get smoke from the tyre, and because it's stopped moving on the road, you get less grip because it slides and over-heats, leaving you with a flat spot. And that's if nothing untoward happens during the lock-up itself, such as the rear snapping on you or stepping out.

Locking up is a thing of the past on road cars, of course, thanks to ABS – Antilock Braking System – so drivers can jam their foot on the brake as hard as possible and the car will do everything for them. But a good driver who understands braking, and can feel the car can probably brake better than an ABS. Personally I'd have ABS taken off my road cars if I could. I know I could stop more quickly without it, and I hate the feeling when it kicks in (all to do with the feel of the car, see?).

In a racing car, braking's tough, because you're on the limit the whole time. You want the car to stop as quickly as possible, but there are grip limitations, and you're always pushing the boundaries of that grip without it locking. And if you brake too hard or you hit a bump on the circuit and the tyre lifts off the road, then it grabs and it's locked and trying to stop a tyre from locking is tough once it's started.

So the first thing you need to master about braking is *when* to brake, and that's up to you, my friend. That part of your racecraft will come down to your personal style as much as anything. This was one of the reasons things improved so drastically between years one and two of Benetton. When I got together with the engineers, knuckled down and learned about set-up, we realised that I was braking harder than Fisi did, and thus if we ran the same ride height – which we had been doing – then I had a tendency to lock up, whereas he didn't

Another thing I did was brake early. Engineers criticised me for it, thinking that I was being a bit of a wuss by braking early. But I subscribe to the Alain Prost school of thought there: brake early and then you can get back on the throttle more quickly.

Either way, the process for braking is pretty much the same, and the process is this: you're full on the throttle and then you hit the brakes hard, something like 130 bar of pressure on the pedal. You can push it harder if you want, and in certain corners you do, up to 140 bar, but if you do that you're wasting your energy. Anything over 130 bar you don't actually get any more braking power because the system can't take it. Plus, you always run the risk of doing what Mark Webber did in 2010 and shearing the brake pedal right off.

So you lift off the throttle, bang on the brakes. Right away you're pulling G. A road car, if you brake as hard as you can, you pull about 1G – if that, probably 0.8 of a G. In an F1 car you'll pull that just lifting off the throttle. Hit the brakes and you pull 5G

Anyway, you lift off, you brake. And then you start modulating the brakes, moving your foot on the brake pedal in order to stop the tyres from locking. At this point downforce comes into play. Remember that? Quick reminder: the faster the car goes, the more downforce it produces, the more it sticks to the deck. But you've lifted off, don't forget, you're reducing speed, you're feathering up on the brake – and now you're super-aware that there's less downforce and therefore less aerodynamic grip.

It's a dance, is what it is. A little foot jig that takes place between brake and throttle: judge the corner, brake, then start coming off the brake pedal as you begin turning into the corner. Keeping the revs up before you get fully back on the throttle.

In long corners, you're on and off the brakes all the way through, trying to balance the car, because throttle causes oversteer whereas braking will straighten the car up, and you're careful not to get on the throttle and brake at the same time, which is something you'd never do in a road car but occasionally in an F1 car to warm them up, but otherwise no. It's called overlapping and it uses too much fuel.

Of course, there's another important occasion for which you need to master braking. And that's overtaking.

Just as cornering is a conversation that takes place between throttle and brake, so overtaking is a negotiation between downforce and the racing line. You never really stop working on your race position so you're in a position to overtake without losing downforce. But more than likely that movement will cost you the perfect racing line.

As I've already said, you don't overtake on the straights as a rule, not unless you get mega slipstream from the car ahead, or you can use DRS or there's a significant amount of difference in your corner exit compared to that of the guy in front, so assuming the guy you're racing is competent, he probably won't mess up his corner exit, and the chances are he's going to have a good racing line as well. Added to that you've got his dirty air disturbing your downforce, which forces you to drive differently.

So, for example, if you go into a high-speed corner right behind the car in front, you lose a lot of your front downforce, so to combat that you have to pull out slightly and take a different line in order to still get a bit of downforce on that front wing, but maybe not as much as the guy in front.

Low speed corners, on the other hand, are where it's at. When you pull out to overtake, you've got the same downforce as the guy in front. What's more, you've caught him up so you're in his slipstream getting less drag and carrying more speed, so you can pull out and when you hit the brakes, you have the downforce, so you don't have to worry about losing grip.

Again, it comes back to the braking. You have to brake later than the other guy, a fraction of a second, the blink of an eye. But enough that you can carry speed through to your manoeuvre, pull out and make a dive down the inside. It may not be the quickest line but it doesn't matter because you're going down the inside and he can't turn in.

And that's it. That combination of reading the race, good throttle control, good braking, an understanding of downforce and racing dynamics, is what it takes to get past the guy in front.

The reason I can do it and most people can't is, firstly, because I know how to brake. I understand how a car works and how to drive it as fast as possible, and the reason I know that is because I started at a very early age, when I was like a sponge, learning from my dad and Dave and Paul Lemmens, keeping some of what they told me and discarding other bits depending on my style, but always listening, never thinking that I knew best.

And secondly, I guess natural talent has something do with it. But what I'd grasped as I came up through the ranks – and this was the hard lesson I learned after the first season in Benetton – is that natural talent isn't enough. You may have ability but you need to develop it.

I think there are certain drivers who have more natural talent than others in Formula One – Lewis, for example – but it doesn't also mean that they're the quickest drivers. It means they've had to work less, but they've still had to work. You're racing against the best in the world; you've got to fine-tune your abilities and you've got to fine-tune the car and the interaction of you and the car as well.

Thirdly, you have to have an inbuilt need to push a car to its limit, and the fearlessness that comes with that. And I know I keep banging on about this, but for me it's always been about feel. I'm a very reactive driver, so say when I come to the corner and brake at a hundred metres out, I'm feeling whether the front's going to lock up or all is fine, or if the rear's going to lock up or if it's working, and I can react to that in order to control the car and carry the speed.

In a way, the ears are more important than the eyes in motor racing. I'm about listening to the engine, keeping the revs high and carrying more speed. So even if I take a wider line, I know I'm going to be quicker. It's the basic racing principle of trying to put the car in the right place. Just like Bowser in *Super Mario Kart*.

38

Jacques left BAR at the end of that season. He and I were on good terms but it seems that he'd burned his bridges with the team. I'm sure he has his own view on what happened, but for whatever reason he ended up leaving one race before the end of the season, replaced by Takuma Sato, a Japanese guy who'd previously driven for Jordan and had a reputation as an exciting, aggressive driver.

Meanwhile, I ended the season in ninth with seventeen points, feeling happier with how things had gone. I had confidence, not only that my career was on the up but also that I could lead the team. I was number one now, Takuma the newbie.

The 2004 car tested well. Designer Geoff Willis had made huge strides with the downforce. Added to that we used Michelins, which were a better tyre.

Sure enough, at Malaysia I got my first podium, then another at Bahrain.

Meanwhile, at Imola I managed to break what you might call my qualifying duck and came in first, which for me was big, in many ways more important to me than that first podium.

Qualifying's not my forte, racing is, but that was my first and I remember every moment of that lap. Qualifying was one car at a time.

Michael went out and did his lap and then I went out, and my time was two-and-a-half tenths quicker than him. This was around Imola, in front of all of the *tifosi*, the Ferrari fans, and I put it on pole by two-and-a-half-tenths, which is a massive gap.

The car worked well, it handled well, and when I watched the lap back what struck me was the sound of it, revving its nuts off the whole way round what was a beautiful, flowing lap. The circuit finishes with a little tough chicane, bounce over the kerbs, across the finish line and I knew right then, as soon as I felt that bounce then crossed the finish line. I knew it was a pole lap.

Immediately, the team came on the radio, screaming in my ear, 'You're on pole, you're on pole,' and that meant the world. I was racing against the best drivers in the world and I'd gone the quickest, faster than Michael in a Ferrari. It meant a lot – and that pole lap goes down as one of my favourite of all time – because I've never been the quickest guy over one lap; I'm much better in a race situation when it's about thinking on your feet through a race. For me, that's my strength: saving fuel, having three sets of tyres and assessing how quickly you can get from the first lap to the first pit stop, rather than just banging it out for one lap.

In the race, however, Ferrari were quicker. I got a great start and pulled away leaving Michael battling with Juan Pablo Montoya in the Williams and I built a good lead for the first lap, which is always something you've got to do when you start on pole: get a massive gap on the first laps, hammer it like you're qualifying.

But then I pitted on lap ten and Michael went a couple of laps longer, pitted and came out in front of me, after which I was always trying to chase him down.

He was just too quick for me, but even so, a great race and a great way to score a hat-trick of podiums.

In retrospect that year was a funny one, because it was just so easy to get a podium. It came easily, and the reason for that was that things went our way. We never had any reliability issues, and other people made mistakes and we capitalised on them. It's another of those F1 idiosyncrasies. If you have a good car, everything's so much easier. You can make mistakes and still have a good race. Whereas if you have a middle-of-the-pack car, you can't make a single error. If you do, you get a shit result. With a quick car, you can fight back from a balls-up.

That December we bowled up to the *Autosport* Awards, which after the FIA Awards is the biggest motor-racing awards ceremony. The top award is the International Racing Driver of the Year, which is voted for by the public, and usually goes to the Formula One World Champion. But it didn't go to Michael Schumacher that year, it was awarded to me.

So that was pretty awesome. I mean, I guess with *Autosport* being a British magazine and me being British that must have helped. But even so, it felt like things were looking up.

Oh, but then…

39

Having finished the season third in the Drivers' with BAR taking second in the Constructors' – a good, no, a *brilliant* year – I chose to leave BAR and move to Williams for 2005.

Why? Bloody good question. The problem with BAR was that it was using Honda engines but it wasn't a works manufacturer team, and we felt that you had to be with a works manufacturer to win in Formula One. Williams was basically BMW-Williams, and they had been doing well. They'd won races with Montoya and Ralf Schumacher and I felt that they were a good bet for the future. Hands up, I was thinking of number one, hoping to move to a team that I thought could further my career and help me become a World Champion.

Little did we know, however, that BMW was pulling out of the sport and Williams would be using a Cosworth engine, which was probably going to be slow. So that was a sudden and unwelcome fly in the ointment.

After that, well, I would go into all the nitty-gritty but you'd switch off, so I won't. The upshot was that BAR kicked up a fuss. The engine issue became a real problem. I changed managers. There was a court case. The judge decided I'd have to stay with BAR for another year.

In October 2004, I parted company with my manager and asked a friend, Richard Goddard, to manage me. Richard was presented with a situation where I'd signed a contract with Williams but didn't really want to go there because of the engine, while BAR wanted to keep me.

I left it to Richard to negotiate, but the end result was that we had to pay Frank to get out of the contract and stay at BAR.

A messy, dragged-out business that took over two years to sort, after which the press were asking, 'How is your relationship with Frank now?' and I was thinking, *Well, he's happy because he's got loads of cash out of it, a good day at the office for him,* while also having the problem of walking back into BAR to endure the narrowed eyes of the team.

No doubt they were thinking, *He doesn't want to be here. He thinks he's too good for us.* Which of course wasn't the case. Well, I suppose it was a bit. But it wasn't as though I regarded BAR as a crap or even lesser team, just that I (mistakenly, as it turned out) believed that Williams might be a better option. Don't forget I'd been racing F1 since 2000. I wasn't a dinosaur but neither was I a rookie. I was ready to move up, to make more frequent appearances on the podium, and challenge for the championship.

The season began and I got a podium at Imola, but then the team was disqualified for an illegal fuel tank. We were barred for three races and had a fine to pay. It was a shock, but in a way it cooled things down for me, firstly because it proved that despite the contract dispute I was still pulling for team BAR, and secondly because the 'Jenson's disloyalty' issue was sidelined in favour of the 'fuck, we've just been disqualified' issue.

Oh, we had so much fun for those three races though. We had to turn up at the circuits during the day but at nights our time was our own, and without having to worry about driving the next day, it was party central.

In Cannes, we went to Naomi Campbell's party. We went to another party, Dolce & Gabbana, I think it was, where I ended up sleeping on the sofa of somebody's yacht for a couple of hours and then getting a taxi back to Monaco, having breakfast, a quick Bloody Mary and then going straight into the TV box to do the commentary on the race. (I did a pretty good job, if I do say so myself.) Kid Rock was at the race. Him and the old man were getting on famously, best pals they were. They'd bonded over a love of Bob Seger, particularly the song 'Like A Rock', which was Dad's favourite. He used to put it on all the time when I was karting. If I'd won a race then we'd be playing it in the Transit on the way home.

We all went out on Saturday night when my dad pulled his party trick: falling over.

He used to do it quite a lot. His speciality was to fall on the table, sending glass and bottles flying, which frightened me to death, because he was diabetic. Most of the time he'd emerge from the carnage completely unscathed. On this occasion, he'd picked up a cut. Good old Kid Rock used his hat to plaster the cut and then they sang 'Like A Rock' together. Of course.

40

That year, 2005, was the one where things went seriously pear-shaped at the US Grand Prix. At that particular moment in time, Formula One was big everywhere in the world apart from in the States (same as now, really) and we were trying to break into the market by racing at Indy, their famous oval circuit.

We weren't using the whole oval, just a bit of it, but even so, our tyres couldn't take the banking and in practice they were blowing up, causing accidents all over the show.

What we worked out was that the Bridgestones were fine, but the Michelins were a liability. Basically, if we were using Michelins – which we were – it was dangerous to race.

Overnight there were discussions like you wouldn't believe. It would take far too long to go into the ins-and-outs of it, but it ended up that we were obliged to start the race even though we didn't plan on continuing it. So the world settled down to watch the Grand Prix only to see the majority of cars start the race and then peel off into the pits and park up, race over. Only a handful of cars raced that day.

The fans were in shock. As you might imagine, there were a lot of hot dogs dropped that afternoon, and it pretty much destroyed us in the States until Austin came on to the calendar seven years later in 2012.

It was during that time in America that we ended up making a documentary for CBS at the Playboy Mansion. This was something organised by James, my PR guy, but as for what happened to the finished programme I couldn't say. What I can remember is that we arrived in LA having travelled from the Canadian Grand Prix. We'd had a party the night before, during which my manager Richard tripped down a hole and sprained his ankle (it's a prerequisite of a Jenson Button party that someone must fall over and sustain an injury) and by the time we stumbled out of that it was daylight, so we went back to the hotel to freshen up, pack bags and leave for the airport.

Travelling with me was Richard (in pain from his sprained ankle) and Richie Williams, my old karting chum, who came to as many races as he could. I was late and kept the car waiting, so by the time we arrived at the airport we were behind schedule. I had no bags so I checked in, passed through Passport Control before them and got through to departures, went to my gate.

Suddenly everything got really busy. No sign of Richard (limping) or Richie. They were taking for ever. I took my seat on the plane. Their seats, empty, were across from me. The plane filled.

'Excuse me, sir,' asked a stewardess, indicating the seats, 'I see you're travelling with two other people. Are they coming?'

I looked at her and I thought, *Should I? Shall I? Oh, go on then...*

Now, before I go on, you've to bear in mind, one, that we'd been at a party the night before so maybe I wasn't 100 per cent sober by this point and, two, we were at that stage of our lives where we played gags on each other all the time, where virtually nothing was off-limits, where everything was funny.

So I looked at the stewardess and as sweetly as you like, as though butter wouldn't melt in my mouth, I said, 'No, I'm sorry, I'm afraid they're not coming.'

'Ah,' she said, pulling a pained face, 'then I'm afraid we're going to have to offload their bags.'

'Oh, I'm sorry,' I said, with a pained face in return, 'I'll be sure to let them know the trouble they've caused.'

The problem was that Richard was in Business Class but Richie wasn't. Being a mate, Richard had waited for Richie so they could board together, but of course they had reckoned without Richard's poorly ankle.

So we took off without them and I got to LA while they sat in the lounge for six hours, during which time Richard fell asleep, forgot about his ankle, woke up with pins and needles and stamped his foot to try and get rid of them. You can imagine the scene.

But I missed that, because I was already in LA. I'd landed and travelled to the house we were due to stay in, which was in Malibu, a beautiful house owned by the guy who invented Inspector Gadget. I grabbed a Corona, sat on the balcony, put my feet up and gave Richard a call. He wasn't happy.

The next day, a load of us including James, Richie and Richard, toddled off to the Playboy Mansion for this documentary. There we met an ancient Hugh Hefner, who shuffled down in his red smoking jacket and didn't even know what time of day it was. I was giving him a signed top and he literally didn't know who I was, or why I was giving him this top. I was thinking, *Oh God, this is going to be the day that Hugh Hefner dies.*

So there I was, hoping Hugh wouldn't die, frankly wondering what on earth I was doing there, wandering around the Playboy Mansion interviewing various people, including his three wives, after which we went to another party, followed by food at the Melrose Diner, where one of our American companions was so tired that he fell asleep in the middle of eating his burger and dropped it all down himself.

And that was LA.

Meanwhile, the 2005 season continued, but it was a bit crap compared to the previous year. Third-place finishes in Germany and Belgium and ninth overall in the championship wasn't quite building on the success of 2004. Yet again I was beginning to feel frustrated, certain that it was my time, yet somehow unable to convert my growing experience and confidence on the track into a sustained title challenge. You have to win things in motor racing. You either keep winning races or you nab a World Championship. Or nobody will remember your name.

To do that, I needed the equipment, so Honda moving into BAR for 2006 was very exciting, not just because they could produce a good power unit but they could put money into the team, help BAR on the chassis side of things, employ the right people. All the things a team needs.

Me, I was greedy for success. I'd been in the points for some time now; I'd had podiums. Now I wanted to win. I wanted to challenge for the big one. It wasn't as though I was being blamed for not winning previously. After all, none of my teammates had won; in fact, I'd outscored them. Even so, there's a perception. Was I a nearly man?

I had a new teammate. Out went Takuma Sato, who on his day could be very good but struggled with consistency, and in came Rubens Barrichello, who'd been alongside Michael for years at Ferrari but rarely given the chance to win because he always had to give it up for Michael.

Like me, he wanted to win, so he came to Honda. So suddenly I had a teammate who was very competitive, very quick, very experienced, and was capable of designing a car around himself. Suddenly, it got a lot more competitive and thus a lot more fun for me. There's no such thing as a racing driver who doesn't like a challenge.

We got to Hungary, where I qualified fourth but was given a ten-place penalty after an engine failure in practice. Michael Schumacher and Fernando Alonso were at the back of the grid with me, penalised for silly things they'd done in practice. We were like the naughty schoolboys at the back of what was a very damp grid.

All to play for, nothing to lose. Wet conditions.

It was my time to shine.

41

That moment of peace. You get it when you first put down your visor, and then you get it again on the grid when the crew have left and it's just you and the other drivers, approaching your moment of truth.

And then, even though there are nineteen other cars revving their engines, it suddenly becomes very peaceful again.

This is your focus coming to you. Your world starts to narrow. At that moment your only thought is of getting the perfect start. Outside of that nothing else seems to exist: just you and the start you need to have. I'm often asked if I miss karting, because it was such a 'pure' form of racing, a true test of driving skill. But the answer's no, because that feeling I'm talking about only exists in Formula One.

And then there's a moment, just as the lights go out, when it suddenly goes almost quiet as the revs drop when you release the clutch and pull away. These days there's more driver input at the start, but back then it was pretty easy to be exact, a series of beeps telling you what to do. Inevitably, your wheels spin, because you get excited, but you try to limit it by holding your foot, keeping your throttle percentage constant and waiting for the wheelspin to subside before applying the throttle again, then going up through the gears. We have rev lights to tell you when to shift, but I don't pay attention to those

– using ear and feel – more intent on looking ahead and positioning myself for turn one.

Turn one is pandemonium. It always is. You don't want to lose position, so you're looking in the mirrors to stay aware of any potential threat from behind, but equally you're focusing ahead, because that first turn is all about gaining position so you're trying to find a gap to go through. At the same time, you don't want to take the gap immediately, because you want to tow up behind the guy, get a good run and *then* pull out.

Which is what I did to the great Michael Schumacher at turn one of the Hungarian Grand Prix. Like me he was desperate to make up places after his lowly start, but he was on Bridgestones and struggling, maybe being a little tentative on the damp surface. I used his caution to my advantage, braking later and sailing past him on the inside.

My first scalp of the race, a mighty one at that, and a great bit of action between me and Michael. He was a tough driver but he was always fair with me. He never took the piss when it came to racing; he'd push me to the limit but never over it. A controversial character, for sure – just ask Jacques Villeneuve and Damon Hill – but it was always fun fighting with him.

Especially when you put him in the rear-view mirror.

The first lap of any race is as vital as it is hard-fought. At Hungary I was in the middle of the pack, where it's most crazy. You're looking at the guy in front hoping he's not going to change line. You get next to him and suddenly he comes across and you've got a car boxing you in on the other side. You're trying to find space, keen not to lose position, trying to make up places, trying not to hit anyone and desperate to stop being hit yourself, because if you break your front wing on the first lap, it's game over.

And that's if everyone gets a normal start. If a car up front gets a bad start and everyone's trying to go around him then it's even worse. He's trying to hold his position, so he starts weaving to keep drivers behind him. You're trying to get past without losing position yourself. You're still trying to think about gaining position, protecting your wing, etc.

It's a scary lap too. The rule in Formula One is that if you have a car on your tail on the straight, you can't move twice. So, for example, if I try to overtake the driver in front, I might go to the left, and he's allowed to move and block me, but he's not allowed to move back.

The idea is to stop dangerous driving and improve racing by offering opportunities to overtake, otherwise cars would simply weave in front of each other for the whole race.

The other rule is you can't move while you're braking in a corner, because if you do that and the guy behind you is trying to overtake he's liable to go over the top of you. So that's banned too.

But the reason the first lap is the most nerve-racking is because that's the lap where the rules go out of the window. There's so much going on. Drivers bank on the fact that any infractions may well get missed, plus our adrenalin is way, way high, heart rate through the roof, you're driving on instinct. But like I say: great fun.

By the end of that lap I was up from fourteenth to twelfth.

By lap two I'd made my way up to ninth.

And then from lap three onwards, I found my rhythm. It's pretty much always the same. That's the point at which the race settles down a bit, but it isn't like we drive round for fifty laps behind each other. You're thinking of the tyres and trying to anticipate your competitors' race plan. Over a weekend, there are different compounds of tyres you can use: the softest are quick for a couple of laps but degrade quickly, while the harder ones last a lot longer. So you're checking out what tyres other drivers are using, trying to work out when they might pit for new ones. I'm constantly talking to my engineers trying to work out when X or Y's tyres will degrade, when he'll need to pit, thinking, *Well, that guy two cars in front, he's on softer tyres, he's going to pit early, we should be able to beat him.* But then you forget about the guy two cars back who pitted early and can now over-jump you in your pit stop. You think that you and your strategist have gone through every scenario beforehand, but there'll always be one you haven't banked on. Or simply a driver with a better strategy.

Around we went. Fernando had the lead but by now I was chasing him from second, both of us clocking up fastest laps, the gap between us fluctuating between four and five seconds.

On the forty-sixth lap of seventy, I made my second stop and re-fuelled but Fernando maintained his lead. However, when he came in for his stop on lap fifty-one his driveshaft broke, and that was it. He crashed out. Race over.

On my third stop I moved to slicks, which was exactly the right time. When I radioed in to ask about my lead I was told it was thirty-five seconds with ten laps to go, and that is a big, big lead by anyone's standards.

Now all I had to do was stay in front, and that's the time you get on the radio and say to the team, 'Guys, is the car okay? Is there anything I can do to look after it?'

Most of the time they say, 'No, just do what you're doing, just bring it home,' so that's cool, but at the same time you're keeping an eye on the fuel.

Prior to the start, we do simulations to gauge how much fuel we think we'll use during the race. It tells you on the dash how much you're using per lap and it'll tell you in percentage terms how much fuel you've used and how much fuel you should have used. If I've used more fuel than I should, it'll be red. Green if I've saved fuel. So say, for example, if you're on lap forty of a sixty-lap race and it says you're minus 5 per cent, that's worrying because you've got to save 5 per cent fuel over the rest of the race, which is five kilos.

To save fuel you have to cruise. You lift off early for the corners, 'lifting coast' we call it. If you'd normally brake at a hundred metres, you lift off and then brake at two hundred to save fuel. Another thing we do is short shifting. So if you normally shift at 13,000rpm up to the next gear, you shift at 10,000rpm instead.

But of course you still need to keep tyre temperature, because if the tyre temperatures drop too low the tyre doesn't work, so you're stuck. There are times when the team say, 'Jenson, you need to save fuel, but keep the tyre temperatures up,' and you're like, 'How can I keep the tyre temperatures up if I've got to save fuel?'

To which they say, 'Just do your best, Jenson.'

Meanwhile, the track itself is changing. As rubber is laid down you get more grip on the racing line which isn't a bad thing, but everywhere else on the track you get 'marbles', which is when bits of degraded rubber flick off the tyres and on to the track. Marbles aren't a problem if you're out in front like I was, but they make life a lot harder if you're trying to overtake. You brake late for a corner, run wide, you go on the marbles and suddenly you've got less grip than you had before. It can take two or three corners before you clean your tyres and get the proper grip back.

It's funny, because at times like that, with all that stuff to think about, driving is the least of your worries. Driving is the bit you know you can do. It's the rest that's tough.

But you do it. And I did it then. I was roaring into the radio – shouting so loudly that during the interviews later I could barely speak I was that hoarse. And the next I knew I was across the finish line in first, and then in *parc fermé* where I unstrapped and leapt out of the car like a man doing star jumps. Nick Fry was there, the first to congratulate me. My cheeks were wet with tears – I'd been crying with sheer elation and hardly even realised it, as I left the car, burst out of *parc fermé* to see the team, and of course my dad, his eyes gleaming with tears as he grabbed me and pulled me into a hug that I knew so well, beaming with pride. There were times it had felt as though we'd never get here, but here we were, my first Grand Prix win.

42

I saw a lot of grown men cry that afternoon. The Japanese were especially emotional. They'd worked so hard for it. And the great thing was that Takeo Fukui, who was the President of Honda – as in President of Honda *worldwide*, not just motorsport – was there. He hardly ever came to races but in a stroke of good luck was at this one. He came up on the podium as a representative of the team.

I'd had four second places, nine third places. They were starting to say that I'd never win a Grand Prix, but at last I had, and I always enjoy podium celebrations – I make no apology for being a demon with the champagne – but, boy, did I enjoy that one.

Next I was told I had to fly straight to China for a sponsor event. Oh my God, are you serious? I have to go to China after winning my first Grand Prix?

Yes they were serious. Positively insistent. Okay, right. Deep breath. *Go.* We dived in a car then transferred to a helicopter and then took a private jet from Hungary back to the UK, drinking champagne, living it up, and then jumping on a plane from London to Shanghai.

In China, it was as though the energy had all been sucked out of me after the race but I did the event there, by which point my girlfriend at the time, Florence, had flown out to China. More celebrations back at the hotel.

Great, now I get to go home.

No. Now you get to go to Japan.

By this time I was seriously overdoing my duty; I just wanted to return home and celebrate, but okay, let's get this over with and go to Japan. So we hopped over from China to the Honda offices in Tochigi in Japan.

'This might be a bit emotional', I was warned, and they weren't kidding. Arriving, we found ourselves at the end of a long corridor that passed the centre of an open office. The office was about five hundred metres long, with desks on either side of it, only nobody was at their desk; they had all stood and were lining the corridor, all of them in a state of excitement somewhere between simmering and boiling over. I'm not kidding, there must have been over a thousand people in that office, all wanting to thank me for giving them Honda's first Formula One win since the 1980s, a guard of honour cheering and clapping as we made our way down the corridor.

It was… *magical.* And I'm so glad they forced me to go to Japan and experience it, because I'll never forget it as long as I live.

It was a special feeling, that win. There were always questions from the people who don't know the sport: when are you going to win? I'd say to them, if you watched the sport and understood it, you'd know the car isn't quick enough to win races. But people outside motorsport didn't see that. They just saw the erstwhile golden boy failing to live up to the hype.

Fair enough, though, I'd taken longer than I or anyone else would have wished. One hundred and thirteen races, to be exact. And though I'd always known that the failure to win wasn't my sole responsibility, and so there wasn't pressure, as such, I'd been getting frustrated by seeing other guys taking all the glory and being unable to challenge for the win myself. Fernando Alonso had been my test driver when I was at Benetton in 2002. He took my seat and he was winning for that team, which was galling.

So the win was enjoyable, but I think mostly it was relief that I'd finally got that monkey off my back. At the same time I tried to enjoy it as much as I could, because I knew the next one wasn't round the corner. We'd still won despite not having the quickest car. But we were also aware that it wasn't going to happen again in a hurry.

And it didn't. Not that season. But fourth in Turkey, fifth in Italy, fourth in China and Japan, and, finally, third in Brazil wasn't too shabby. The season in 2006 ended up being a really good one.

I should have known better. It all went to shit in 2007.

43

At the end of the year, Chrissy and I took a boys' trip to the MTV Music Awards in Copenhagen. We partied. A lot. We met Daniel Craig, and this was just when he'd been announced as the new James Bond, so that was thrilling, and a good chance for us to wheel out our Sean Connery impressions.

When we were all partied-out we took a plane to Belgium, back to where I won the European Championship, for two days of karting. It was good but for the fact that after the first day I went to bed with sore ribs. Didn't think much of it, got up and did some more karting. After that I was in serious pain. I'd been wearing a rib protector but I'm a tall guy and all that bouncing around in the kart had fractured two of my ribs.

This all came to light after I'd flown back to the UK, the upshot being that I missed all of winter testing in the new car. I had to rely on Rubens' report, and his report was…

The car is shit.

Problem? Honda had fired Geoff Willis. That was the wrong move. Especially as his replacement, Shuhei Nakamoto, was not nearly as well versed in F1 as Geoff had been. Sure enough, the car was a mess, aerodynamically all over the place. Neither I nor Rubens could do anything with it, and as a result we'd spend most of the season propping up the back of the grid.

To add insult to injury, this was the year that Honda decided to adopt a new 'green' way of working called Earth Dreams, which was done with the best of intentions but was fatally misguided. Firstly, they changed the livery of the car. They painted it as the planet Earth, to symbolise the fact that we were saving the planet. They didn't have sponsors stickered on the car – the first time such a thing had happened since 1968 – but instead sponsors could 'buy' the car and use it as part of their marketing strategy: 'the car is the star' was the buzz-phrase at the time.

Added to that they changed all the monitors to make them low-emission; we had to make a big show of changing light bulbs wherever we went; we had to plant a tree for every lap we did, which meant that we spent the whole season being photographed planting trees.

All good in principle – don't get me wrong. Just a bit of a ball-ache in practice, and maybe just a bit, dare I say, *pointless*. When you consider the carbon footprint of Honda, F1, and motor racing as a whole, it was like Bernard Matthews campaigning on behalf of vegetarianism.

Of course, this was something that journalists were quick to point out, barely disguising their mirth as Rubens and I wriggled like worms on barbed questions. Wouldn't a more effective way of saving the planet be to withdraw from Formula One altogether? they said. Maybe even stop making cars? 'The car's not very competitive anyway,' they'd add. 'Wouldn't it be more green just to stop racing?'

It was hard to disagree with the logic, and certainly for me it took every ounce of diplomacy and loyalty I had not to simply agree with the journalists.

Elsewhere the rise of a rookie called Lewis Hamilton at McLaren-Mercedes was making waves. This was his first season in F1 and he won at Canada (my gear selection problem put me out while I was still on the grid) and then went on to win the next one, America (I had a wretched race). He'd go on to notch up nine consecutive podium finishes that season, second in the Drivers' Championship to Kimi Räikkönen.

The ascent of Lewis was a real good news/bad news situation for me. The good news was that the press no longer amused themselves by asking questions about Honda's green policy. The bad news was that they amused themselves by asking questions about Lewis. How did I rate his chances? How did I feel about him? Diplomacy won the day, but of course I was sore. Who wouldn't be? People were going wild over a British driver and it wasn't me.

Rubens and I could only hope things would improve for the 2008 car, but if anything things got worse. On the one hand, I finished sixth in Spain and I changed a lot of light bulbs. On the other hand, Rubens and I spent the season battling with an aerodynamically unstable, unreliable car with a fancy picture of the planet Earth on it. At least he had a podium at Silverstone. I was only in the points once all season.

It was the first year since 2001 that my teammate had scored more points than me, and it was a big dent in my competitive pride. I knew that I could and should have done better, but I also knew that some of the fight had gone out of me. The year 2006 had been so good that I'd started to… *hope*, I suppose, maybe even think in terms of challenging for the championship. For that to be followed by two such lame years was tough to take. The car was difficult to drive and it didn't suit my style, so I probably wasn't pushing it as hard as I should have been. Meanwhile, I was having to stand by and watch Lewis do really well.

Having almost won the championship in 2007, he did it for real in 2008, and it was tough for me to see that, not because I begrudged him his success or was especially jealous of him, but because we were both British drivers and our backgrounds and trajectories had been so similar – my dad had tuned his kart engines, for God's sake. I knew that given half a chance I could be just as competitive as him. He'd got a seat in a winning car while I was struggling to make the top ten. His success was a painful reminder of the one rule in Formula One that no amount of good driving will overcome: you can't win in a bad car. Not me, not Lewis, not Ayrton Senna.

I knew I was a good driver. Rubens had finished second in the World Championship several times, so we knew he was a good driver too. We should have been competitive but we were let down by our equipment.

There was a glimmer of light at the end of the tunnel. Lewis mania meant the press weren't quite so interested in me now. But when they did bother to ask me questions they were no longer amusing themselves by asking about Honda's green commitment or reminding me that he was the new Brit golden boy.

Now there was yet another topic of conversation. All about something big that was brewing at Honda.

44

Honda gathered the entire team into the factory in Brackley. The announcement was that big. Everybody had to be there to hear it. Chief executive Nick Fry was like, 'Ladies and gentlemen, please welcome your new team principal, a man who needs no introduction…'

And in walked Ross Brawn. And everybody went bananas.

Why? Because as a technical director Ross Brawn had *won* things. He'd been with Williams, Arrows, and then Benetton, where he'd won a Constructors' and two Drivers' Championships, and next at Ferrari where he'd won six consecutive Constructors' Championships and five Drivers' Championships with Michael Schumacher. And now he was coming to save us at Honda.

He began work in November 2007, sadly too late to do anything about the 2008 car. Instead he set about moulding the team in order to be competitive in 2009, and although we trudged through a wretched 2008 there was at least a sense of looking forward. The team had a noticeable spring in its step once again.

So when the 2008 season was over, I took off to Lanzarote with a few friends in tow. Chrissy came, Mikey and my trainer John Brame. It wasn't a piss-up; we were there for base training in preparation for the coming season, which I was taking very seriously indeed. Why?

Because the car looked good. I'd seen it in the wind tunnel, looked at the numbers.

It was one of those years that designers love, when there's a huge regulation change. Ross had done a great job of choosing a good engineering team, and they in turn had spotted a very useful loophole in the regulations, allowing what they called a 'double diffuser'. The diffuser is a device at the back of the car that helps the passage of air from underneath and out the back, converting it from the low, downforce-creating pressure beneath the car to the normal pressure of the outside air, and thus reducing drag at the back. What Ross's team had created was a kind of 'double-decker' version that would make this process way more efficient. It was a massive step forward.

As you can imagine, excitement was building around the team but most importantly within it as we woke up to the idea that we might – just might – have a very competitive car on our hands, and in me and Rubens we had the drivers to capitalise on that. Everybody knew that he and I could drive. Just give us the right car and we'd be challenging for the front, no doubt about it. Now at last it looked as though we might have the car to do that.

So, yes, 2008 had been a tough year (well, you know, all things being relative) but we'd ended on a high. We were fit, healthy and excited about 2009. We had Christmas coming up, which I was excited about; there was a real snap in the air.

And then, arriving back in Gatwick from Lanzarote, I got a call from the big man. The man we call God. My manager, Richard Goddard.

We were at the baggage carousel, waiting for our luggage, when I checked my voicemail. It was proper doom-laden stuff: 'Jenson, please call me. We need to speak immediately.'

So I did, knowing from his tone that something was up. 'It's not good news,' he said.

'Okay,' I said, 'well, that could mean anything—'

'Honda are pulling out of Formula One,' he said. 'They're pulling out of the sport altogether.'

And again I knew – just from his tone – that there was no 'but' coming. 'Honda are pulling out… *but* Ferrari want you to drive for them.' 'Honda are pulling out… *but* I'm just pulling your leg to get you back for stranding me in Canada.'

None of that. Just, 'Honda are pulling out.'

This was 2008, remember, the time of the credit crunch. Everyone was tightening their belts. Even so, I couldn't quite get my head round it, reaching out on autopilot to hoist my luggage off the carousel, trying to find the words.

'Well…' I started. 'What does that mean?'

'It means the team doesn't exist any more, Jenson. It means we don't have a drive for 2009.'

'I'm out of a job then?'

Silence.

45

My advice: if you're going to be on the receiving end of bad news, a potential job loss say, then do it anywhere else but Heathrow, in full view at the baggage carousel.

'Oh, wicked,' I snapped, not really taking it out on Richard but yeah, taking it out on Richard. 'That's exactly what you want to hear when you arrive back from training camp.'

'Well, listen,' he said, 'I'm looking at other options now, so don't worry, we'll get something, there's a few positive things.'

But I wasn't really listening. My head was spinning, trying to make sense of everything, thinking that I'd been racing for nine years and won one race. One, as in, *just one*. And that one was supposed to be a start, a beginning of the next stage, like the second act of the superhero movie where he's mastered his powers and is off to kick supervillain butt because now we had Ross Brawn and a double diffuser.

Only, what we didn't have, all of a sudden, was the backing of one of the world's biggest automotive companies. Which meant there were going to be a lot of people out of jobs, including me. It was December, four months before the season was due to start. Contracts are worked out in September. *Latest*. It didn't matter what Richard said. He was probably only saying it to be nice anyway. There was no way I was going to find a drive for 2009. Not any kind of drive worth having.

We were glum as we made our way out of the airport. 'Why not sit out a season, Jenson?' was the question nobody asked, because Chrissy, Mikey and John all knew the score: there is no such thing as a sabbatical for a Formula One driver. You're only as good as your last race.

We did a lot of talking over the next few days. One option was to race for Toro Rosso, Red Bull's junior team. I loved them; they had and still do have great spirit and attitude, but I knew I'd never get close to a podium in their car. What's more, they wanted me to bring money in the form of sponsorship to help fund the team, which was singularly unappealing.

The other option was to find a buyer for Honda. In the immediate aftermath of Honda's decision to pull out, Ross wasn't interested in heading up a consortium. Instead we found ourselves the subject of interest from Virgin, with Richard Branson thinking he was going to ride in and be the saviour of Formula One. We weren't keen on that idea, mostly because we thought Branson was a bit of a turkey, but you know how it is, any port in a storm, and talks continued in that area.

Meanwhile Ross Brawn and Nick Fry weren't taking calls. We were biting our fingernails, wondering what on earth was going on. And then at long last they got in touch. 'We're going to buy the team.'

Honda were really good about selling up. Rumour had it that they gave the team enough money to pay everybody off generously, and in fact that pot was enough to keep the team running for at least another year, maybe two, without a major sponsor. That was Ross and Nick's gamble: keep the team going, and bank on success with the new car.

Me, I had just signed a new three-year contract for big money, including bonuses. I was entitled to a large settlement but it was put to me that if I didn't accept a lower one, then we couldn't go racing.

So that's what I did. I took a settlement for the Honda contract and signed a new one with Brawn for relatively little money.

Next problem was the fact that Honda were taking their ball home, which in this case meant they were taking their engine home too – so suddenly we had no engine.

The team spoke to Mercedes about getting a power unit. They also had to speak to Martin Whitmarsh, who ran McLaren at the time, to ask if it was okay that we had Mercedes engines, because it meant we would have been a competitor of McLaren. Luckily he said yes.

The engine didn't fit initially. It was a different fitting so they had to put a spacer in between the tub and the engine, which you wouldn't do normally, but without that we couldn't go racing. By the time that was ironed out it was late in the day, well into the start of 2009.

Other teams were testing. Barcelona. Jerez. Most teams had already had two test sessions before our car was even ready to go out on track. When eventually we got everything together we took it down the road to Silverstone, except for some reason we weren't allowed to use the main track, or even the smaller track. They put us on the little school track, Stowe. There we set up a tiny little awning to try and keep off the worst of the weather, which was foul, freezing cold, and stood there stamping our feet as the engineers readied the car.

It was very quiet. I remember it well. An atmosphere of industry and restrained tension. Nobody knew if the car would work, that was the thing. The double diffuser was new. We'd bodged a Mercedes engine into it. The numbers were good but everybody knew that numbers in a wind tunnel are just a guide. You don't *really* know what a car is like until somebody's driven it, and nobody had driven it yet. That's why we were at Silverstone, freezing our nuts off.

Rubens was there, too. I don't know the details of his contract, but I know that like me he'd had to renegotiate and no doubt taken a hit.

But if you think we were standing there grumbling, stamping our feet and thinking dark thoughts about the other teams in Barcelona then you'd be wrong. We were praying the car would work. We were thanking our lucky stars that we had a drive.

At last everything was ready. The engineers stood back. *Your turn, Jenson.* The moment of truth had arrived.

46

They started her up, and I left for my installation lap. When I came back in, the mechanics and crew crowded around the car as I flicked up my visor. They're always keen to see your facial expressions at a time like that. They want to look into your eyes while they interrogate you.

'Guys,' I sighed, 'it was just an installation lap. You can't tell anything from that.'

Shoulders fell. *Sure, right.*

But of course I had an inkling. Just an inkling, mind you. I was keeping my fires under control, didn't want to give anything away just yet. But I had a good feeling, a feeling that was more like an itch at this stage, almost a premonition, but a feeling nonetheless.

So then I went out to begin a proper run, and on my first lap it happened, something special.

I'd been looking for something wrong with the car. You always are. You need to identify problem areas: weird vibrations, strange balance, anything in need of work. But there was nothing. The gears were smooth, the braking was perfect. The car felt comfortable, it seemed to flow around corners, and the engine felt powerful, much more so than the Honda engine.

In short, it just felt… *right*. It felt a part of me.

After twelve laps I came in. 'We're ready to go testing in this,' I grinned, and in a second the tension that had hung over us all morning lifted to be replaced by beaming faces, relief written on every one of them.

Off we went to Barcelona for testing, which is like a mini curtain-raiser for the season, where all the teams get together and the general public are allowed access.

There at the Circuit de Catalunya, the scene of so many of my life's tuning points, we found ourselves surfing on a sea of goodwill. Nobody likes to see a team leave Formula One, and we were the guys who had averted that disaster: the plucky privateers rising from the ashes of Honda.

For us, Ross was a talismanic presence. At Brawn he wasn't an engineer or aerodynamicist, he was the leader of the team, but he was able to bring all that championship-winning knowledge and experience to the table. And despite the fact that there was an enormous amount of pressure on him, he wasn't at all highly strung about it. There was no screaming or shouting from Ross – great for me because I really don't respond to that. He just had that calm authority that meant people listened to him.

And his cars won trophies, which meant interest in what we had in our garage was sky high. Our crew had put screens around the front of the garage but photographers dangled arms over the top and started clicking away in the hope of getting a fluky shot of the car. They were leaning over the balcony above trying to glimpse inside, desperate to see it, not just because it was a Ross Brawn creation, but also because they knew it had a troubled history. We were late with its debut; word had leaked out about the engine-fitting problems. Could it be the Brawn magic touch had failed him? Maybe we had a cobbled-together jalopy lurking behind those screens.

I went out for my first run, wondering if my feelings in Silverstone had been an illusion, fearing that sheer relief or the freezing cold had coloured my judgement.

But no. The car was even better. They'd made some tweaks in the meantime and the weather was warm, so it was running beautifully. Again I felt at one with it, came back into the pits, into the garage to see my race engineer, Andrew Shovlin, a very bright guy who had race-engineered me at BAR and then come with me to Honda and Brawn. All told he was my race engineer for five years.

'What do you think, Jenson?' he asked.

I was still keeping my excitement in check at that point, replying, 'I'm pleased. It's got good balance. To be honest, I'm just happy that we're here and we're able to go out and do some laps in it.'

He went boggle-eyed, like I didn't quite understand what he was saying. 'Jenson you're sixth-tenths quicker than anyone else.'

I looked at him. Briefly the world stopped spinning on its axis. *Six-tenths quicker.* The other teams had already been in situ for two days; this was my first lap.

Cautious I said, 'Are we running low fuel?'

He said, 'No, we're running fifty kilos.'

Moments later, I was on the phone, telling my dad, Richard, Chrissy, anybody who answered that the car was great. And not just great but bloody great. Maybe the best car I'd driven in Formula One.

Later that day, I went out again and I overtook Lewis. I flew around the outside of him on turn three, and that was sweet. In the afternoon I collared Rubens only to learn that he'd been having exactly the same experience as me, both of us barely able to control our excitement, the whole team buzzing with it.

After that we started running high fuel, just so the other teams wouldn't know how much speed we had. And not only did we have pace in hand, but we didn't have a single reliability issue. No bodywork that needed altering, no valve that needed replacing. It looked like a work of art and it drove like one too.

Leading up to the first race of the season, Melbourne, we worked on the car, Rubens and me. He was good at that – probably the best teammate I ever had in terms of understanding and improving a race car. I remember after his first day of testing he'd walked into the garage and started telling the engineers all about the car. I was like, *You're going to need to step up your game, JB.* Here was a guy I could learn from.

Regarding the car one nagging doubt remained. Just the one. We hadn't done any race simulations, nor had we been out on any long runs. There was Barcelona, then more testing at Jerez and we topped the timesheets on both occasions, but there was still a question mark hanging over the car's stamina. Would it stay reliable for an entire race?

Now I come to think of it, there was a second doubt: we hadn't really practised pit stops.

So that's two doubts. But one thing we were absolutely sure about was the car's performance. And what we knew, of course, was that we had more performance than we were letting on. After we did so well in testing the rest of the paddock collectively came to the conclusion that we were testing with low fuel, hence our excellent times, when in reality we were doing the opposite, as any sensible team would, in order to keep our powder dry, so to speak.

That was the position when we arrived in Melbourne. We wanted to do well in qualifying, of course, but even if we did, would that mean anything when it came to a full race?

47

The Australian Grand Prix is a good one. It's the season opener, so it always feels that bit extra-special, and Dad loved it. Every year in Australia he'd get together with a bunch of Formula One cronies and have a big get-together, a huge meal to welcome the season. And by then, of course, the old man had *a lot* of friends in Formula One; he was as much a part of the paddock furniture as Murray Walker and, like Murray, he was somebody that everybody in the paddock loved.

It was partly his huge coterie of friends that had led to him being nicknamed Papa Smurf. Well, that and the fact that in around 2004 he grew a beard that was snowy white, and some joker (okay, me) decided he looked like a dead ringer for the little blue guy. Somebody gave him a little Smurf that he'd started carrying at races and taking its picture.

No doubt he had it in Australia that year. He wasn't around for testing – I made him stay away – but he'd leave home in Monaco and join me at Melbourne every March, regular as clockwork. It was like we came alive.

That year was extra-special, of course. We came with high hopes and great expectations. Practice went well and to say qualifying was a success is an understatement. We absolutely stormed it. I was first and Rubens was second on the grid. A brilliant start by any measure. Truly this was a sensational car.

That night we decided to get a bite to eat at Nobu in Melbourne. This was me, my girlfriend Jessica, Richard, Dad and a few others. In we walked, and who should be there but Ron Dennis, the McLaren supremo, who didn't look at all pleased to see us. We greeted him warily as we passed his table.

He leaned back in his char. 'I think you should be thanking me,' he said, rather imperiously. 'You wouldn't have that Mercedes engine if it weren't for me.'

Now, of course this wasn't strictly speaking true, because the engine had been arranged through Martin Whitmarsh, but it was the wrong time to play Mr Pedantic, and besides I didn't want to rub salt into the wounds, given that the McLarens were back in fourteenth and fifteenth on the grid. So I smiled sweetly, thanked him and moved on, hoping that all this confidence in our car wasn't premature. Quick in testing is one thing; quick in qualifying another. But what about those doubts? We still hadn't raced it yet. We could end up pushing it around the track for all we knew.

So anyway, we took our seats, and I can't remember how far we'd got through the meal when we became aware of a kerfuffle at the door and turned to see that His Royal Highness Sir Richard Branson was arriving.

And he was very, very drunk.

Now, by this time we'd already had our fill of Sir Richard, because earlier in the day he'd arrived at the circuit with all the pomp and ceremony of a returning hero. With a bevy of flag-bearing dolly birds in his wake, he'd marched up and down the paddock, waving, grinning and giving the thumbs up to his adoring public, who were, in fact, wondering what he was doing there in the first place. The reason, of course, was that he had a couple of stickers on our car. A million bucks' worth of sponsorship, which is a lot of money but in F1 sponsorship terms, chicken feed. And yet he was behaving as though he had bank-rolled the whole thing.

I can't say he'd won a lot of admirers with that stunt, but at the end of the day he's national treasure Sir Richard Branson, famous publicity seeker, so you cut him some slack. It'd be like hating a dog for barking at the telly. They can't help it. It's just what they do.

What he did in the restaurant was less excusable. However, before I go on, it's only right and proper for me to point out that he apologised for what happened that night, and even said that he gave up drinking for months afterwards. Not only that, but the press had a field day at the time and no Branson blush was spared. With all that penance paid you might think that he's done his time and by rights I should leave out this story.

But I'm not going to.

So anyway. Our saviour, Sir Richard Branson, pal in tow, lurched over to our table, awkwardly high-fiving everyone, and then plonked himself down and started behaving like a party-starter. I had to make a toilet visit so I didn't see what happened next, which was that he leaned over to Jessica and told her, 'Stop staring at me.'

She pointed out that she wasn't staring at him.

'Stop staring at me,' he insisted.

Although Jessica was a model she was quite shy, so this was making her feel uncomfortable. Especially when Sir Richard followed up his blatant flirting by putting his hand on her face.

I'm still in the toilet, remember.

'Look, I think you better leave,' warned my manager Richard, 'or you're going to get chinned when Jenson gets back.'

Actually, I'm not in the habit of punching knights of the realm in Nobu, so there was never any real danger of that happening – certainly *not* the night before a race – but even so I was furious to return and find His Excellency with his hand on my girlfriend's face.

'Hold on,' I said, 'that's enough. That's well out of order.'

But he was so hammered that he simply didn't understand what the problem was. The next thing we knew he'd stood up from our table and tottered over to a party of ten, where one of the diners, presumably unaware of quite how drunk he was, handed him a baby, hoping to get a picture of him holding it.

At our table we were giving each other horrified looks, unable to believe our eyes as the incredibly leathered Sir Richard not only proceeded to pick up and cuddle the baby, but stagger around the restaurant with it, gradually getting more and more careless. Various people were trying to talk him out of it. 'Richard, please put the baby down. Step away from the baby,' until at last he returned the child, and shortly after that left the restaurant – to everybody's great relief.

At our table we were looking at each other incredulously. 'I can't believe this,' said Richard. 'We've got to work with that knob for the rest of the year.'

48

Unlike most races that start at two or three o'clock, the Aussie GP kicks off at five, so we'd always have a bit of time to kill in the morning before going down to the circuit. A whole crowd of us, including the old boy, used to drive down to the beach for coffee at the Stokehouse restaurant. It was a great time just to hang out, chat, get your head together before the madness of the race, and, in the case of that particular year, talk about the antics of Sir Richard Branson the night before.

It's also where my focus began to come in. Generally speaking, I'm a pretty easy-going guy, but get me at a race and you might not think that because I'm all about getting my focus.

Sometimes Dad would annoy me, just by saying something, could be anything, and I'd snap at him. Same with Richard. Those two got it in the neck more than most. It's not like I'd shout and swear, chuck coffee cups and throw Naomi Campbell-style tantrums, but I could be a bit short on occasion.

Mum found it difficult to understand. Whenever she came to a race she wanted to be with me all the time; she'd have sat in on meetings if she could have done. She couldn't quite get that I would be different at a race. She just wanted to ruffle her little boy's hair. The slightly uptight, semi-stressed, focused-on-other-things bloke in a racing suit was an imposter as far as she was concerned.

Focus – that was for racing. Stress – that was for the other stuff. Interviews. Sponsor meets. All the stuff, ironically, that gets in the way of your focus. That's why having coffee at the Stokehouse was such an important part of the Melbourne ritual. It took you away from the track until absolutely necessary.

What was different about 2009 was the expectation. Sitting at the Stokehouse – Jessie was there, my dad, Richard, Mikey, Chrissy – I found that I zoned out of the Branson talk, letting my thoughts go to the race. It was a calmness that I felt, a little sampler of the peace to come. In motor racing it's common to feel that you're fighting your equipment rather than working with it. I didn't feel that with the Brawn car. I knew the guys sitting around the table at the Stokehouse would never let me down. I felt the same way about the car.

We arrived at the circuit to find a full house glittering in the sun and crackling with atmosphere. In the paddock the team was relaxed, but that wasn't something that came easy; we'd had to force it upon ourselves for fear of being swamped by our worries. There was, for example, lots of pre-race stuff we simply hadn't done. We still hadn't practised starts or pit stops; we didn't know how the car was going to feel in the race; we didn't know how many laps we were going to be able to get in before we'd have to stop for fuel.

On the other hand: *we were racing, baby.* Four months previously we weren't even sure whether we'd have jobs, and now we'd rocked up to the opening GP of the season with a car that was outpacing everything else on the grid. Toyota and Williams had double diffusers as well, but even they couldn't touch us. All signs pointed to us hitting the sacred sweet spot. All I had to do now was capitalise on it.

And so to the race, where Rubens had a shocking start but mine was good, and before I knew it, I'd pulled a good gap. Glancing in the mirror there was no sign of Rubens, and I felt the usual set of conflicting emotions about that: I wanted him to do well, but on the other hand I *really* wanted to beat him.

I drove a good race. Smooth. Fast. Pushing the car to its limits, nailing the kerbs, as pure a drive as I'd had since karting. We got to the last stint and Sebastian Vettel in the Red Bull was getting close. The team were on my radio. 'He's catching you. Half a second per lap.' He was on softer tyres than me, and he was faster. *So much for this double diffuser*, I was thinking. Danger was averted when he and Robert Kubica crashed and were both out, the safety car was deployed and the rest of the pack caught me. But when I looked in my mirror it was Rubens I saw behind me; he'd been able to fight his way back through the pack.

And that was how it ended. A sedate trundle behind the safety car over the finish line. Not exactly the most thrilling or glorious way to win a race, but frankly, we didn't care. This was Brawn's maiden Grand Prix, and we'd just scored a one–two. On the pit wall the engineers were going wild. Ross was jumping up and down. I came in the pits, stood on my car and gave it the number-one fingers to all the mechanics, photographers and journalists who were watching. My dad was there. Big hugs from him. Right behind me was Rubens, and together we headed up to the podium. I remember looking across at him and nodding, and him nodding back, and we both knew that we'd done all right. First time out. What a way to start the season.

Afterwards, I had the trophy in my hand. No way was I letting go of it. 'Come on, guys, let's not throw this away,' I was saying. 'This is probably the best opportunity we'll ever have to win the champion-ship,' which might sound premature, it being only the first race of the season, but I don't think it was. You hear teams say things like, 'We didn't think about the championship until the end of the season, we just concentrated on race wins,' but I call bullshit on that. Right after that first win, I was looking at the championship. I was thinking, *This is my chance.*

49

Other teams kicked off about the double diffuser, of course. This is the way in Formula One. One team does something, the rest of the teams kick up a fuss about it, and the FIA is obliged to investigate.

'It's a shame this double-diffuser business is getting in the way,' I said to Ross one day. We were walking around the car at the time.

'It's fine,' he said, pushing his glasses up his nose. 'In fact, it's good. It means everybody's looking at the double diffuser and they're not paying attention to what else is on the car. Plenty of little tricks on it.'

Nothing illegal, but the job of a designer like Ross is to find and exploit loopholes. On the track we pushed the cars to the limit; off the track, they push the rules to the limit. That's the 'formula' in Formula One.

Second race, Malaysia, was a wet one. The rain was coming down so hard we could barely see, and once again we crossed the finish line behind a safety car. But once again I managed to do it in first place, having put it on pole the day before.

In China, Flavio Briatore, my great friend from Benetton (sarcasm alert), told the media that he couldn't understand why I was leading the world championship. He was just pissed off because he couldn't get the double diffuser banned. He also described me as a *paracarro*, which is a sort of concrete bollard. No, me neither.

Things went a bit pear-shaped (but only comparatively speaking) in China, where I qualified fifth. Yet again it was a wet race, which was fine by me. I passed Fernando and Rubens to put myself behind the Red Bulls, which were a formidable pair by anyone's standards. Sebastian was still the new hotshot back then – him and Lewis in the McLaren – and it was only his second season in F1, having raced with Toro Rosso the year before that. Slightly contradicting what I said earlier about never winning in a Toro Rosso, Sebastian had done exactly that the previous season. I guess that's the exception that proves the rule – it remains their only race win. As for Sebastian, he's probably the hardest-working driver on the grid in terms of his time with the team. He reminds me of Michael Schumacher like that, while Mark Webber, in the other Red Bull, I knew quite well because he had been the test driver at Benetton. He was like DC in style and temperament, and he was another one who did his homework.

More to the point, they were both in a good car that season, which made them a real threat – especially Sebastian, who was still proving himself, still hungry.

Sure enough, despite a good battle with Mark in China, I couldn't hold him off and ended up on the bottom step of the podium.

Then came Bahrain, where I qualified fourth – not great – but did well in the race and won it, which meant I was back on the top step again, with Sebastian and Jarno Trulli keeping me company. No doubt about it, Sebastian was going to be my main competitor for the season, him and Rubens. Right from that first win in Melbourne I'd acquired the mindset that anything less than a win was not good enough. I loved the car – me and the car were *like that* all season – and I knew I could drive it well.

Of course, what comes from that knowledge is a kind of internal pressure. As soon as you drop off from winning it feels like failure, which is a strange feeling. The logical bit of your brain is saying, *Come on, you came second, that's a bloody good result,* whereas your gut instinct lies there unimpressed, curling its lip and saying that second isn't good enough. Not when you came first in Melbourne and Malaysia.

Barcelona, I won again, a good little battle with Rubens, who had an issue with the team because we changed strategies halfway through the race.

'I can't believe you gave him the best strategy,' he fumed, even going so far as to lambast someone from the team while we were actually on the podium.

Seeing him do that I thought, *I'm getting to him,* which is exactly what you want to do as a rival driver. He was a friend, but he was also a competitor, so it was important for me to stay strong. To see a weakness in him was encouraging, as sharklike as that sounds.

At the same time I understood why he was so upset. It wasn't true that I'd been given a 'better' strategy, just a different one that had paid dividends in this particular instance.

'If I get a whiff of team orders I will hang up my helmet tomorrow,' he said, no doubt with frustration carried over from years at Ferrari, where Michael Schumacher's contract had stated that he was number one, and he should get all the new parts ahead of Rubens.

Now Rubens wanted to compete for the championship on level terms. Me? I was happy about that. I prefer to be challenged by a teammate. I'd say that I probably even *need* it to stay competitive. Bring it on.

Meanwhile, with five races of seventeen down, I was leading with forty-one points out of a possible forty-five, while Brawn was topping the Constructors' table with sixty-eight points, well clear of second-placed Red Bull. Lewis, meanwhile, was having a torrid time at McLaren, having only managed to score nine points.

At Monaco, Red Bull introduced a double diffuser on to their car, which meant we were all on level pegging.

Monaco's amazing in qualifying, when you're driving with low fuel and new tyres. The race itself? A bit of a procession, if we're honest. You can't deny, however, that it's very glamorous.

Through testing, the pace was good. The Ferraris were the closest challengers to us all the way through Q1 and Q2 but they're just the knockout rounds. Five cars get eliminated in Q1, and then the next five knocked out in Q2.

By Q3 it was down to ten and I was a long way down that ten, hopes of qualifying on pole were fading – and did I mention how important it is to qualify on pole at Monaco?

But then I had one of those laps where everything just went right, where I felt like I was flowing around the circuit, rather than driving around it, feeling a rare kind of symbiosis with the car, as though temporarily unable to tell where I ended and the car began.

And when the lap was over, it was as though I emerged from a kind of blissful trance, a state of focus and transcendence. You'll know the feeling if you run, cycle or take part in any solo sport. You go into your zone. I never really mastered qualifying laps. I was always more Prost than Senna in my approach to a race weekend, thinking of set-up and overall strategy rather than pulling off a jaw-dropping lap time.

That lap though, That was my Senna moment. I was on pole.

For the race I got away in the lead and pulled a good gap. Behind me was Rubens who was following closely. Too closely. Because as you know from your downforce lessons the problem with staying on the car in front is that you lose that precious aerodynamic grip.

Sure enough, I could see that Rubens was damaging his rear tyres. In response, I took it easy on my own tyres on corner entry, accelerating gently to minimise wheelspin, and generally keeping mine in better condition than his. By the last section of the race I had backed off in order to preserve the tyres, but the weird thing about Monaco is that backing off can actually be quite dangerous. You tend to make more mistakes when you're not on the limit because you're not fully focused, and at Monaco you need that focus because the circuit seems to get narrower the more tired you get. Not only that, but I had vivid memories of my accident there. I knew only too well that you only need one slip-up and you're in the wall.

But I did it. And to cross the line in first place at Monaco is like winning the World Championship. In all the excitement, I totally forgot that Monaco differs from other races, when instead of leaving the car in *parc fermé* you drive around the last corner after the race, do a victory lap then down the start/finish straight and stop at the line. The reason for that is that Prince Albert of Monaco is there waiting for you.

But I forgot all that. I parked the car, all excited, only to have an official piss on my chips. '*Excusez-moi*, monsieur, you haff parked in ze wrong place.'

'Oh, really?'

He said, 'You're supposed to be over there.'

I was, like, *Oh, of course.*

So with my helmet on, still holding my gloves, I ran all the way down the pit straight, five hundred metres or so, waving at the crowd and the mechanics, feeling a bit of a Charlie having parked up in the wrong place, but not that much of a Charlie, to be honest, because I'd just won Monaco so eat that, suckers, and arrived to find two cars already parked up, Rubens and Kimi waiting for me, Prince Albert laughing his dogs off.

'I'm so sorry I'm late,' I said breathlessly, shaking his hand, getting a hug in return. 'Did I miss anything?'

Oh, and then the National Anthem. Proper proud. Then the champagne moment, where I jumped down from the podium, started spraying everybody, gave Ross a good soaking, all the team hanging off the pit wall.

It was a special celebration. Mum and Dad were both there, trying to fight their way through the crowds. A real *Rocky* moment as I eventually reached them and gave them a big hug.

Not that the fun ended there. Oh no. When you win the Monaco Grand Prix you're invited to a black-tie dinner to sit with Prince Albert and his girlfriend (now wife) Charlene. Richard sorted me a suit from Dolce & Gabbana so Jessica and I went, and I found myself sitting opposite Prince Albert, Jessica beside him, a really fun evening.

'So, Prince Albert,' I said, as the meal drew to a close. 'What are you doing now?'

He pulled a 'going home' face.

'Oh no, you can't go home,' I insisted. 'I'm meeting some friends at the Amber Lounge, they've got a table, come with us.'

I was thinking, *This is going to freak Richard and Dad out, when I turn up to Amber Lounge with Prince Albert of Monaco in tow.* No way was I taking no for an answer.

'I can't—' he started.

'You're coming to the Amber Lounge,' I insisted. Fortunately, I had support from his girlfriend, Charlene, and Jessica did her bit, too. And so off we went, just us four – and a whole platoon of bodyguards.

Just as I expected the guys were gobsmacked. What's more, Prince Albert turned out be quite the clubber. Had a few drinks, got down on the dance floor. He's got some real moves, has Prince Albert. Nobody bothered him, he just had a ball.

At one point, Richard dived over the back of a sofa, nothing too acrobatic, just meaning to sit down, but he got his foot caught and landed on the Prince's back. 'Oh, sorry,' said Richard, and gave the Prince a matey slap on the back, only to have bodyguards descend on him, proper hands-inside-jackets tackle.

Next morning, we expected to be hungover but in fact we felt fine. 'I know,' I said to Jessica, 'let's go down to La Note Bleue on the beach, have a nice spot of lunch, maybe a glass of rosé.'

Arrived, got a text from the boys: 'Where are you? We're coming down.'

Next thing you know there are eight of us piling through magnums of rosé. Four or five hours we must have been there, pretty hammered by the end of it, but up for more fun. But where can you go for fun on a Monday afternoon in Monaco? We called a friend, the manager of a club called Zebra Square, who opened the club just for us and welcomed us with a gargantuan bottle of champagne, removing the cork by swiping it off with a big sword. When that was gone he brought another one out. Maybe even another.

It was thanks to that day that we coined the idea of Super Monday – a day after a race where we, you know, 'relax'.

Trouble was, it would be a while before we could enjoy another one. My winning streak was about to judder to an awkward stop.

50

I won the Turkish Grand Prix, sharing my podium with Sebastian and Mark of Red Bull. By now I had a fairly unassailable lead. 'You've built me a monster,' I yelled over the radio. 'Thank you so, so much.'

The next race was Silverstone, my home race, where all my family, friends and everybody from the team would be in attendance. As you can imagine, I really wanted to win. And to be fair, having come first in six out of my first seven races, I was well within my rights to think I would. This after all, was *my* season.

In practice, I was a lot slower than Rubens. Couldn't understand why. It wasn't until the next day, qualifying, that we worked out it was to do with tyre temperature. It was cold in Silverstone, that was the problem. June in England and we were treated to a high of sixteen degrees Celsius.

'It's your style, Jenson,' said Shov, my race engineer. 'Rubens is much more aggressive than you; he's getting the heat in his tyres.'

'So what do we do?'

The answer was hope for a sudden heatwave or try to change my driving style, both of which required divine intervention. Instead I soldiered on and had to settle for sixth on the grid. Rubens was second, and with him were the two Red Bulls.

The Red Bull car had been given an Adrian Newey-inspired makeover, it was looking good, and we were beginning to cast nervous glances in their direction. As a driver, my biggest rivals that year were Rubens and Sebastian, but although Red Bull were a long way behind in the points, there was still just over half the season to go and they had a confidence about them that was unsettling.

In the race I got a good start but was blocked by Massa in the Ferrari and lost a place. I spent most of the rest of it trying to get past Jarno Trulli. By then I'd worked out how to race on the tyres. But it was too late. I came home in sixth.

Like I say, winning recalibrates your attitude to it. By the time I retired from racing altogether I would have been more than happy with sixth. In the context of that 2009 season it felt like I might as well not have bothered turning up.

Not only that, but my poor British GP was followed by a Red Bull one–two at the Nürburgring in Germany, while me and Rubens had to be content with a fifth and sixth respectively. That meant two first and seconds in a row for them, which put them within twenty points of us.

Back to Hungary, scene of so much jubilation three years previously. This was the race at which Felipe Massa was struck by a spring that came off Rubens' car in qualifying. This particular spring weighed about a kilo, and the impact of it on Felipe's visor – twice the force that a bulletproof vest is designed to withstand – knocked him unconscious and caused him to put the car into the wall.

For a time it looked a bit touch-and-go for him but he was okay, thank God. It made a mess of his helmet and visor, but those things are tough – tough enough to save Felipe's life and eyesight, although he wouldn't race again that season.

Because the spring had come off Rubens' car they changed the relevant part on my car as a precaution, which cost us in qualifying and meant I only drove one lap instead of two, and with a heavier fuel load into the bargain. I qualified eighth.

As for the race? Sigh. I finished seventh. The surprise of the weekend was Lewis, who up until then had been having an abysmal season, coming through to win, as well as offering notice that he planned to be in the mix for the rest of the year.

Personally, I felt as though we'd lost our way at Brawn. It wasn't as though we were going backwards, just that everybody else had been catching up and we'd stopped spending money on the car. Richard had heard the budget for the car was £7m but they only spent £700,000 of it. Their attitude was 'it's not broke, so let's not fix it', which was… unusual, let's say, because normally you'd be putting new parts on the car at every race. Developing the car is such an important aspect of what we do as a team, but apart from the stickers it looked exactly the same at the end of the season as it had at the beginning.

Valencia was a disappointing race for me, although Rubens won, which was great obviously (gnashes teeth), and both the Red Bulls were out of the points, which did a lot to slow their charge.

On to Spa, and again Belgium was a bit cold for the car and I couldn't get sufficient heat into the tyres. Remember how at the beginning of the season I was in love with the car, praising its smoothness and flow, vibing on its power? While the relationship hadn't soured, it had certainly cooled. For reasons that may well have been partly psychological, I was finding it difficult to drive and impatient with how flaky it was in the cold. The honeymoon period was over. I qualified fourteenth, retired a DNF from the race.

Scores on the doors? I was first with seventy-two points; Rubens second with fifty-six, Sebastian third with fifty-three. In the Constructors' we led Red Bull by 128 points to 104.5.

Monza was better, a one–two for Brawn, though not in the formation I would have liked. Singapore was the only race of the season with neither a Brawn nor a Red Bull driver on the podium, Lewis bagging that one. By now there was only us and Red Bull with any theoretical possibility of winning the Constructors'. Me, Rubens and Sebastian were the three in contention for the Drivers'.

Japan. Another fairly mediocre result (Rubens seventh, me eighth) but it left Brawn a point away from the championship, while I was eighty-five points compared to Rubens on seventy-one.

No problem then. After all, the next race was only Brazil, Rubens' home track.

I was stressed, I admit it. On the bright side the weather in Brazil would suit my fussy car but otherwise I was seriously worried that the championship, once mine for the taking – nailed on, as they say – might actually be snatched from my grasp, sacrificed to my sudden lack of pace.

Going into the race the situation was this: Red Bull were still in with a shout of winning the Constructors' but needed their drivers to finish first and second, both in Brazil and the next (i.e., last) race in Abu Dhabi, as well as relying on us not to score. Not impossible, then, but highly unlikely. Barring some kind of disaster, Brawn had the Constructors' in the bag.

On the Driver's side, things were a lot less cut-and-dried. I needed to finish within four points of Rubens to win the title at Brazil. Sebastian needed to finish first or second to stay in the running and take things to Abu Dhabi.

So, yes. The championship was mine to lose, and as a result of that it was a very stressful weekend in the lion's den, where the patriotic Brazilians were making their feelings known. Booing me. Swearing at me. They do like a gesticulation, do the Brazilians. Jessica had wanted to join me but knowing what the reception might be like I'd asked her to stay away – and good thing I had.

At one point we visited a restaurant and a bunch of turkeys from a TV company set up a stepladder outside the door so that I'd have to walk underneath it in order to reach the street.

We pushed it over. Don't look at me like that. I know it was a bit petulant. Maybe not in the spirit of what, after all, was just a TV station prank. But there you go. I offer my moment of bad behaviour as proof that things were really getting to me before that race. Any other day I would have laughed and played along. Not then.

Testing went okay but then, for qualifying, it was wet and we – as in the team – messed up on the tyre selection, meaning that everybody else did quick laps while the best I could manage was fourteenth on the grid. To make things worse, Rubens qualified on pole. Pole. *Jesus*.

As I trudged to my car after qualifying, I tried to block out the jeering of Brazilian fans.

'Hey, Jenson, how you doing?' It was a friendly voice so I turned to say hello.

Only to see a grinning kid giving me the finger.

51

Journalists would say things like, 'Don't you want to win the World Championship?' as though they genuinely thought I was throwing it away for a bet.

What do you fucking think, you idiot? I wanted to scream.

Have you lost your nerve?

No, I haven't lost my nerve.

Have I?

Okay. Calm. Calm.

It was getting to me, the pressure. Those questions. Maybe I was throwing away the championship. Maybe I had lost my nerve? The night before I'd dreamed that I was going to have a terrible qualifying session and sure enough I had.

And yet there was still that conversation taking place between my logical brain ('You're ahead; *they* have to catch *you*.') and my gut instinct ('You've bottled it, you idiot.').

I consoled myself by remembering that Sebastian had had a fairly torrid qualifying as well – worse than me, in fact – and would be starting at sixteenth. I totted up for the umpteenth time and told myself that the maths favoured me and that even if things went tits-up tomorrow I could still win the championship.

Do they all *have these doubts?* I wondered. All the drivers who have been in my position and prevailed. Were they, too, tortured by the fear of failure?

I joined the old man in the hotel bar for a drink. 'Dad, I've got to win it this weekend,' I told him, and I remember this so clearly. He smiled at me. He could see that it was getting to me, that I was… not on the edge, not quite, but approaching the edge and braking late. The smile said, *You'll be all right, Jense.*

Friends arrived: Chrissy, James, Richie, Richard. The whole crew. We had a meal and I relaxed a bit and then went to my room. That night I had another dream, and in this one I won the World Championship. It should have been a nice dream, really, but it wasn't, because when I woke up I hadn't won the World Championship.

The next morning I went through my usual pre-race routine with Mikey, finding my focus and staying there. I hadn't lost the lead, that was the thing. And while it was true that I'd failed to maintain my early season dominance, neither had I fallen away. Every single point I'd earned was vital in keeping me ahead of the pack.

Even so, the next few hours could see me losing my title.

Certainly the Brazilian fans were desperate for me to fail. The jeering had continued when I arrived at the circuit. Kitted out and ready to race I steered the car to the dummy grid, parked up, got out and took off my helmet – only to be greeted by a chorus of boos from the pit-straight grandstand opposite. A load of British journalists were there and came over to show support. Dad, too, who turned, grinned and gave the finger to the grandstand. That got them going. They all started cheering after that, and I realised that it wasn't really malicious, the booing, they didn't hate me, they just wanted the other guy to win, and that's the only way they knew how to help him.

As if he needed it right then. After all, their hero was on pole and I was back in fourteenth. If things stayed that way then he would be within two points of taking the championship in Abu Dhabi. *My* World Championship.

No two ways about it, I needed points.

Lights out. I made a better start than Romain Grosjean in the Renault and made up a place right off the line. The first lap was mayhem: Heikki Kovalainen, Sebastian Vettel, Giancarlo Fisichella, Jarno Trulli, Adrian Sutil, Mark Webber and Fernando Alonso were all involved in minor scrapes.

Kovalainen pitted, followed closely by Räikkönen, who needed a new front wing after tangling with Webber. Kovalainen finished his stop, but was released with a fuel hose still attached to his car. Behind him came Räikkönen, whose exhaust ignited the fuel, causing a fire on the track. All came under control and both drivers rejoined and finished the race.

And since nobody was hurt, I can safely say that, for me, the first-lap pandemonium was a godsend. Thanks to various drivers pitting, not to mention the appearance of the safety car, I'd made my way up to ninth. Just outside the points.

'Let's go, let's go,' I was saying over the radio, turning it into a virtual chant, hyping myself up, keeping the car on the limit and ready to make bold moves.

'Come on, JB, you can do this,' they urged, all the time giving me info and updates on Sebastian and Rubens.

I overtook Kazuki Nakajima next, going into turn one. Next lap, also on turn one, I braked late and took Sebastien Buemi by diving down the inside, super-aware that Sebastian Vettel was on my tail the whole time.

I stopped on lap twenty-nine, having been in second for five laps, and came out sixth but trapped behind Kamui Kobaysahi, doing maths in my head: Rubens was in third; if things stayed the same he would only score three points more than me and he needed five to keep his title challenge alive.

Then, with eight laps to go, Rubens had some kind of tangle with Lewis and went into the pits with a puncture, falling to eighth. I was in fifth.

Which meant, if it stayed the same, the championship was mine. Sebastian was ahead of me but it wasn't enough for him to stay in the fight.

I got on the radio to Shov. 'Do I need to do anything? How's the car?' A strange calm had come down on me. The championship was in my hands but then again it wasn't, because if something went wrong with the car I was back to square one. For some reason that combination of factors made me feel pretty zen, and I relaxed. You might even say that I began to enjoy myself.

'Just keep doing what you're doing,' said Shov. He started to count down the laps but I had to ask him to stop. I was enjoying the race. It was one of the few moments in my career when I've let my mind go elsewhere, thinking about all that had happened that year, everything I'd gone through: the wins, the bad races, the bad press, the good press, the crowd in Brazil.

I came out of the last corner, got on the throttle at full power, knowing that all I had to do now was cross the line, feeling the car, every gear shift, loving being in control, wanting to prolong and savour the moment.

At the finish line was Felipe Massa, who hadn't raced since his accident but had made a decent recovery and was waving the chequered flag, wearing a big grin that was matched by my own. The team were on the pit wall, cheering and clapping, I was singing Queen's 'We Are The Champions' into the radio (a good rendition, I thought), saying, 'We are World Champions,' yelping, screaming, thanking the team, making myself hoarse from shouting.

I did a final slow-down lap, which was particularly sweet, because I knew I'd won, the team knew and the crowd, too, but also other drivers, who came alongside, giving me the thumbs up, clasped fist, showing support. I got an especially warm greeting from Rubens, which was great, and really showed what an utter gent he is. More than anyone else, I knew how much he would have loved to have won. He would have been *gutted* that he came so close only to miss out. Relations between us weren't always great that season but at that moment in time he found the generosity of spirit to say well done and it meant a great deal.

I'd finished fifth, so I didn't get a podium celebration, which was a shame but not unknown – Lewis didn't the year before – but on the other hand at least I didn't have to prowl around the green room, get given a cap to wear and make small talk with the other drivers: 'I really thought you were going to catch me on that last lap.' Instead, as I jumped out of the car in *parc fermé*, I was greeted by the sound of the crowd cheering, which knocked me for six. They'd spent days jeering me and I'd beaten their guy and yet they were gracious and supportive in defeat. Gotta love the Brazilians.

Photographers were gathering. I was looking for familiar faces, wanting to share the moment with the team, with my mates and with

Dad – and with Ross, of course, not forgetting the fact that I wasn't the only champion decided that day; the points meant that Brawn were crowned Constructors' champions – in their maiden season, a proper fairy tale.

Brawn mechanics made their way through the photographer scrum towards me. Mikey, my physio, was there with a drinks bottle, picking me up in a massive hug. Off came the gloves, and I emerged from within the helmet the World Champion, giving it the number-one fingers for the photographers.

And then I saw Dad. There he was in his pink shirt and shades and in the next instant we were in each other's arms, father and son. Our journey together had begun with a junior bike one cold morning and brought us here, to the World Championship. We'd given each other such an incredible experience and I could feel all that pride and joy pouring off him. He was crying and they were filming and I knew he wouldn't want pictures of him crying to be broadcast around the world, so I held him close for longer, for as long as I could, until it was starting to look weird, and then finally let him go.

52

'About time,' said Bernie Ecclestone as we met while I was still floating on a cloud of elation. I ran down the paddock to see Richie, Chrissy, James and the team. 'Finally,' said Ross drily as I arrived.

Someone handed me a Union Jack. Flashes were blasting away as I posed with it. Then came a press conference and it was so easy. Most interviews you do as a racing driver, you sit there and process the answer for a moment: what can I say? What can't I say? But the answers just flowed out of me, an outpouring of emotion. I felt like I'd been answering questions about being a World Champion all my life, it just came so naturally.

It was all a bit of a blur, to be honest. I was surfing a wave of total joy. The funny thing is that when you win a Grand Prix it's a feeling of pure adrenalin and excitement. Nothing compares to it for total in-the-moment emotion. Winning the World Championship was different. The primary feeling there is one of relief. You've just finished the longest, hardest slog of your life. Even now, however many years later, I can wake up in the morning and think, I'm World Champion, and it brings a smile to my face.

We did the debrief. Most pointless debrief ever. Everybody was already necking champagne, spilling it on their laptops. The celebrations continued until we all piled into cars to make our way back to the hotel and then onwards to a big celebration party.

But I got to the party and it was too overwhelming, so I had a drink, said goodbye to the guys and headed back to the hotel. There I sat in my room for three hours, just mulling things over in my mind.

Later, we at Brawn would discuss the season in depth. We talked about the reasons for my run of disappointing results and could never quite put our fingers on why that was. Was it the pressure? The increased threat from Red Bull? It had taken Rubens a while to get used to his car but when he did he began to catch me up.

As Shov said, 'The pressure doesn't make you drive better,' while Ross put it down to struggling with tyre temperature, to not being aggressive enough.

The important thing was that I had hung in there.

The double diffuser was an advantage, of course. But it makes me laugh (translation: it pisses me right off) when people say that we only won the World Championship because of it. We weren't the only team to have it at the beginning of the season, and those teams who adopted it later couldn't catch us. Some of my drives that season were bloody good. Coming from fourteenth on the grid to fifth in Brazil wasn't too shabby, for a start. It's worth pointing out, also, that we didn't develop that car during the season.

'Finally,' was what Ross Brawn said, and that definitely fed into all the relief I felt. Nigel Mansell had 176 starts before he became World Champion in 1992; it took me 169, the second longest.

That night, however, as I sat in my room with the party going on some floors below, what I thought about most was that journey – the one Dad and I had made together. A childhood dream of becoming World Champion. I fell asleep, and when I awoke the next morning, the dream was real.

53

Next stop after winning the World Championship in Brazil was the Bluewater Shopping Centre in Kent, complete with a troop of Button Babes, loads of well-wishers, the model Jodie Kidd and pop singer Joss Stone. I was like, 'A sponsorship event at a shopping centre? Are you kidding?'

They weren't, and, one private jet later, I was in Kent, where my job was to grin for photos (lots of number-one fingers), take passengers for a ride in a super Mercedes and participate in a Scalextric challenge. The whole time I was thinking, one, *This is really surreal* and, two, *I could do with a kip.*

But World Champions don't sleep, especially when there's important celebrating to be done. Next stop, London, where I joined the boys for a night on the town, ending up in swanky Mayfair club, Jalouse. More well-wishers – I *love* well-wishers – but not so many that it got boring. The perfect amount of well-wishers. Lots of dancing, champagne and in every way a great Jenson Button night out apart from the fact that nobody fell over and hurt themselves.

In the early hours, we stumbled out, and were about to climb into a Mercedes V-Class people-carrier when up pops a pap. 'Quick picture, Jenson, and I'll let you get on your way,' he said ingratiatingly.

Bitter experience told me that he wouldn't stop hounding me even after I'd done what he asked. But hey, I was the new World Champion, I was a very happy three sheets to the wind and I'm a nice guy. Who knew? Maybe the pap was too. Perhaps he was the only living pap in London who would keep to his word.

'Right you are.'

But of course he was just as crooked as the rest of them, and after we clambered in the V-Class and took off, he jumped on a scooter and began following, snapping away as he did so. Quite an art riding a scooter and taking pictures at the same time, but we weren't in the mood for admiring his pap skills; we were more concerned that he was following us to where we were staying, which we didn't want.

At the same time we were chatting about something we'd seen on YouTube, where a famous person had nicked a pap's car keys to stop them following them.

Next thing we knew as the car came to a standstill at some lights, James jumped out of the car, ran over to the scooter and whipped out the keys. He clambered back in the car and then, about half a mile down the road, launched the keys out of the window.

Yes, I know. Not big or clever. The pap was just a guy trying to do his job. I'm aware of all the arguments. But in mitigation, we were pretty hammered and very pissed off. And after all, the guy had lied to us. That's a bad thing.

Next morning, poor old James woke up with a head on him, fuzzily playing over the events of the previous night and wincing when he got to the bit where he chucked the car keys out of the V-Class window.

He phoned Jules Gough, my lovely PA, to tell her that she might get a phone call regarding this particular incident, and sure enough, she did, and it was the police, who wanted to speak to James, who told them what he'd done and that he did it out of a concern for public safety, what with the guy running loads of red lights, and also that the guy had assaulted him, because there had been a bit of argy-bargy on the night.

The cops said, 'Great, okay, we'll call the guy and find out if he wants to press charges', so James said, 'If he wants to press charges, then I'm going to press charges for assault', and they came back and said that he wanted to let it go.

Which more or less wound up my WDC celebrations – for the time being, at least, because we had the small matter of the final race in Abu Dhabi, which I enjoyed like never before. Spinning off in practice? Who cared? Not me. I was having fun.

Sebastian won but the real action was between me and Mark for second and third. The Aussie won that one, but at least I got to join the two Red Bulls on the podium, where Sebastian turned to me, fixed me with that look of his, a cross between quizzical and bemused, and said, 'It is nice enjoying ziss podium viz you. It iz good.'

He was right. It bloody well was.

I can't remember exactly when it was, but it was around that time that I found myself alone with the old man, reminiscing about the season.

'Dad, there's something I need to tell you,' I said.

'What is it, son?'

'One night, years ago, we were driving back from a kart race. You and Pippa were in the front. I was asleep in the back.'

He looked a little wary. 'Go on.'

'I wasn't really asleep. I heard what you said.'

His face was grave. He so rarely looked that way. 'What did I say, Jense?'

'You said, "I don't think he's got it."'

His face crumpled. 'Oh, Jense, I'm so sorry. It was just that…'

'No, No, Dad, I'm not telling you to make you feel bad. Don't you dare feel bad.' He was shaking his head, feeling bad about it, but I wanted him to hear me out; I wanted him to know. 'Really, Dad, I promise. I was bit lost then, having doubts, not really enjoying the racing. Hearing you say that, it was exactly what I needed at the time. I was determined to prove you wrong.'

He smiled. 'Well, you did that, Jense. You really did that.'

PART THREE

'You arrive with dreams...'

54

I'm World Champion. What do I do now?

It was a thought that had troubled me that very first night in Brazil, when I'd excused myself from the party to go to my room. This, after all, was the achievement of my life's ambition, a thought that had driven me since childhood. There's only one way to go from there. I knew that even if I were to win another World Championship I'd never top that feeling. I could go on to win five more on the trot and each one would be a pale imitation of the first.

How, then, to avoid that feeling? That was the question.

The answer didn't materialise right away. First, I needed to decamp to Dubai, where me, my manager Richard, and the rest of the crew rented a place at the end of 2009. During our stay we were visited by Ross Brawn and Nick Fry who wanted to talk future plans.

'We'd like to sign you for the next few years,' they said over coffee on the terrace.

Great, we thought, and waited for the next bit. There's always a next bit. It's the next bit that's interesting. Obviously, we had a little shopping list of things we wanted from them, the most important of which was a commitment to developing the car over the course of the season. We wanted a repeat of 2009 but not a word-for-word repeat, if that makes sense.

Either way, what they said next rendered virtually all of my concerns redundant.

'Mercedes are going to buy the team,' they announced. 'Next season we'll be called Mercedes Grand Prix. We're replacing Rubens with Nico Rosberg and we'd like you to drive alongside Nico.'

I looked at Richard.

'So Mercedes will be funding the team?' I asked, thinking that meant an awful lot of money for development.

Tumbleweed. Ross and Nick clearing their throats and studying their shoes. 'Not exactly,' said Nick. 'Mercedes will buy Brawn, but it's up to us to find the sponsorship to fund the team.'

Richard and I said we'd have a think and bid them a fond farewell, but we were rolling our eyes the second we closed the door on them. Finding a sponsor for the team was a big ask. You're talking about hundreds of millions a year. And why on earth would Mercedes buy the team then fail to invest further in it? For the answer to that you'd have to ask Mercedes, of course, but the theory at the time was that they were being cautious about their re-entry into Formula One. For years they'd been an engine supplier in partnership with Ilmor, but they evidently wanted a quiet entrance when it came to being a constructor again. It seems crazy now, of course, when they've been so dominant for the past few years, but that was the state of play in 2009.

And it wasn't a very appealing prospect, if I'm honest.

It was while relaxing on a sun lounger in Dubai, with a chilled drink close by, that I decided I didn't want to make life easy for myself.

That was the answer I'd been seeking since that night in the Brazil hotel room. Winning the World Championship was a relief, it was a release ('About time.' 'Finally.'). But in that second half of the season

I'd misplaced the sheer joy of racing. I wanted that back, and to get it back I needed a new challenge, and by that I don't mean the challenge of schmoozing new sponsors for Brawn. I needed a new challenge on the track and I had an idea where I might find one.

'Are you sure?' asked Richard, when I told him my hare-brained plan.

'I'm sure,' I told him.

Next thing, Richard was on the phone to Martin Whitmarsh of McLaren. 'Hello, Martin, do you have a seat available next year?'

'Possibly, why?'

'Jenson's shown interest in driving for you.'

'Really?'

'Yeah, are you surprised?'

'Well, I didn't think Jenson would leave Brawn. After all, Brawn are the World Champions. *Jenson* is the World Champion. It's surprising you'd want to upset the applecart.'

'Yeah,' said Richard, 'but your car was the strongest car at the end of 2009. They won a couple of races and he feels that yours is the team that he wants to drive for.'

It's absolutely true that I'd been eyeing up McLaren's car. Though their MP-24 had begun the 2009 season in pretty poor shape they'd been quick to respond to the double-diffuser challenge and continued to develop and improve the car through the season, so much so that by the end of the year they were winning races. It was that effort in turning around the car that had really caught my attention. Of our competitors that season it was either them or Red Bull, and we knew there were no seats at Red Bull – Sebastian and Mark were safe there. But we knew that Heikki Kovalainen hadn't quite delivered for McLaren; he was the first to admit that he'd had a torrid year, so that chances are they'd be looking for someone to partner Lewis.

And that was the other thing I liked about McLaren. They had Lewis Hamilton, who had won the championship in 2008, the year before me. I wanted him as a teammate.

Thus far in my career I'd had mixed fortunes with teammates. From that moment when Frank had offered me the job and Ralf pulled his diva act I'd recognised that your teammate was also your biggest rival, and so it had proved. Ralf always came across as a bit insecure to me, as though he feared he was being usurped, and he never quite treated me as an equal, which might have been my age or the language barrier. His strength as a driver was that he was quick over one lap, and it took me a while to get to his level. Once I did, he thawed a bit.

It had been the same story with Jacques, of course. I had to prove myself.

Then there was Fisi, who drove so much better than I did, but rather than revel in his superiority, had actually been very supportive. Good old Fisi. Later, Jarno Trulli had been a bit more quiet, kept himself to himself, as though he wasn't a big fan of the Formula One circus, how I imagine Kimi Räikkönen must be.

Lewis, though. Well, you could come up with all sorts of psycho-babble reason why I wanted to partner him, but it would boil down to one reason: I am a sportsman. I feed off competition and I wanted to pit myself against the fastest driver on the grid, a World Champion. I wanted to see if I could beat him.

If I were to partner Lewis, then McLaren would be the first team to start a season with the last two world champions as their drivers, the first pairing of two British world champions since Graham Hill and Jim Clark at Lotus in 1968. All the stars were in alignment.

'We'd love to have you in the team,' said Martin as he gave me a tour of the factory in Woking. My eyes were on stalks at trophy cabinets that seemed to go on for miles like some kind of gleaming optical illusion; racing cars everywhere – a huge room filled with McLaren's Formula One cars all draped with crinkly plastic sheets. So many number ones and names of the greats: 'Senna', 'Prost', 'Hunt'. You can sit in the 1988 MP4/4 driven by Senna and Prost, the most successful single-season car ever.

For a racing nut it was like wandering around heaven. What am I saying? For a racing nut it *was* heaven: just like Williams, McLaren were a cornerstone of Formula One; also in common with Williams it had two figureheads, Ron Dennis and Martin Whitmarsh, both of whom were legends in the sport. I'd always found Ron a slightly unusual character in ways I found difficult to put my finger on and we never quite gelled in all the time we worked together, but I had acres of respect for him and his achievements, and at the end of the day he was a racing man through and through. I loved that about him.

Besides, it didn't really matter that we weren't bezzy mates. He'd already stepped down as team principal by this point, handing the reins to Martin, who I got on with like the proverbial burning abode.

Discussions continued. We certainly didn't bail on Brawn just like that. But we knew that there was practically no work being done on the 2010 car, and anyway, they seemed reluctant to talk to us, with phone calls going unanswered, emails ignored. In reality, the Mercedes deal meant they'd taken their eye off the ball and they didn't really have the time to give to me, but I was like, 'Guys? Hello? I'm over here,' and wondering just what on earth was going on.

It all added up to a sense of not being wanted, and being the sensitive little flower I am, I need to feel wanted. Joking aside – and more to the point – I was keen to be in a competitive car.

'I think you're making a career mistake going up against Lewis,' Ross told me, as negotiations reached the point of no return. News had leaked out and there were plenty of paddock folk dropping their chips in surprise. I, the World Champion, was leaving the World Champions to go and race a World Champion. But my mind was made up. It was true that Mercedes was shaping up to be a good bet for the future, and with the benefit of hindsight we now know that's the case, but I was thirty years old by then, no spring chicken in F1 terms; I couldn't afford to prop up the back of the grid for three years while they developed a decent car; I needed one there and then. I was only going to get that at McLaren.

Ross and I were both at Buckingham Palace that December. He received an OBE for services to motor racing and I was awarded an MBE. He'd mellowed by then; he understood that I was a racer at heart and that I wanted to go where the racing was best.

Nick Fry, though. *Whoa.* While Ross was pretty sanguine about the whole thing, Nick went ballistic. After one phone call I knew he was going to kick off, and when it came to going to Brackley and telling them in person, I was ready for a confrontation. Put it this way, I made Richard stay away, for fear of proper fisticuffs taking place. (Put your money on Richard in that situation, incidentally; he's a karate black belt and there's no one in the world he's scared of apart from my older sister, Tanya.)

So anyway, I went on my own and Nick was furious, literally shaking with anger as he started shouting at me.

As we all know, I don't do being shouted at, and he was really laying on the decibels, going way past the point at which Richard would have chinned him.

And then he stopped all of a sudden. 'Why are you laughing?' he snapped.

'I'm not laughing,' I said.

But I was smiling.

'You're smiling.'

It was true, I was smiling. One of those nervous I'm-thirty-years-old-but-this-man-is-shouting-at-me smiles that you can't help and the more you try to stop it the bigger it gets.

Red-faced, Nick yelled, 'And you can wipe that smirk off your face.'

Put it this way: any lingering doubts I had evaporated at that precise moment in time.

55

'You're mad going to McLaren,' they said. 'That's Lewis's team.'

Was it? Was it really? Let's look at the stats. In 2007, when me and Rubens were driving a Honda with a picture of the planet Earth on it, Lewis had made his debut in Formula One, partnering Fernando Alonso, who at that point was reigning World Champion and one of the most phenomenally talented and instinctive drivers the sport has ever seen.

Lewis beat him that season. Only just – they had the same points but it went to countback, and Lewis, with more second places than Fernando, won. But even so. He beat Fernando. And that same season, his first in Formula One, he scored more podium finishes than any other debutant in F1 history and came second in the Drivers' Championship. He finished one point behind the eventual winner, Kimi.

The next season, 2008, Lewis won, pushing Ferrari's Felipe Massa into second, becoming the youngest-ever holder of the title, the first black driver and the first Brit to win since my sister's playmate Damon Hill in 1996.

In 2009, he'd had a terrible start to the season but rallied and dragged McLaren to third in the Constructors' Championship, himself fifth in the Drivers'. In both 2008 and 2009 he had left his teammate Heikki Kovalainen for dust.

So on the one hand, they were right. It *was* Lewis's team. What the bloody hell was I doing?

But on the other hand, a team isn't just one driver, and I was grizzled enough to know a few tricks when it comes to ingratiating myself with my new colleagues. Nothing especially cunning, just spend a bit of time with the guys, make sure there's a mutual respect there. It was something that had taken me a few seasons to work out, but having done so, it was a tactic I'd taken with me throughout the years and it had always served me well.

Meanwhile, Lewis was very friendly and welcoming, and presumably confident enough in his status at the team that he didn't need to feel put out.

At first, anyway.

My first race as a McLaren driver was the Bahrain Grand Prix, where despite my car bearing the coveted number one, I only qualified eighth to Lewis's fourth. Ferrari dominated the race – a one–two for Alonso and Massa – with Lewis in third and me only just in the points in seventh. Bit shit, really. I probably didn't take things to the limit. Must pull socks up.

Sure enough, in Australia I qualified fourth behind the Red Bulls and Alonso's Ferrari. The next day it rained just before the start and I began to fancy my chances. Things went a bit pear-shaped at turn one. In front of me Alonso turned in and I had the choice of either braking and causing a pile-up behind or clipping him and spinning him.

I chose option two, and in the next second Alonso was facing the wrong away, most of the cars behind reacting quickly and steering around him apart from one – Michael Schumacher, who had joined

Nico Rosberg at the new Mercedes and was effectively driving what would have been my car. He clipped Alonso and damaged his front wing.

Michael came in for a new wing and eventually took a point. Alonso, meanwhile, had been knocked into last place but mounted an incredible fightback to finish fourth. Me? I'd lost places in the early laps but I was doing my best to feel the car in the conditions, and although it was still wet, I was convinced it was time to go in for slicks.

Lap six and I came for slicks, heart sinking when I saw that the pit lane was still soaking wet, thinking, *This could be really embarrassing.* Still, once the tyres were on it was too late to change my mind and I left the pits, almost immediately running into trouble when I nearly came off at turn three.

Big mistake, I was thinking. Big mistake. Rookie error.

But then I started to pick up speed. The track was drying; other drivers were coming in for slicks and I started making up the places I'd lost after my poor lap one and pit stop. I'd worked out the dry lines on the track, whereas other drivers were still looking for them, and made a couple of overtakes until by lap eleven I found myself behind race leader Sebastian Vettel.

I stayed there, hunting him down, hoping for a chance to pass and planning to jump on any mistake he made when lady luck did her thing and sent him into the gravel, something to do with a loose wheel nut.

After that it was all about looking after those tyres. I nursed them all the way to the finish line and my first win with McLaren – their nineteenth winner – and the thirteenth driver to have won a Grand Prix for three different constructors.

Malaysia was blah. Lewis was sixth. I was eighth following a gargantuan battle with Alonso.

China, though: different story. It was just starting to drizzle as the race began, and there was a crunch at turn six that caused the safety car to come out. As ever, drivers used the opportunity to pit, and both Sebastian and Mark for Red Bull switched from slicks to intermediates.

I was doing okay. My slicks still had loads of grip despite the wet so I decided to stay out for the time being, and it was one of those decisions for which I'd come to be very grateful, because I'd soon made my way up from fifth to second.

Lewis, meanwhile, was getting into it with Vettel. There was a moment when they were both released from their stops and were racing in the pits (Lewis yielded) which is a big no-no, and they tussled on a couple of corners as well, which cost them both time.

Meanwhile I had climbed to second and was hunting down Nico Rosberg, who slid on lap nineteen, giving me the lead.

Now the call for intermediate tyres was made and I came in. But there was still drama to come. Jaime Alguersuari hit the wing of his Toro Rosso, leaving debris strewn all over the track. Out came the safety car again, and as you know, that's like a virtual restart.

For five laps we kept sedately behind the safety car, which came into the pits on lap twenty-five. I had control of the field and I slowed it right down, bunching everyone up behind me (Mark Webber came off as a result; he was furious about it), Just keeping them slow, biding my time, until…

Bang. I got on the throttle, shot forward with Rosberg right behind, Kubica behind him, Lewis back in seventh.

Behind me, though: *jeez.* Lewis overtook Kubica then Rosberg and from lap thirty-nine onwards it was me and him and he was making life very difficult for me. For a while it looked as though I might pull away and build on a ten-second lead, but my tyre went off, and from then on I was wrestling with the car, desperately trying to keep him off my tail.

I hung on, and when I came in first, it put me ten points clear of Rosberg in the Drivers' Championship and feeling pretty good about my decision to move to McLaren. I'd wanted a challenge. No doubt about it, I'd got one. Game on.

56

Damn. In Spain I finished fifth (Lewis third). I went into Monaco still in the lead for the championship but had to retire when a mechanic left a bung in the air intake and my engine overheated. As a result of that I lost the championship lead big-style, with Webber, Vettel and Alonso all vaulting me.

Even so, I remained ahead of Lewis in the points.

Did he like being beaten by his teammate? Probably not, but he's a competitor and I'm sure that like me he relished the challenge. That's why we do what we do. Personally, he was fine with me, no issues at all at this stage of the game, but you could just tell he was a little bit peeved. That thing about it being *his* team? It was right on the money. And if you ask me, he was finding it difficult to get a handle on the fact that it was *our* team now.

The thing was that I came with baggage in the form of my mates, Richard, and my dad, all of whom liked a laugh and tended to dominate any room they entered. My dad, for example, used to collar my engineer, Dave Robson: 'You're doing a great job, Dave, you're doing a great job, look after my son, you're doing a great job, just don't fuck it up.'

Prior to joining McLaren I'd been worried that the atmosphere might be a bit lacking. Ron, after all, had a somewhat dour reputation

– his obsession with the colour grey might well have been an outward manifestation of his personality – so it was good that we were able to come in and lift the place, add a bit of much-needed levity.

We were in good company, of course, because this was the time that Red Bull, under Christian Horner, were also establishing themselves as a bit of a party team. Ferrari were fun then, too, and overall it was a good atmosphere in the paddock, with McLaren right in the thick of it.

But like I say, I'm not sure that was to Lewis's taste. I don't think that *I* was to his taste, if I'm honest. Plus things then took a bit of a turn for the worst in Turkey that year.

There were two real talking points in Istanbul. First, the Red Bull drivers had a collision that led to a huge falling out within the team; secondly, me and Lewis almost had a collision that led to a minor falling out between us.

What happened was that after the two Red Bulls wiped each other out, it was Lewis and me on course for a one–two, the only question being, who was going to be number one, and who was going to be a number two.

So with the lead to ourselves, I closed in on him until we were just a second apart.

What I didn't know was that he was being asked to conserve fuel. As I came up behind him he radioed in to his team, saying, 'Jenson's closing in on me, you guys. If I back off, is Jenson going to pass me or not?'

'No, Lewis, no,' came the reply.

But of course I didn't know any of that, and slipped past him. That made him mad and he came back at me, pulling alongside and staying side-by-side as we roared through turns thirteen and fourteen. Crossing the start–finish line you couldn't get a credit card between us – the official gap was 0.0s – but he had the inside line going into turn one. For a scary moment it looked like there might be another Red Bull double-wipe-out situation as our tyres rubbed coming through turn one, but he managed to get past me to claim the win, me in second.

Then on the podium there was what the media called some 'frosty' body language and a 'muted' celebration. In fact, he came straight out and asked me about it: 'Did you pass me against team orders?'

He was the winner. Jesus.

'No,' I told him, 'I did not pass you against orders. I was never told not to pass you.'

That sent him off thinking that the team were taking my side against his, though he never did explain why they would want to do that, given that we were on course for a one–two and, apart from our respective race engineers, nobody in the team would give a flying fuck who came first and who came second.

It was a bit weird, slightly unnecessary – the team later came clean and said he'd simply been given incorrect information – and a little more proof that all was not well behind the smiles.

Canada was another one–two, which put Lewis in the lead with 109, me second on 106. Red Bull were still very much in it, though, and Sebastian took first in Valencia (this at the race where Mark sheared off his brake pedal), while Lewis and I finished second and third.

Mark won at Silverstone, Lewis second, me fourth. Nine races to go and we were out in front of the Constructors', while Lewis was first and I was second in the Drivers' with both Mark and Sebastian breathing down our necks. There was still all to play for.

In Germany I qualified fifth, Lewis sixth, and then we finished fifth and fourth, with Ferrari taking a one–two. We maintained our places on the leader board but were biting our lips, painfully aware that our rivals were finding pace just as we seemed to be losing it.

Sure enough, Hungary marked a turning point, with Mark taking the win, Lewis retiring, me coming home in eighth. Red Bull crept ahead of us now.

Lewis won at Spa, while I got nobbled by Seb at the chicane for a DNF. At first he tried to say I'd braked early, which I hadn't, then later amended his story, saying his balance had been unsettled by a bump, and even called me later to say sorry.

Now Lewis had 182 points, Mark 179, Sebastian 151, and I was fading on 147. At Monza I took the lead for the first thirty-five laps and had hell's own job fending off Alonso, who was a tough and cunning an operator as you could possibly imagine, especially in that situation. Matters weren't helped by the fact that I'd flat-spotted a tyre by locking up, and the vibrations were insane.

In the end he had a better pit stop and the faster car. We finished three seconds apart, and the Italian fans, the *tifosi*, went batshit crazy.

So, having said that Alonso had a better stop than me, I'd better say a quick word about mechanics before they get the hump, because what you cannot do is underestimate the importance of stops in a Grand Prix, and to get it as fast as they do – and it still amazes me how fast they are – they need to work at it. They prepare just as rigorously as drivers when it comes to diet and fitness.

At McLaren we were always trying to find new and better ways of improving pit stops. We'd pioneered a method of having wheel nuts mounted within the wheel rims themselves, so there was less likelihood of a mechanic dropping the nut. We managed a record-breaking 2.6s stop, which is sensational for the static time in which all four wheels are changed. And later in the year the boys got that down to 2.31s.

I've trained with mechanics and, believe you me, they work out hard. They need to be strong, for a start; those wheel guns are heavy and the kickback is immense, as well as the fact that it's dangerous – the wheels are hot and there's the constant risk of fire. Each member of the team trains and prepares for a different role, and they're constantly monitored under test conditions to see if one member of the team is physically better suited to another task. Often they're the difference between a good race and a bad one, and they so rarely get the credit for it. Big hand, please, for the mechanics.

Lewis retired at Monza then again at Singapore while I managed fourth. He was fifth at Suzuka. I was fourth.

Korea, I finished twelfth, which pretty much dashed my title hopes for that season. The only positive of that weekend was that I went to a restaurant and somebody in the restaurant thought I was Sebastian Vettel. I didn't want to put them straight, because they were so friendly, but then I tried to get the bill and they'd paid for me, so I left happy.

That was the only highlight of the Korean Grand Prix – that I got a free meal because someone thought I was Sebastian Vettel.

57

In Brazil, I had what you could safely say was a cruddy qualifying session, managing eleventh on the grid. I was slightly cheered up by seeing a cute dog on the journey from the circuit back to the hotel.

We were in a little A-Class at the time, and this being Brazil we were being driven by an armed police driver, Daniel, on a three-lane highway. Rising above us on either sides were the terrible São Paulo shanty towns they call the favelas, a higgledy-piggledy collection of mostly makeshift homes scattered on the hillsides as though tossed there by some unseen giant hand and left for someone else to tidy up. Their inhabitants live in grinding poverty and life is cheap; that the favelas could even exist is a terrible blight on São Paulo and Brazil.

Worse still was the city's awful cosmetic attempt to try and hide them. Talk about turning a blind eye. This was a journey we'd made many times over the years, of course, and over the last few visits we'd noticed flats springing up on either side of the highway, obscuring our sight of the slums.

We'd stopped at traffic lights, about a couple of rows back from the front, and I was casting my eyes over the flats, knowing what terrible poverty lay behind them, when I caught sight of the cute little dog, ambling along by the side of the road. Like I say, just seeing it took my mind off qualifying.

'Guys, look at that dog,' I said. 'How do you think they survive in all this poverty?'

The next thing I saw was a guy holding a baseball bat. He'd appeared from inside one of the flats, probably having come down from the favelas and through the back of the flats. The reason I thought he was from the favelas and not a resident of the flats, was because of the baseball bat, and the reason I thought he was bad news and not simply a keen baseball fan, was because the bat was studded with nails.

The others saw him too. They'd been expecting to see a cute dog. *Let's indulge Jenson, he's had a bad day's qualifying, poor love.* But instead what they saw was Baseball Bat Guy. Worse he was joined by at least four other men, all of whom were armed, either with handguns or submachine guns.

Oh, and they were making their way through the traffic. They were ignoring the other cars. They were making their way directly towards us.

Later we were told that criminal gangs pick out cars with likely victims, people like us who have nice watches, laptops and so on. The A-Class wasn't an especially eye-catching vehicle – you don't flaunt wealth in Brazil – so it's entirely possible that we'd been identified in advance, maybe even at the circuit. The way they do it, apparently, is by marking your car with chewing gum.

What happens next is that the gang appear, carrying guns. Ah, but our Merc had bulletproof glass. Another necessity of living in Brazil, and another reason I'd asked Jessica to stay at home (and thank God I did). But that was where the nail-studded baseball bat would come in handy. The glass is made bulletproof thanks to a film over the window, but swing a bat at the window and the glass stars, the film is broken and hey presto, it's no longer an A-Class with bulletproof windows, it's just an A-Class with a bunch of cowering Brits inside.

Besides, if the baseball bat approach fails to work for some reason, they can stick the barrel of a gun into the seam of a door and pull the trigger. The bullet will pass into the cabin and the cowering Brits inside will give you anything you want to stop you pulling the trigger a second time.

What I'm saying here is that bulletproof glass is about as much use as a chocolate teapot in São Paulo; what you need is a bulletproof car. And we didn't have one of those.

Like I say we didn't find any of this out until later. At the time, what we saw was five armed men advancing on the rear of our car – very definitely our car.

'Daniel.'

Our driver twisted in his seat, saw the threat and reached to his belt for his gun. *Oh sweet Jesus they're going to have a shootout*, I thought, but Daniel thought better of it. His hand went from the gun to the gearstick.

'Hold tight,' he said, and floored it.

The A-Class shot forward, into the gap between the two cars in front. It was too narrow. A howl of metal was testament to that. The scraping of car on car and the protest of wing mirrors torn from their moorings. Cars to our left and right were shouldered aside, and we saw angry, uncomprehending faces as the A-Class scraped between them and then lurched forward, finally coming free of the surrounding traffic.

Getting free had punctured a tyre and buckled one wheel but we weren't stopping. Behind us the baseball bat guy and his mates had broken into a run, hoping to capitalise on our damaged vehicle and still catch us.

'*Go*,' we were shouting, somewhat redundantly, because having executed a pretty nifty bit of evasive driving, Daniel was clearly in no mood to stop, and we had enough speed to pull away from our pursuers.

Drawing alongside us were the cars we'd damaged. Angry faces. 'Stop. What are you doing?' But Daniel had wound down the window and was telling them the score. By now the men on foot had given up the chase, and about half an hour later a whole convoy of cars pulled up to the hotel, where insurance details were exchanged.

By now Daniel had filled us in on the possibility that we'd been singled out for robbery. We didn't check the car for chewing gum, but either way I was straight on the blower to the team, demanding a police escort for getting to the circuit the next day. After that we piled into the bar for a stiff drink and ended up telling a load of journalists what had just happened to us.

The next day, it was already a big story, and after we'd got our police escort to the circuit and made our way into the paddock, virtually everybody we met wanted to know what had happened to us. For a while we'd been worried that people might not believe us that a submachine gun had been involved, but then it emerged that a couple of guys from Sauber had been threatened with a submachine gun, too, so everybody believed us, we were getting the full lucky-to-be-alive treatment.

All, that was, apart from one.

In the paddock you've got all the team, lorries backed on to the garages on one side, and on the other side, the big team motorhomes where drivers hang out, bigwigs are entertained and so on. We'd reached the McLaren motorhome, piled inside and were gathering ourselves when who should walk in but Bernard Ecclestone.

Quick bit of context to this next conversation. Over the years there had been an awful lot of moaning from teams about the dangers of Brazil and, perhaps understandably, Bernie had always tried to play it down. Just as the Brazilian government turned a blind eye to the favelas, so Bernie did with the armed guards and bulletproof glass.

'Hello, Jenson,' he said.

'Hello, Bernie,' I said.

'What's all this I hear about you and some locals?'

'They were chasing us, Bernie. They had guns; they had a submachine gun.'

He pulled a lemony face. 'Come on, seriously, do you think it was really dangerous?'

'Of course it was dangerous. They were armed. It was *very* dangerous, Bernie.'

Now he came over all philosophical. 'There are victims in life, Jenson,' he said, 'and you've got to know whether you're a victim or not.'

He left and we looked at each other, gobsmacked.

There's a postscript. At the end of that year, Bernie was pretty badly beaten up by muggers who took his Hublot watch as he left his offices in Knightsbridge. A photo of his bruised face was used in a Hublot advert: 'See what people will do for a Hublot,' so full marks to Bernie for capitalising on that one.

Not long after, he sent me the photo in the post, with a card that said, 'I'm sorry. It seems like we can all be victims at one time or another.'

Which was nice of him.

Trouble was, in the meantime I'd sent him a bitchy Christmas card addressed to 'Bernie, the victim'.

They must have crossed in the post. Oops.

*

After all that Brazil was an anti-climax. True, I improved on my eleventh grid position and finished fifth, but it wasn't enough to keep me in contention for the title. Mathematically, I was out. Red Bull, meanwhile, were whooping it up, having secured the Constructors' title, though they couldn't party as much as they'd like because they still had to focus on the last race, Abu Dhabi, in just a week's time.

That left Fernando and Mark as the bookies' favourites going into Abu Dhabi, with Sebastian and Lewis the outsiders. Come the race and Ferrari made a tactical error, focusing their efforts on stopping Mark. The upshot was that Sebastian came through and nicked it. Thus, the Drivers' title went to Red Bull. Meanwhile, Lewis was second and I was third, so at least I had a podium to end what had been a great season.

And looking back over it, of course it was a shame that we'd started so well and then fallen off, but second in the Constructors' and fourth (Lewis) and fifth (me) in the Drivers' wasn't too shabby. To be honest, the Red Bulls were so fast from the start of the year and very difficult to beat; indeed, this would be the beginning of a period of total domination for Red Bull.

Personally speaking, though, I was happy. I'd come into the season wanting to relocate my love of racing, hoping the challenge of partnering Lewis and driving for McLaren would be the catalyst for that, and that's exactly what had happened. Was it more important to me to win races, maybe retain the World Championship? Or was it more important to me to beat my teammate? I managed neither, so in a way the question's irrelevant, ask me another. But if you were to insist then I'd have to smile mysteriously and point you to the bit where I say that the competition between teammates is the purest kind of racing that exists in Formula One, because that's where it stops being about you and your engineers and your design team versus him and his engineers and his design team. It's just you versus him.

As for Lewis, I still think he was a bit freaked out by the way things at the team had changed.

Again. Let's be clear about this. He was smiley and friendly. But as everybody says about him, he's very friendly and polite and full of respect for the sport and his fellow competitors, but there's stuff going on beneath that surface – stuff you only occasionally glimpse. That scene on the podium, for example. He can be quite unpredictable in his responses to things, gets an idea in his head and you think, *Where on earth did he get that from?*

Or maybe it was simply the case that he'd had things his own way for too long. Before I came trailing Team Button, my pink-shirted dad, swearing at the engineers and mussing up the mechanics' hair, he'd been top dog, hot new British driver at a British team – outpointing the great Fernando Alonso to boot.

Oh well. Maybe our relationship would improve in 2011.

Certainly things were looking good as far as the car was concerned. I mean, I don't know about other drivers but I never stop marvelling at the engineering of an F1 car, which to me is like a beautiful mix of science fiction and magic, and that was certainly true of the 2011 car, the MP4-26.

For a start, it had very cool-looking sidepod inlets and though the double diffuser was now out – banned by the FIA – it incorporated a system of hot blowing, where the exhaust fired even when you were off the throttle in order to maintain downforce. Our KERS system was good, too. KERS is Kinetic Energy Recovery System and works a bit like a dynamo, storing up energy from the brakes that you can then use to aid acceleration on the straight.

Like I say, it's magic and even as a driver my own understanding was limited. I did, however, have more driver input than I had on the previous year's car, so I came to it with increased confidence and a feeling that this was 'my' car.

Meanwhile, the rules had made it legal to use DRS in qualifying, as well as for overtaking during the race itself. Red Bull concentrated on getting their DRS right for qualifying and pre-season testing seemed to indicate that that was where they'd have the edge.

So it would prove at the first race, Australia, where Sebastian was on pole position, Lewis second and me fourth behind Mark. Sebastian won the race, which was pretty much the story of that season, while Lewis was second and I was sixth.

I was second in Malaysia, behind Sebastian, while Lewis laboured in eighth after a problem with a jammed wheel nut. In China I was called in to pit and accidentally stopped in the Red Bull pit. Thank God for the helmet to spare my blushes. I managed to pull forward just in time, as Sebastian came screaming into the pits behind me. Lewis ended up winning that race. Me? Fourth.

Turkey was one of the best races of the year and the reason was that Lewis and I had an almighty battle for fourth. I make no bones about it, I loved going head-to head with him, even when he got the upper hand, which he did then. The Red Bulls took a one–two in that race, but just behind Sebastian in the standings was Lewis while I was behind Mark in fourth.

Could we catch the Red Bulls? They were already forty-three points ahead of us in the Constructors' and had a real spring in their step.

Could I catch Lewis? Just watch me try.

In Spain I performed a mighty cool overtake on Webber and Alonso. An opportunistic move, they'd been fighting each other but I took them both by surprise and passed them in the space of a lap. This was me really enjoying my racing now.

Sebastian was on pole in Monaco ahead of me but I kept on his tail and capitalised on his delayed pit stop in order to take first, staying in front until I had to stop again. With the pit-stop strategies confused I had to be content with second, but for Monaco that's no disgrace.

Then came Canada.

58

Rain. That was Canada. A rain that started like a persistent drizzle, promised more for later and delivered it in torrents.

The safety car was deployed right away and we tootled behind the Mercedes for four laps. When it came in after four laps Sebastian took off and pulled clear of Alonso. Around we went in sluicing rain until by lap six the order was Sebastian, Alonso, Felipe Massa, Nico Rosberg, Michael Schumacher, me, and then Lewis.

Lewis tried to get past me on lap eight and came out to my left, trying to take me through the corner. I didn't see him. Focused on trying to cut through the rain and half-blinded by conditions in which all you can see are balls of spray and rooster tails, my mirrors were useless as I moved across to take the racing line out of the corner, unaware that Lewis was coming up that side. His right front wheel came level with my back wheel then…

Bok. We clipped and he was off into the pit wall, his race over with what they thought was broken rear suspension.

'What was he doing?' I yelled over the radio, privately wondering how Lewis would react, because like I say, he could be unpredictable that way.

The rain was coming down like stair rods now. Out came the safety car, making its second – but by no means last – appearance of the race.

Meanwhile I'd picked up a drive-through penalty for going too fast behind the first safety car, so I had to serve that through the pits. After doing that I was fifteenth, but undeterred I started making up ground and lapping really quickly, the fastest man on the track I later discovered. I was also the most motivated. This race had put a fire in my belly. Things weren't going according to plan and I liked that.

Oh, but now the rain started coming down again and it was *chucking* down, covering the track, quickly making it impossible to continue.

The race was red-flagged. Too wet to continue, it ground to a halt, and we formed up on the grid in current-race order.

We'd be there for two hours, so I had plenty of time to get out of the car, dart across to hospitality and find Lewis.

'Mate, sorry, I didn't see you.'

'Don't worry,' he said, 'it's not your fault. I shouldn't have put my nose there.'

And that was that. Despite the fact that our collision had put him out of the race he was totally cool about it. Go figure.

Later, of course, his fans were saying that I did it on purpose to put him out of the race, but we're in complete conspiracy-theory territory there, because it's just not something a driver would ever do – mainly because there's a massive chance that you're going to get hurt doing something like that, or at the very least damage your car.

So anyway, having made my peace with Lewis I jumped back in my car ready for the restart. Off we went and the going was less treacherous; there were even dry lines forming on the track.

I was making good progress when I made contact with Alonso in the Ferrari who spun out, a prang that damaged my front wing and gave me a puncture.

Once more I came into the pits – my fourth stop of the race – where mechanics performed a lightning-fast swap of my front wing and wheel, and then off I went, *again*.

By now I was…

Where was I?

Last.

Not only that but I was half a lap behind everybody else with thirty-three laps to go, and if anything else went wrong I was in serious danger of being lapped by Sebastian.

But I loved it. I got my head down and began my charge, driving as smoothly and as fast as I ever have and beginning to make my way back up the field: taking the racing line, braking late. Using the downforce. Working the throttle. Playing my McLaren like it was a kart and I was a kid again. Nothing to lose but everything to play for. Having fun.

I felt that the circuit was drying, and in another of those sixth sense decisions I pitted early for dry tyres, one of the first to pit, which put me in a great position.

I passed Kamui Kobayashi, after which I was fourth behind Mark Webber, Michael Schumacher and Sebastian Vettel.

On the last chicane I passed Mark Webber by going on to the wet on dry tyres, which is something you just don't do but I had to be brave. Next lap I overtook Michael Schumacher and now, incredibly, I was in second. From last to second. An incredible drive, which, even if it ended there, would still be one of the most memorable of my career.

But now I was chasing Sebastian. I'd gone from fearing he'd lap me, to chasing him. The laps were running out but I was gaining on him at the rate of one second per lap. Part of me was screaming to settle for second, don't push it too hard now, don't risk everything when you've come so far.

Another part of me – the louder part – was screaming, *Go for it, go for it, push it, take it to the limit.*

And that's what I did. I stayed on Vettel's tail, getting closer and closer to him until we rounded the fast right-hander and on to the last section of the lap, two long straights, and I thought, *If I can just get close enough to him…*

I was less than a second behind him now.

If I can just get close enough, I can tow past him on the straight with DRS, the flappy wing thing.

Little did I know, I didn't need the DRS. I pushed him through the right-hander and on the next corner, a left-hander, he was paying too much attention to the mirrors and ran wide.

I jumped on his mistake, diving down the inside and taking the lead, completing the manoeuvre before I could even believe what I'd done.

And now I was in front. From last to first with less than a lap, just seven corners to go.

Don't mess it up, I was thinking. *Don't mess it up.*

Stay to the dry line.

We were both on slicks. Straying off the dry line might be fatal for me now. I drew on all that grounding, everything I'd learned coming up: keep it smooth and delicate. I was checking my mirrors, paranoid he might catch and overtake me at the death, my heart leaping when I saw that he just wasn't close enough to make it happen, and unless the bottom suddenly fell out of my car or the man in the plastic raincoat from Hockenheim made a reappearance and ambled across the track in front of me, I was going to win this race.

And I did.

After five hours of racing, the longest race in Formula One history, having started, restarted, had two accidents, six pit stops, battled my way up from last, and led only half a lap of the entire race, I came in first.

59

What I love to do is watch old races and qualifying sessions. Not to see my driving (well, not much) but for that bit they always show on TV when the picture flicks to the reaction of your team or your friends and family.

I love all that. There was a great shot of my mates hugging when I won the World Championship in Brazil, an image I'll treasure for ever; and so many times I've seen Dad's face, that mix of pure pride and barely restrained elation, like he's about to burst with it. The TV cameras usually manage to catch a sudden change in his facial expression that always makes me giggle and fill up at the same time.

Seeing it later means I get the best of both worlds. I witness the celebrations but I also get to be the guy in the car, which in my case means bursting my race engineer's eardrums. After Canada I was yelling, 'That was a helluva race!' at him, but to be fair it was perfectly justified on that occasion. Canada was special. One for the record books.

Even after a race as mad as that, there's a protocol to follow. After the chequered flag comes a slow-down lap before you take the car to *parc fermé* (unless, of course, it's Monaco and you're on the podium, ahem).

Parc fermé is basically an area where all cars must go directly after the race. It's a kind of quarantine, the idea being that the cars can't be

2010 – how do you respond to winning the World Championship? In my case,
I moved to McLaren to take on one of the F1 greats, Lewis Hamilton. Here we are
battling at Suzuka *(Top, © Getty)* and celebrating at Abu Dhabi *(Below, © Darren Heath)*.

Canada 2011 in the rain,
one of my greatest races.
I won having started,
restarted, had two
accidents, six pit stops,
battled my way up from
last, and led only half a
lap of the entire race.

(Above and below © Getty,
right © Darren Heath)

I marked my 200th Grand
Prix in Hungary with a
win (in the rain of course!),
before winning in Japan
where Sebastian Vettel
hunted me down like a
Terminator, finishing just
a seond behind. In the
Championship, sadly, our
positions were reversed.
*(Above and left © Getty,
below © Darren Heath)*

Racing in Belgium in 2012. *(© Getty)*

Pink for Papa. I raced in pink to honour my dad (right) who died in 2014.
He was always the life and soul of the party and immensely popular in the
F1 paddock. After his death, racing was never quite the same for me.

(Above and below © Getty, right © Darren Heath)

'Team Button' at Abu Dhabi 2016 – my last 'official' race. L-R: James Williamson, Chrissy Buncombe, Jules Gough, Caroline Goddard (Richard's wife), my mum Simone, me, Brittny Ward, Richard Goddard, my sister Natasha and Mikey Collier (wearing my helmet). *(Above © LAT, below © Darren Heath)*

touched or tinkered with by the team, while officials from the FIA check for legality issues.

For drivers, it's also a good time to have a word with your competitors. If you've had a wicked bit of competition then it's time for a congratulatory pat on the back. But if he's been a dick then it's the moment to have a word about it. Technically speaking it's probably *not* the best moment to have a word if he's been a dick because you're both so high on adrenalin you're likely to say something you might regret. But that's what we tend to do anyway, for better or worse.

Then it's weigh-in, which if you're one of the top three, usually takes place in the green room immediately prior to the podium. Your physio will be there – Mikey in my case – handing you a towel, a drink, and a cap to hide your sweaty hair, and then you go to the podium, remove your cap for the anthems, spray the champagne, have a great time.

If you're not one of the top three you go straight into your interviews, which are held in something we call 'the pen'. You've probably seen it: it's like an enclosure at a farm park, except with Formula One drivers instead of goats, surrounded by journalists waving microphones at you.

Those interviews are always tricky, again because you run the risk of saying silly things you shouldn't (mind you, if that happens you can always use the 'adrenalin excuse' afterwards). You see someone like Max Verstappen doing it, maybe coming out with the odd thing in the heat of the moment that would have been better kept between him and his dad. It comes with experience, I guess. You learn to calm down, breathe and try to remember that you're not just speaking for yourself, you're speaking on behalf of five hundred other people in the team.

I'm not one who finds it difficult to watch my interviews; I think it's quite instructive to get an idea of what works in a broadcast interview and what works in print. Sarcasm, for example, is always a bad idea in a print interview. Giving facetious answers can make you look like a moody git, even when you're being asked silly questions.

For example, if an interviewer says, 'How do you feel about crashing out on the first lap?' I naturally want to reply, 'How the hell do you *think* I felt about crashing out on the first lap?' But I don't because, firstly, I don't want to look like a moody git, and secondly because I realise that it's not for the journalist to say how you feel; they want to hear it in your own words. I'm also aware that they're hoping I'm going to break with protocol and say something really controversial, but sorry you'll have to wait for Max if you want that.

Overall, though, I reckon the important thing is to show emotion. I think I'm pretty well known for giving a good answer to a question, however daft it is, because I understand that it's an important part of the job, and for those moments in the pen I'm a team spokesman, their ambassador.

Same as being on the podium. I've got no time for drivers who stand up there with a long face because they didn't come first. *You're on the podium, mate, you're living the dream, let's see some teeth.*

Daniel Ricciardo's one of my best mates left in the sport, and he's podium gold. He's got this shoe thing he does, a 'shoey', where he takes off his boot, pours champagne in it, drinks it and then makes other people drink it as well.

X-Men actor Patrick Stewart was on the podium in Canada and Daniel got him to do a shoey. Patrick Stewart – Patrick Stewart! – drank out of Daniel's sweaty racing boot. He's done it to Gerard Butler as well.

I was on the podium at Silverstone 2017 – just asking the questions, my only time on the podium at Silverstone (sniff) – and I was so grateful that Daniel wasn't there, because personally I wouldn't drink champagne out of my girlfriend's sweaty trainer, let alone Daniel Ricciardo's. But there you go, it's part of the moment, the fans love it. It makes the sport what it is.

60

I was sixth in the Grand Prix of Europe at Valencia. Not great, but in the points at least. Unfortunately it was followed by a dismal Silverstone, where a malfunctioning wheel gun left me with a loose wheel nut and a DNF. Lewis came fourth while Fernando took the win for Ferrari.

In Germany I had to bail again, hydraulics failure the villain on this occasion. Lewis came first and was now ahead of me on the leader board: 139 points to my 109.

Onwards to Hungary, which would be my 200th Grand Prix. Turned out to be a good one too. Lewis and I were second and third on the grid respectively, with Sebastian in top spot. But looking at the weather on Sunday, it threatened rain.

Sure enough it bucketed down. Sebastian slid on turn two and Lewis duly slipped past into first. Meanwhile as the track began to dry, and I decided the time was right to go on to supersoft slicks and pitted. When Lewis did the same we were in front and on course for a McLaren one–two.

Needless to say, I wanted to be the number one, and I thought I had a good chance if I nursed my tyres. If I could do that and still gain on Lewis then I should be able to take him.

On lap forty-seven the heavens opened again, and ahead of me Lewis spun. I passed him as he was facing the opposite direction. A moment later I was about to lap backmarker Adrian Sutil when I was yellow-flagged and forced to slam on the anchors. That gave Lewis a chance to get his arse in gear behind me, and by the time we went into the next corner he was right on my tail.

As was now customary, the race became a duel between me and my teammate, the best kind of racing as far as I was concerned, both of us pushing it to the limit. Between laps forty-seven to fifty I was in the lead, and then Lewis snatched it back on fifty-one. On lap fifty-two, the team were urging me to pit for intermediate tyres, 'Come in, JB, come in,' but I wasn't so sure, because even though the grip wasn't quite on point, I was still fast and feeling in control of the car.

'Let's wait,' I urged them in return. 'Wait.'

Hallelujah, it was the right decision. Not long after came the message, 'Lewis is coming in, just stay out and the race is yours, JB.'

So I did, and it was. Lewis dropped to fourth and I crossed the line a comfortable three-and-a-bit seconds ahead of Sebastian. It was a great race – a really *fun* race – and a brilliant way to mark my 200th F1 appearance.

As far as that goes, we'd already had a small celebration in the McLaren motorhome on the Saturday night. However, the night before a race is not exactly the best time for a party, and as a result it was a fairly sedate and civilised affair. We decided to make up for that on the Sunday.

After the race we were given a police escort to the airport, which isn't as unusual as it sounds, because in Hungary we always got a police escort, even though I'm not aware of Hungary being especially dangerous. There was one particular race where, as well as the police motorbike up front, they gave us blue lights for the top of our car, which was pretty cool. We were doing a sponsor event, so we did that and were on our way back when the police escort went the wrong way, leaving us alone.

The blue light was still on so I decided to have a bit of fun, racing through lights, beeping my horn, proper *Starsky and Hutch* tackle. Cars were screeching to a halt at crossroads, the whole bit.

And then the police bike caught up with us. I slowed right down as he pulled alongside us, looked in and shook his head very slowly. I slotted in behind him again and we continued on our way, with me feeling like a naughty little boy.

But anyway, back to my 200th GP and this particular police escort on the Sunday was a nutter. He was literally driving head-on at traffic clearing it out of our way so we could make it to the airport.

We got there. Hopped on a private jet – very flash – and were meeting Richie at Zuma in Knightsbridge for 8.30pm. What a life, eh?

Spa was a good race. It often is in Belgium. At one point I was nineteenth, but despite the loss of downforce from a damaged front wing I managed to poke it back up to fourth, with only Alonso and the two Red Bulls ahead of me. Sebastian and Mark were quick and there was no catching them, but I managed to get past Alonso for third – which was especially sweet since I'd been so shite in qualifying.

At Monza, I found myself in sixth, and then fifth when Mark spun out. Michael Schumacher and Lewis were duelling ahead of me, but once again I capitalised on the fact that they were preoccupied with each other and sprung an attack, passing first Lewis and then Michael. By the end of the race I was second behind Sebastian, and moved up the leader board, ahead of Lewis but behind Sebastian and Fernando.

Sebastian won in Singapore, after which he only needed one point to claim the WDC. I was second with 185. Mathematically it was still possible to catch him. In reality? Not a chance.

So it proved. Even so, Suzuka was another great one.

61

Prior to the Japanese GP in Suzuka I signed a new three-year deal with McLaren, which, while handsome, was nowhere near the £85m reported by the press at the time. I wish.

During the race itself I was second on the grid and alongside Sebastian at turn nine when he cut in front of me so violently that I had to go on the grass just to avoid hitting him. He knew I was there, no doubt about it, despite what he said later – our eyes practically met as we drove side-by-side.

He avoided a penalty, much to my irritation. What's more, the near-miss had cost me a place when Lewis pounced, making us second and third by the end of the lap. There followed a long period of musical chairs as various pit stops shuffled the order. By the final laps I was out in front but I had trouble in my mirrors. Behind me were Fernando Alonso (two-time World Champion) and Sebastian Vettel (one-time World Champion), both of them hunting me down mercilessly, like a pair of Terminators. As the laps counted down I found myself low on fuel and against all my instincts was forced to take it easy, nervously monitoring events behind as my pursuers got nearer and nearer. In the end I came over the line in first, running on fumes, and breathed a huge sigh of relief.

My win did nothing to upset the championship, though. Getting in the points was enough for Sebastian, who became the youngest-ever back-to-back champion. Me? I was number two but over a hundred points in his wake, fighting off challenges from Fernando, Mark and Lewis behind me.

I was fourth in Korea, where a rock damaged my front wing and lost me downforce. But that weekend was overshadowed by some terrible news from the US: my old karting rival Dan Wheldon had been killed during the IndyCar World Championship in Las Vegas.

His death sent a ripple through the racing community. Dan was a popular guy and a great racer. He was always the one to beat in karting and in Formula Ford. Such a great talent and a great fighter. For him to go like that – at thirty-three, and in an absolutely horrific crash – was as shocking as it was sobering.

His funeral was in the States but we were able to attend a wake in the UK, and that December we got together in Milton Keynes, his birthplace, for a very special charity kart race. A nice way to remember him.

By now, Red Bull had been crowned Constructors' champs, while by finishing second at the Indian Grand Prix and then third in Abu Dhabi I'd scored enough points to ensure that Lewis couldn't catch me, which was very satisfying indeed, a personal milestone reached and the final vindication that I'd done the right thing by leaving Brawn for McLaren.

In Brazil I finished on the podium with the Red Bull guys. I was happy with that and could rest easy that I'd had a good – hell – *great* year. Winner of three Grands Prix, twelve-time podium attendee, second in the World Drivers' Championship, second in the Constructors'. It doesn't get much better than that.

And sure enough, it wouldn't get any better than that.

62

The 2012 car was yet another otherworldy creation. By now hot-blowing had been banned – teams find a loophole, the FIA closes it, repeat till fade – so the exhaust system was completely different in that it now had to direct exhaust gas away from the diffuser.

One way around that – another loophole in a way – was to use what they call the 'Coanda' effect, where air will adhere to a curved surface, to train gases towards the diffuser anyway, even though the exhaust was pointing away from it. See? Magic.

So, all looked good with the car and I was a happy bunny. Lewis, not so much. Though I'd enjoyed the 2011 season, and I'd especially relished my battles with him, he was simultaneously having a much less friendly rivalry with Felipe Massa, things coming to a head in the inter-view pen after Singapore, when Felipe tapped Lewis on the shoulder, made a sarcastic comment, and Lewis responded by snapping, 'Don't touch me again.' *Ouch.*

Now, if that was rugby or football, the pair of them would have been on the floor of the pen brawling. But racing drivers have good self-control, so that's about as tetchy as things got.

However, it did highlight a Lewis tendency, which was to let himself get rattled, and he was acquiring a bit of a reputation as a hot-head.

Earlier in 2011 he'd been very public about a meeting with Red Bull's Christian Horner, as though wanting to remind McLaren that his stock was high. At Monaco that year he'd either accused the stewards of picking on him for his colour or made an ill-advised Ali G-inspired 'is it cos I is black' joke, depending on who you want to believe.

As for me and him, we remained friendly, though we were never best buddies. That year we voiced cartoon versions of ourselves for an animated series, *Tooned*, which portrayed us as bantering rivals. The rivalry was real – and much more healthy than the one he had with Felipe and later with Nico Rosberg (I never lobbed a hat at his head for one thing) – but there wasn't a great deal of banter.

To be honest, I was pretty zen. I'd proved myself as World Champion; I'd showed that I could outpoint Lewis (and until Nico Rosberg's WDC in 2016 I was the only teammate to do so). I just wanted to enjoy my racing.

And so to the season, where a win for me in Australia – Sebastian was second, Lewis third – was followed by Malaysia, where I damaged the nose of my car, made three pit stops and found myself at the back but unable to repeat my Canadian epic and make it upfront. Result? Fourteenth, my first no-pointer since Korea in 2010.

In China I made up places from a sixth-on-the-grid start and tucked in behind Nico Rosberg in first and Michael Schumacher in second. After one pit each I was in the lead. I had one more stop to make, however, and it went wrong on the thirty-ninth lap when a botched pit stop cost me six seconds. I should have won but I had to make do with second.

Bahrain I was fourth to Lewis's second. Spain, I just couldn't get the temperature into my tyres – déjà vu – and finished ninth. Upfront nobody was able to string two consecutive wins together; indeed the season was notable for the fact that seven different drivers won the first seven races, which set a new record at the time.

It was Mark's turn to win in Monaco, but I spun trying to get past Heikki Kovalainen and retired with a puncture.

By now I was feeling frustrated, a situation not helped by events in Canada, where I came sixteenth, struggling with tyres, and Lewis won.

I was still having tyre difficulty at the European Grand Prix in Valencia but managed eighth, followed by more blah at Silverstone – tenth. Lewis came in eighth, and by now both he and I were finding it tough to understand why the car didn't seem to be performing as well as it had at the beginning of the season.

For the German Grand Prix at Hockenheim, we had an upgrade on the car, while I'd also been spending a bit of time in the simulator in a bid to improve my tyre-warming technique. All was looking good in the race and I finished second. Unfortunately Lewis marked what was his 100th race with a DNF, but even so we were still feeling pretty happy with our upgrades.

Lewis won again in Hungary, while I was cheesed off that the team kept bringing me in for stops and then sending me out into heavy traffic, the upshot being that I ended up in sixth.

So that's where we stood going into the mid-season break, when I was able to indulge my 'other' pastime – a hobby that had swiftly become something of an obsession...

63

I'd first dipped a toe in triathlon in 2007, when I was having a hard time with Honda. Frankly I needed something, *anything*, to take my mind off events on the track. We'd been in Lanzarote training, got involved in a regular Monday mini-triathlon and, before I knew it, I was training with the triathlon in mind.

Since getting into Formula One I'd turned into a diet-and-fitness freak, and I particularly liked the way one would complement the other. When I was trying to keep my weight down for driving, for example, I'd be a total low-carb fiend (tell you who takes a load of sugar in his tea: Lewis Hamilton, that's who), making sure my body fat stayed right down. Training for a triathlon, on the other hand, I'd be less worried about body fat and more about muscle, so I'd need carbs, and I'd go from eating protein for breakfast to porridge. It can make flitting between the two disciplines quite tricky but I enjoy that aspect of it almost as much as I enjoy the triathlons themselves. I love the transitional elements, going from swimming to biking and then running. The swim is good for your upper body and core, the bike is legs and core, and the run is an all-over workout. So what's not to like?

Plus I love the autonomy. As you've already heard from me so many times, if you've got an under-performing car there's nothing you can do with it; as a driver you end up feeling powerless. With a triathlon, on the other hand, it's pretty much just you, your fitness and your stamina. Coming from F1, where you're at the mercy of engineers, engine suppliers and a million other factors over which you have absolutely no control, that was majorly refreshing.

What I soon found was that one helped the other. Training for triathlons was helping me with the mental side of Formula One. Rather than risk the temptations of bars and restaurants in Monaco and London, I'd drag my friends out to Lanzarote for training breaks. Pretty soon, triathlons became a major preoccupation, and being an all-or-nothing type, it wasn't long before I decided to have a crack at hosting my own.

In 2010 we'd set up the Jenson Button Trust as a way of making charitable donations to causes close to my heart. A couple of years later, I competed in a triathlon called Lavaman in Hawaii, which has a music-festival feel, with a barbecue and bands following the event itself. I thought that was pretty cool – so much better than doing sweaty fist-bumps and then sloping off home for cocoa and *Strictly Come Dancing*. And so in 2012, I decided to do something similar, only instead of Hawaii it would be in Luton. Awesome.

And that's what I did with my mid-season break that year. We held the first-ever Jenson Button Trust Triathlon, which was a roaring success apart from what we'll call the 'Wetsuit Error'. As in, I had forgotten mine.

For a while I decided I wouldn't bother with one. After all, it was a very hot day. Did I really need one? What I soon worked out, however, was that the reason all the other competitors wear wetsuits is because they make you a lot faster, not forgetting the fact that however hot it is on a summer's day in Luton the water can still be very cold, and… oh, look, it's just better to a wear a wetsuit, okay? And I was the chump who had forgotten to bring one.

Solution? Borrow Jessica's wetsuit. It was a tight fit but I could move and that was the important thing. Off I went, on the inaugural event of my own triathlon. First event, the swim.

I hit the water and right away the wetsuit shrank. And I'm not talking a bit, like slightly uncomfortable and a little embarrassing. I'm talking about being unable to swim. Or breathe.

After a moment or so of thinking that I was going to die, and the next event to bear my name would be the Jenson Button Memorial Triathlon, I managed to undo the wetsuit in the water and gulp air into my lungs. By the time I'd flopped out of the water, however, it was game over. Pretty mortifying when it's your own triathlon and you've named your team 'Ichiban', the Japanese for 'number one'.

Undeterred I've bought my own wetsuit since, and the triathlons have continued – we held our sixth Jenson Button Trust Triathlon in 2017 and it was a great success. My passion for the sport has only grown.

I get weirdly nervous when I compete, much more so than I ever did in F1. But again I like that side of it; it's good to climb out of your comfort zone. I also enjoy the family aspect of it. My sister Samantha has raced a couple of triathlons. So has Natasha. Other members of the family are getting into it too. In other words, it's all good.

And so back to that season, Belgium, and what would turn out to be one of my desert island races.

64

Spa was one of those races where nothing went awry. The car worked; I couldn't put a foot wrong. It was like, *Oh my God, this is so easy* from first practice Friday to the race itself on Sunday.

Not many of those weekends happened in my career. I don't think they happen often in *any* driver's career, but that weekend the stars were in alignment.

Well, on the track at least.

Off it, things took a slightly weird turn. Qualifying had gone well on Saturday. I was flying with the car, really enjoying it since the upgrades and stuck it on pole – my first pole for McLaren and my first since Monaco in 2009.

Meantime, Lewis qualified seventh. He'd been using the old rear wing, thinking that he could make use of the extra downforce it would give him, whereas I'd gone for the new wing.

Afterwards, and I didn't find this out until later because I'd never got round to following him on Twitter, Lewis posted a series of tweets concerning the difference between his qualifying pace and mine.

'Damn, WTF!!' he said in his first one, 'Jenson has the new rear wing on, I have the old. We voted to change, didn't work out. I lose 0.4 tenths just on the straight.'

There were a couple more tweets as well, the final one being a show of support for me, which was decent of him.

So far, nothing much to see here. Personally I wasn't gasping in horror and clutching at my pearl necklace concerning his use of 'WTF'. I like to see drivers expressing themselves; the sport needs more of it. No doubt a bit of bad language makes sponsors nervous, but that's really up to Lewis. Also, he didn't seem to be whinging about the difference in rear wing so much as expressing regret that the decision hadn't worked out.

Despite the tweets being seized upon by the media, who were desperately trying to catch Lewis out at the time, the team were fine with them, and he wasn't asked to take them down.

And that would be the end of our story were it not for the fact that the next day he tweeted a screengrab of our respective telemetry – in other words our technical readouts – which showed his lack of straight-line speed compared to mine.

Quite what was in his thinking at this point, I honestly couldn't say. I don't think anybody disbelieved him that he was losing straightline speed compared to me, but the point of running extra downforce is that you make it up in the corners anyway. Besides, it wasn't as though the team had held a gun to his head and forced him to use the old wing.

Or maybe they had. Maybe that was the issue. Certainly any displeasure he was showing was aimed at the team, not me, but I ended up being collateral damage because you don't make telemetry public. You just don't. As well as the speed differential, the screengrab also showed set-up information that you don't want being made public: ride height, braking and acceleration rates – the kind of things you work hard to keep hidden from your rivals. (And I'll let you into a secret, the telemetry he posted was from the simulator, not our actual racing telemetry, although apparently he didn't realise that. Double oops.)

I made my feelings known about that. The official version was that I was 'disappointed'. Had I gone with my unofficial reaction it would have made 'WTF' seem very tame indeed. But at the same time I knew it wasn't personal. Bit dumb maybe. But not an 'I hate Jenson' thing so much as an 'I'm fed up with McLaren' thing.

Anyway, the race. The start was dreadful when at the first corner Romain Grosjean in a Lotus squeezed Lewis, lost control, hit Sergio Pérez and then became airborne, taking out Alonso at the same time. A nasty accident – Grosjean almost took Alonso's head off – and one that saw four drivers out of the race, including Alonso who at that time was top of the leader board.

All this was happening behind me, of course. I'd had a good start from pole and stayed in front for the entire race. The regulations say you've got to stick with the wing you used in qualifying, and the decision to go for low downforce was the right one; the car felt great, my drive was good, and I ended up finishing well over fifteen seconds ahead of Sebastian in the Red Bull. What we call 'a dominant win'.

Lewis used the lower downforce wing for the next race, Monza, and we locked out the front row. Unfortunately, while he went on to win, I retired with fuel pressure problems. Singapore, I finished second, Lewis was a DNF.

A few days after Singapore, it was officially announced, ending months of speculation, that Lewis was leaving to partner Nico Rosberg at Mercedes. Joining me as his replacement would be Sergio Pérez.

That was a shame for me; I'd really enjoyed our rivalry. Off the track, however, he was still being a bit weird. After Japan, he had another one of his weird Twitterfart moments: 'Just noticed @jensonbutton unfollowed,' he wrote. 'That's a shame. After 3 years as teammates, I thought we respected one another but clearly he doesn't.'

Of course the flaw in his logic was that I'd never followed him in the first place so could hardly be accused of lacking respect by unfollowing him. And, anyway, I *did* respect him.

Fair play, he realised his mistake and put it right: 'My bad, just found out Jenson never followed me. Don't blame him! Need to be on Twitter more!'

Needed to be on Twitter a bit *less*, if you'd asked me. But no harm done other than advertising to the world that we weren't quite as close as our animated *Tooned* counterparts suggested.

In India I finished fifth but set fastest lap. Abu Dhabi fourth. In the United States – a return after the debacle of 2005 – I finished fifth. Red Bull secured their third Constructors' Championship on the trot. Next stop Brazil, where Lewis took pole and I was second, a tenth of a second behind him. Like me, Lewis is a driver who can excel in the wet, and together we led on a very slippery track.

On lap six I overtook but he came back at me on lap seven, recovering the lead. Then, as was often the case during our head-to-heads, I got past him again.

Not long after that, Nico Hülkenberg joined the chase for Force India. Lewis went ahead on lap forty-eight. On lap fifty-five he was held up by the back markers Heikki Kovalainen and Timo Glock, which gave Nico a chance to slip by him. Unfortunately (well, for them) they made contact, Nico spun, Lewis went out with a damaged suspension and I snatched the lead.

Behind me Nico picked up a drive-through penalty for the incident with Lewis and dropped to fifth as result (bit harsh, since it was what we call a 'racing incident') and now all I had to do was try not to slide off in swiftly worsening conditions and lead the Ferraris of Fernando and Felipe home.

I made it, and finished the year with my third win of the season and fifth in the Drivers' Championship with 188 points, just behind Lewis on 190. That meant that over the three years we'd been teammates, I had outscored him, with 672 points to 657. I counted myself more than happy with that.

There were no big goodbyes between us, but I look back on Lewis as one of the best and most challenging teammates I ever had. After all, he's a brilliant, mercurial driver. Of everybody on the grid, he's the guy who really has that 'gift'. Like me, I think that he probably coasted on that talent at first, and like me, I think it might have taken him a while to realise that he had to work at it, and despite having won a championship at McLaren he was still getting to grips with that.

The thing was that nobody could beat him on natural ability and he knew that, so I think it threw him when I beat him in 2011. And – theory alert – that may well have been at the root of his problem with McLaren, a mistaken belief that they were favouring me over him, and that's why I was winning, when in fact the simple truth was one that I'd learnt myself a decade before: you need to augment your talent by working at it, by learning your racecraft and helping the team to develop a car around you.

That's the truth of it. There was nobody out to get him at McLaren; he was adored by the fans and racing fraternity alike. His speed and skill alone made sure of that. But, seemingly, he could never get it out of his head that he was being marginalised.

As people, we had a lot in common. There was our shared karting history, not to mention the fact that his dad was a customer of my dad. And unlike a lot of drivers in Formula One neither of us came from an especially wealthy background; we'd achieved what we had through talent and a lot of grafting.

So I regret that despite our similarities we were never really friends. When we spent time together it was nice, and he'd always strike up a conversation with Dad, and we'd hang out a bit, but at the same time there were an awful lot of awkward and uncomfortable silences, and often I'd think, *What's going unsaid here?*

Maybe something, maybe nothing.

What's good to see is that Lewis has really come on over the last few years. He's matured, in other words; he's become a bit of a statesman and a great representative of the sport worldwide. He's built on all that talent and hard work and he's a more rounded character as a result. No doubt about it, he's one of the greats.

Which made it all the more satisfying to beat him, not just in 2011, but overall in points during our three seasons together.

In a way, it was a shame to wave that phase of my career goodbye, but I'd joined McLaren wanting to recover that pure joy I'd found in racing and in that respect, thanks to some of those scintillating duels with Lewis, it was job done.

65

The 2013 season was, shall we say, 'different'. For a start I had a new teammate in Sergio, better known as 'Checo', a driver they called 'The Mexican Wunderkind' and a graduate of the Ferrari Driver Academy.

At the risk of sounding like a retired sergeant-major, there is such a thing as paying your dues, and Sergio's problem was that he came in like a bull at a gate. Me, I'd been around for years at this point, I could remember when all this was fields, and I could certainly remember a time when new drivers had a lot more respect for the older ones.

Does that make me sound like a retired sergeant-major? It does? Oh, who cares. The fact is that our relationship didn't start well for those reasons and it got worse before it got better. However – spoiler alert – it *did* get better so this is one story with a happy ending.

Which is more than you can say for the rest of what was by any standards a pretty disappointing season, and compared to the previous one (fourth and fifth in the Drivers', third in the Constructors') pretty disastrous for the team.

Firstly we had another new car.

At the beginning of a season most cars are new, or at the very least a major development on the previous year's model. Engineers will have been working on it for the best part of six months. That's the nature of the beast.

However, rather than develop the 2013 car ahead of a regulation change in 2014, McLaren decided to build an entirely new car, which was a brave but ultimately foolhardy move because we just couldn't get it right, and as a result, we would struggle all season to stay competitive.

Our car's shortcomings first became apparent in Australia when we discovered that it was unstable over the Albert Park bumps. Sergio and I were a good three seconds slower than Sebastian Vettel's Red Bull in practice and that was how it stayed for qualifying. I managed ninth in the race.

Sensing that we'd made a tactical error, Ron pressed for the team to bring back the 2012 car, which opened up a rift between him and Martin, who thought that the 2013 car could be fine-tuned and made to work.

As a compromise, some of the 2012 car's features were reintroduced – the exhaust, for one – but it didn't make much difference, and as the poor results began to tot up (I was seventeenth in Malaysia, fifth in China, tenth in Bahrain) the 'has McLaren lost it?' reports began to appear. Pundits noted that we were losing sharp technical minds to Mercedes; sponsor Vodafone had jumped ship; there was even the odd suggestion that Martin should step down as team principal and Ron might return to the position (and looking back that might have been where the seeds were first sown in Ron's mind).

In Bahrain, we had a meeting with Stefano Domenicali, who was then the team principal at Ferrari, about a possible drive there. As you can imagine, it was all kinds of tempting. The tifosi used to say to me, 'Hey, Buttoni, when-a you gonna come drive for us,' and although it would have meant a move to Italy and the challenge of learning a new language, I was certainly up for giving it proper, serious consideration.

Ultimately I was spared haivng to make a difficult when Stefano moved on – that very weekend, in fact. Was it something we said?

During the race itself, Checo pulled a couple of aggressive overtaking moves on me that properly wound me up. 'Get him to calm down, will you?' I snapped over the radio and had a few words to say to the press afterwards.

As ever, the meaning of my words was distorted so that my single outburst about that one particular instance of Checo's 'dirty driving' became me calling him a 'dirty driver' – two very separate and distinct things. With hindsight, though, Bahrain was probably the weekend that things got interesting between Checo and me, because I found myself surprised by just how competitive he was. He certainly proved his speed at that race.

Mind you, I was pissed off at him again in Monaco for another rash passing move. Kimi Räikkönen was another one he upset. Never one to mince his words, Kimi said that Checo 'should be punched in the face' for a particular move that ended up with him putting his car into the wall.

Canada and Britain were shite, with twelfth and thirteenth places to show for my efforts. I was sixth in Germany and seventh in Hungary, but by far the best thing about that race was the bash we threw the old man for his 70th birthday afterwards. We flew Natasha, Samantha and Tanya out to Budapest and had a good old knees-up that continued on Sunday night when we rented a private jet and flew back to Monaco for yet another party.

It was a magical family weekend. One to treasure. And believe me – take it from one who knows – you really do treasure memories like that.

66

At Spa the car decided to perform and I qualified sixth and also finished sixth in the race. Remember what I was saying about adjusting your expectation in F1? Sixth was good that season.

It was followed by tenth in Italy, seventh in Singapore, and eighth in Korea. In Japan a load of drivers who'd flown from Korea got together. Let's see, who was there? Most of the grid is the answer: Mark Webber, Nico Rosberg, Felipe Massa, David Coulthard, Fernando Alonso, Lewis Hamilton... in all it was thirteen Formula One drivers and a couple of Super Formula drivers, Andre Lotterer and James Rossiter.

Finding ourselves thrown together and in the mood for a bit of fun, we phoned a bar and asked them to stay open late, which wasn't hard when they heard who was in our party.

Things soon got messy, as you might imagine, one of those nights when everything's going well, old rivalries are forgotten and none are being created afresh or renewed. Formula One drivers don't often get the chance to let their hair down together – it's usually with the team, which is the way it should be, of course – but every now and then it's cool to get together, shoot the shit with your fellow competitors, and... watch them make drunken fools of themselves.

During the course of the night there was a format for getting a drink. To buy a round you hit a drum with a stick at which point everybody was given a shot.

It was getting into the early hours, the party was still in full swing, and it was my turn to get the drinks in, but for some reason (i.e., drunkenness) I couldn't find the drumstick so I decided to hit it with my fist.

'Do it again, do it again,' urged Felipe Massa, who picked up the drum so I could give it an even bigger wallop. Which I did.

I knew the second it happened that I'd done myself a mischief. Obviously with my huge experience of drunken mishaps, I'm aware of the fact that alcohol tends to dull the pain, but even so the agony was intense right away.

'Oh God,' I said, holding up my hand the way zombies do. DC lurched into action, asked for some ice and we iced it for about twenty minutes. My fellow drivers showed their concern by leaving in search of a nightclub, but nursing my wounded hand I decided to call it a night. Good thing I did. Back at the hotel, I found myself on my bathroom floor, cradling my painful hand while vomiting into the toilet. Not a good look.

'You've broken your knuckle,' said a doctor the next day, looking at an X-ray. 'You'll have to put it in a cast for two weeks.'

'Not sure I can manage that,' I told him. 'I'm driving a Formula One car in the Grand Prix in four days' time.'

Rolling his eyes, he said, 'I'll see what we can do.'

I was expecting something bionic. But in fact his idea of 'seeing what we can do' involved strapping it up, giving me loads of painkillers and hoping for the best, which frankly I could have done myself.

By the time Thursday rolled around, I was thinking, *This is all Felipe Massa's fault*, and the team were advising me not to race.

'Oh come on, it's fine,' I lied, through gritted teeth. 'It feels all right.'

In fact it felt as though my hand were being slowly tightened in a Black & Decker Workbench. At the same time my fellow drivers were showing a spectacular lack of sympathy. Their hangovers had long since cleared but I was carrying mine around on the end of my arm. The only one who didn't seem to find it funny was Nico Hülkenberg, but that's only because word hadn't reached him yet. We met in the paddock and shook hands – me forgetting, him not knowing – and oh my God, the pain. I've never known anything like it.

'Fucksake, Jense,' yelled my dad when he found out. Not surprising. Meanwhile, the team's simulator driver, Oliver Turvey, was bussed in as a potential stand-in, but the team decided they were going to try Kevin Magnussen, who would have been making his F1 debut.

In the event, I was determined not to let the small matter of a broken knuckle stop me and insisted on racing. Come the day I strapped it up, dosed myself on painkillers, gritted my teeth and drove. Not a bad result, either. I came ninth.

What I realised later, of course, was that Martin had wanted Kevin to drive so that he could get a feel for him. He was already thinking about a replacement for Checo.

The knuckle thing was probably the most exciting thing to happen that season (tenth in America, fourteenth in India, twelfth in Abu Dhabi, please make it stop). I felt I was driving well but we just didn't have the tools to challenge Red Bull – or any of the other frontrunners for that matter.

My best race was the last one, in Brazil. I qualified fifteenth, a place behind Checo, but made a great start and eventually managed to climb to fifth.

At the close of the season I finished ninth overall, with a meagre seventy-three points. 2009 seemed an awfully long time ago.

The bad season meant that the writing was on the wall for Martin. Ron wanted to run the team again and that was that. Martin was out.

For me, that change of leadership wasn't great. Martin was a world-class businessman and he was able to separate business and friends. Ron was different. Cut Ron and he bled McLaren. There was no distinction between the McLaren side of him and any other side. There *was* no other side. And while I got on okay with him, he wasn't a friend the way Martin was. I found his style of working a bit 'old school'. I wouldn't go as far as saying that he ruled by fear, but almost. It was Ron's way or the highway.

Martin has gone on to good things. He's now the CEO of the Land Rover BAR America's Cup team, but his departure from McLaren was sad and his presence – not to mention that of his lovely wife, Debbie – was sorely missed.

Even so, everything was eclipsed by what happened next. Everything.

67

There's a restaurant in Santa Monica that I have to pass in order to reach a bike shop I use. I can hardly bring myself to look at that restaurant. I don't like to think of the last time I was in there.

It was January 2014 and I was returning from Hawaii via Los Angeles. Every year from 2009 onwards a bunch of friends and I had spent Christmas and New Year in Hawaii training, the idea being to have a break and return fit, refreshed and ready for the new season.

That year we'd decided to spend a few days in LA on the way back. It was there that we found ourselves in the Santa Monica restaurant for lunch: me, Mikey, Chrissy and a Japanese friend of ours, Yu, having a bite to eat and discussing possible cycling and running routes. We were hanging out, enjoying each other's company, oblivious to what lay just around the corner.

Mikey's phone rang, he took the call and it was impossible not to notice the change that came over him. His face fell from relaxed and companionable to grave in the space of a second. Other conversation died and I leaned towards him, looking at him, like, *What? What's wrong?* as he removed the phone from his ear and looked across the table at me.

'JB,' he said, 'it's Richard on the phone. We need to talk outside. He has something to tell you.'

I remember thinking that whatever the problem, it must be something bad involving my career, because why would I need to go outside for that? Even then I could never have anticipated how bad.

Mikey and I stepped out to the sidewalk where I leaned against a windowsill and he handed me the phone.

'Jenson, I'm so sorry,' said Richard. 'It's about your dad.'

Richard and Dad had been out for dinner the night before. After their meal they stopped in for a nightcap at La Rascasse, a bar the mechanics love to visit during Grand Prix weekend. The party bar, if you like.

It was busy that night. Always is in La Rascasse, where my dad and Richard were both familiar faces. As they chatted, Richard offered Dad a bed for the night, to save him having to go back to his own place, which was in Cap-d'Ail, just over the border into France.

Dad said, 'Yeah, thanks, mate, I might well do that,' but Richard formed the impression that he'd rather go home. The fact was that Dad liked being in his own space. He liked his routines and being around his own stuff. Also, he might well have needed his insulin.

While in La Rascasse, Richard took a call. It was a call about me, some bit of business that needed attending to, and he stepped outside to deal with it.

The conversation took longer than expected, and by the time Richard had finished and returned to the bar, Dad was gone.

There were some guys there they both knew. 'Where's he gone?' asked Richard.

Shrugs. 'Oh, he just got up and left.'

This wasn't particularly unusual for Dad. His diabetes meant that he tended to get tired quickly. It was perfectly normal for him to just leave like that. He did it when he'd had enough, to avoid all the palaver of saying goodbye, save bothering people. It was just his way.

However, when Richard rang to check on him the next morning, he couldn't get hold of him. Even so, the alarm bells weren't ringing just yet. One of Dad's favourite jaunts was to take his Ferrari down to Italy for the day and meet up with friends for coffee. *He's probably done that. Silly old sod's probably left his phone in the car*, thought Richard.

The alarm bells came later. Richard became more concerned with each unanswered call, and so at about 7pm, he pulled on a pair of tracky bottoms and a sweatshirt and set off for Dad's house. His plan was to find the old boy, tell him off – 'Answer your bloody phone' – and dispel that nagging worry.

Dad's house was built on the side of a cliff, and to get to it you had to enter through a front gate at the foot of the incline. That gate was pretty much impregnable. It had been reinforced after a burglary attempt. Once you were inside, there were about sixty steps up to the front door, which was quite a climb. I used to find it hard myself. By the top your legs were on fire.

When Richard arrived that evening he found Dad's keys dangling on the outside in the gate, which was odd. One of those moments where you think, *Might be something, might be nothing*. Richard was remembering the break-in attempts and, deciding he'd better check to make sure everything was okay, he let himself in and began the climb to the front door.

He found Dad's body on the steps.

There was blood and at first Richard thought that Dad might have tangled with burglars. Subsequently we'd discover that wasn't the case, but there was a lot of initial confusion, and after Richard's wife,

Caroline – who's half-French – alerted the authorities, Richard himself became a suspect; he had to call a lawyer and they wouldn't let him phone me. In the end he told them, 'Listen, I'm going to call my mate to tell him what's happened. You'll have to arrest me if you want to stop me. It's up to you.'

And that's when Mikey's phone rang.

There was no delayed reaction; it hit me straight away. I put that down to my job, the way I lived, something about the ability to absorb a sudden and shocking turn of events, being able to quickly process matters of emotional intensity. There was no period of disbelief or numbness. It was just there.

My dad was dead.

He'd been planning to make me a book for when I retired, a scrapbook of my career to date. He'd been collecting pictures taken when I was just a kid in karting, right through my Formula Ford, moving on to Formula Three and of course in Formula One. I don't know if he'd ever intended the book to be a surprise, but if so then his resolve had weakened as soon as he began hunting through the archives. Right away he'd been emailing me, unable to contain his enthusiasm. 'Look at this. Look what I've found.'

And of course I was in Hawaii, thinking, *Oh, it's a different time zone; I'll email him when I get back.*

I can't tell you how much I regret that now – the fact that I didn't reply to his email.

He was happy at least, doing something he loved. I take some comfort from that. But on the other hand, that very frame of mind made his death all the more shocking, because he hadn't been unwell, or under the weather, or unusually preoccupied. He was having the time of his life.

I had to phone my sisters. Doing that was as bad as hearing the news myself. I phoned Jessica. She'd been arguing with Dad around that time but they got on really well. She was as distraught as everybody else.

How could it have happened, they all wanted to know. How could he have met his death that night?

The answer is that we don't know for sure. All we have are fragments. And given that the police investigation has ended having drawn a blank, we will never be 100 per cent certain what took place. We know that Dad returned to his car. But we think that somewhere between La Rascasse and the car he fell and hit his head.

As I've said, his balance wasn't the best. In Monaco, the escalators don't work until you step on to them, and even then they're not very reliable. Sometimes they don't go at all; sometimes you're halfway down and they suddenly shudder into action. They catch a lot of people out.

Maybe Dad, that night, was one of those caught out. Maybe he fell. Certainly when we saw CCTV from the car park, he had blood on the back of his head. There was also a little blood found on the headrest of his car. The most logical explanation is that he fell foul of the escalators.

Nevertheless, he made it to Cap-d'Ail, and at about 3am arrived at his house.

Again, we don't know how it happened, but what we do know is that having let himself in, the gate shut behind him and his keys were on the other side of it.

Now he had a problem. The only way to open the gate was from inside the house – you buzzed it open. But he couldn't get into the house because his keys were on the outside of the secure gate.

There was a little granny flat, a tiny one-room apartment, halfway up the stairs, and judging by some blood on the pillow he lay down in there for a bit.

Then, for whatever reason – perhaps because he needed insulin and had a brainwave about getting in – we think he decided to have another crack at gaining entry to the house.

Wearing his shirt, underwear and socks, he climbed the remaining steps, probably using the torch on his phone to light the way. Whatever the brainwave, it didn't work, because he had turned away from the door and was returning down the steps when he slipped, fell forward and hit his head for a second time. This one proved fatal.

The days after the phone call were a blur. We returned to Monaco, joined the rest of the family, tried to keep things together as we concentrated on organising the funeral, operating in a kind of daze, wanting to wake up from this awful dream.

At the same time I had a sore spot on my leg. I didn't know how, why and where it had first appeared, but it was like a little painful area on my knee. Didn't think much of it. One night we had an evening out – a mad night with alcohol a catalyst for our tears – but the next morning I woke up and my leg was in agony.

I called my mum who was in the same hotel, the Metropole.

'Mum, can you come up to my room, please? I think there's something wrong.' I was looking at my leg as we spoke, seeing for the first time how swollen it was. Moments later she was at the door. I answered it and promptly collapsed.

Somehow I'd picked up blood poisoning. They thought it was from swimming in the sea in Hawaii. I'd cut my foot and my body didn't have the strength to fight the infection.

My mum called the rest of the family to the room. I fainted again. The next thing I knew I was being carted off to hospital and all sorts of drips were going in me. They were taking it seriously. If the infection's reached the bone then that's bad, I was told. Like, amputation bad.

So that was a sweaty few hours, while they ascertained whether the poisoning had indeed reached the bone. It hadn't and I was free to leave, except I couldn't walk because the pain was so bad; every time I moved the poison would shift.

In the end I made it to Richard's house, and that's where I stayed for the next few days, sorting out funeral arrangements. The pain was intense – like nothing I'd ever experienced, before or since; to keep it at bay I had to raise my leg above the level of my head. Showering was agony. Using the toilet, oh my God.

Even so, it didn't take my mind off things.

68

Dad's funeral was held at the Sainte Devote Church in Monaco, which is the church at turn one of the Grand Prix. It was so fitting because of all the races he loved the Monaco Grand Prix the most, even more than Melbourne. That one was *his* race.

So many people from Formula One came to the funeral: Ron Dennis, Martin Whitmarsh, Ross Brawn, Frank Williams… even Prince Albert and Princess Charlene were there. He would have been over the moon but it didn't surprise me at all. Dad was one of the most popular and familiar faces in the whole of F1. He loved a good natter. Whatever team you were in, if you'd had a bad day, you could seek out the old man and be assured of a glass of red, a bite to eat, a good old gossip and a laugh. He had a red pass, which allows you to go anywhere on the circuit, including the dummy grid. They're like gold dust; only drivers and key personnel get them, but Dad wangled one from Bernie, and as a result he knew everything that was going on in all corners of the paddock, which made him a great bet for a chinwag.

So the funeral was tough. God, it was tough. For a start, I could hardly walk and yet there was no way in the world I was going to shirk my responsibilities as a pallbearer. Just you try and stop me. I gritted my teeth, expecting tremendous pain. But I suppose certain emotions take over; the body assumes control to makes sure you get through it. That same internal autopilot helped me deliver the eulogy – the hardest, most painful speech I've ever had to give.

Dad would have loved the fact that Prince Albert of Monaco was in the front row at his funeral. *Loved it.* He would have loved the fact that his funeral was at turn one of the Monaco Grand Prix; he would have been thrilled to see all the people who turned up that day.

I'm not sure about the choice of funeral vehicle, though. He always said he wanted to slide into his grave, locked up, sideways in a cloud of tyre smoke. What he got instead was a Volvo estate.

Fucksake, Jense.

69

People said that after Judy Murray my dad was the most influential parent in sport. That may be so. But to me he was the old boy, Dad, Papa Smurf. He was the leader of my gang. He plotted me a route through life, a way of being; he showed me that you should work hard at something and excel, but never lose sight of why you're doing it in the first place.

He didn't always get it right, of course – we could get on each other's nerves just like any other partnership – but the important thing was that he got it right most of the time. He got it right when it really counted and most of all he made sure every decision was mine – or at least that I felt that every decision was mine. He guided me, not by cajoling or insisting but by coaching and nurturing. He made it so that I only ever got in the driving seat out of a love for racing. He made it fun.

And that was the thing about Dad, maybe the main thing, his legacy: *he never stopped having fun*, even when the numbers got big and the stakes were high. He always had a smile for everyone, from the mechanics to Bernie Ecclestone. He was always laughing.

From the Colorado Beetle of his racing youth to the familiar pink shirt of the paddock, he couldn't help but bring life and colour to wherever he happened to be. He always looked as though he was having a great time, and it was contagious. Life without him was like laughter had been banned or music had ceased to exist. All colour had drained away.

'You haven't mourned him enough.'

That's what Richie says. And he's right because today feels just the same as it did that first day. The shock has faded but the sense of loss is as keen as it was that afternoon in Santa Monica.

And maybe Richie is right. Maybe I haven't mourned enough, or for any prescribed period of time. But when do you stop? How do you mourn someone anyway? What am I supposed to do? Wear black? Look glum? Be extra-specially sad when Bob Seger comes on the radio? How would that help? It wouldn't help bring him back.

Instead I did what I do: I went back to work testing with McLaren.

There I found the team changed in the wake of Martin's departure. Things weren't quite the same. Ron was back in the harness, but he didn't seem to have the same handle on the business as he did before. A lot of the personnel in the team had changed, and as a result the way we did things had changed, but Ron seemed to have remained the same and it made him somewhat out of step, not just with the team, but the whole sport. His was a firm hand on the rudder, but maybe not as steady as it had once been.

Added to that we were licking our wounds after McLaren's worst season since 1980, plus the naturally aspirated V8 engines had been replaced by 1.6 litre V6 turbos; it was all change, and not for the better.

But all of that paled into insignificance beside the fact that for me things just weren't the same without Dad. My love of racing remained but my love of Formula One was lacking, and in my career as in the rest of my life I found myself treading water, going through the motions, looking for meaning and purpose but failing to find it.

A couple of months after Dad's death I proposed to Jessica and we were married ten months later – then split up less than a year after that. This was the emotional rollercoaster I was riding at the time: trying to get my head together but without much success. We rented a house in Saint-Tropez, and in August 2015 we were burgled when intruders pumped anaesthetic gas into our air conditioning, broke in and took stuff as we slept, including her engagement ring. They never caught the guys who did it.

The aftermath was terrifying, of course, imagining intruders creeping around our house as we lay out cold, thinking of what might have happened had we woken up, for example, or if the intruders had had more on their minds than material gain.

Somehow the event formed part and parcel of what was a dark period for both of us, and the fact that the burglars used anaesthetic gas seems ironic in retrospect. For a long time I felt as though I were permanently under its influence, sleepwalking though life.

70

At McLaren I had a new teammate, Kevin Magnussen. I'd had my fallouts with Checo, and a lot of what I said about him during the season was true – he did need to calm down – but we'd ended up getting on got on really well, and some of our races together were great.

I had a great connection with Kevin. He was a straighforward guy. Trouble was, he was learning the ropes the hard way; he'd been thrown into the deep end having Ron as a boss and a World Champion as a teammate in his first year, and though he was competitive for the first half of the season, he found it a lot tougher in the second. I'm someone who feeds off having a competitive teammate, and sadly it didn't quite happen.

Nor did it help that the car wasn't great. It understeered because it lacked frontal downforce, and although it had a stable rear-end, we never achieved a balance between the two.

The first race of the season, Melbourne, was hard without Dad, just as I knew it would be. The guys he used to meet for his annual dinner told me they'd still be having it, in order to honour his memory, which is exactly what he would have wanted, of course. But all I could think was that he wouldn't be there with them, cackling over dinner, knocking back red wine and swapping racing tales.

Meanwhile, the paddock was full of well-wishers, and everybody was great, offering commiserations and sympathy, wanting to tell stories about him. But at the same time it made things so much more difficult because each encounter was a reminder of his absence.

In the race, Kevin was third and I was fourth, and for the first time in my racing career I was grateful not to have to go on the podium. Not that it was a problem for the rest of the season, mind you. We were scraping points, but as for getting up there and spraying champagne? Forget it.

At Silverstone we launched a 'Pink For Papa' campaign, selling T-shirts to raise money for the Henry Surtees Foundation, which was founded by legendary racer John Surtees in memory of his son to help people with injuries caused in auto accidents. At around the same time, John Surtees himself unveiled the John Button Suite at the Buckmore Park kart track, with pink-painted walls and one of Dad's shirts in a frame. It was an especially fitting tribute because Dad and John were always close, and Henry had used Dad's Rocket engines in his Comer Cadet kart when he began racing.

And these were all developments that I greeted with delight and honour, and yet I found myself mentally floundering in a season that felt like a memorial to him. I was numb with grief and stunned by a sudden and profound loss of passion for the sport.

What's more – and as much as I tried to hide it – my lack of verve was only too evident. Watch interviews from that period and you'll see what I mean. As a result, the press were beginning to speculate about my future, with the rumour being that Fernando would be coming in to partner Kevin. Suddenly I felt as though I had to justify my position in the team; each race felt like an audition. I wanted to stay – or so I thought at the time – but I was being made to feel insecure at McLaren. That feeling didn't exactly help matters, let's put it that way.

More and more I found myself looking back on my career and realising that I didn't feel the way that I guess Sebastian and Lewis must feel; I didn't have a need to win title after title. I'd reached Formula One, won races, become World Champion, and earned the right to be thought of alongside the legends. That hunger within me was satisfied.

And anyway, to do it without Dad? To win and not have him there? It almost didn't bear thinking about.

To cope with everything – the loss of my dad, my uncertain future at McLaren, a mediocre season – I developed a strategy. I told myself I was going to live in the moment. Don't worry about the future; it'll take care of itself. And though I can't say it was the solution to all my problems, it definitely helped me separate what was important from what was not.

Meanwhile, in December 2014, it was announced that I would be staying at McLaren and my new teammate for 2015 would be Fernando Alonso. Dad would have loved that, I thought, on hearing the news. He loved Alonso's driving.

Even so, the less said about 2015, the better. I finished a hugely frustrating season in sixteenth with sixteen points, Fernando seventeenth with eleven. We rarely got out of Q1 and my best results were sixth in America, eighth in Monaco and a brace of ninths, in Hungary and Russia. Fernando took fifth in Hungary and tenth in Britain. The rest of the time, blah.

Towards the end of the year Jessica and I decided to call time on our marriage. It was amicable; we both realised that things hadn't been right and that it had been a mistake to marry in the first place. That December

I met Brittny Ward through a mutual friend and we started dating. She's gorgeous and bright and so grounded that I fell for her right away and thanked my lucky stars that she felt the same way. Meeting her was pretty much the only uptick in what was otherwise a fairly dismal period.

Oh, listen to me. It wasn't *all* bad. Although my taste for F1 was AWOL, I still loved racing. In 2015 I was invited to Lydden Hill, one of Dad's old stomping grounds and the spiritual home of rallycross. DC came along and we had a right laugh filming for the BBC and bombing around in a rallycross car.

What's more, my competitive spirit hadn't deserted me. I'd still feel as though I'd won the race if I beat Fernando, which meant I always had something to race for, and he was a great competitor. In fact, I'd say that over the years Fernando had been one of – if not *the* – toughest competitors I'd faced, both as a teammate and a rival at other teams. Lewis was unbelievably quick and could pull a lap out of the bag just like that; him and Ayrton Senna were the two quickest guys over one lap, maybe ever, but Fernando was the more rounded driver. I'd know, even if I outqualified him, that he'd still be tough to beat in a race. He's nice on the outside, really affable and approachable, but beneath that he's a very, very tough competitor who'll do anything to beat you.

In all, a good teammate to have and bloody tough to beat. I enjoyed the two years we spent together and I'm pleased to say that I'm still the only teammate to beat him over a season.

The problem was that I soon grew fed up with racing just one guy.

My head wasn't together. My heart wasn't in it.

71

'I plan to retire at the end of the year.'

We were at Spa in Belgium, August 2016, and my mind was made up.

Ron looked at me and I could tell he was trying to gauge how serious I was. 'Retirement is not a good word,' he said carefully.

'It's what I want.'

Ron tends to go round the houses when you talk to him, and this time was no exception. He talked at length about how I was a little old for a driver (at the time I'd had more race starts than anybody else on the grid, ahead of Fernando and Kimi) but how I was in great physical shape.

Which was true.

'But I can tell you're drained,' he said. And that was also true.

He said he understood why I might want to retire, but thought it was a mistake. 'I think you should take a year out and think about it, do all the things that you want to do and come back fresh,' he said, adding that Alain Prost had returned from a sabbatical as an improved driver in 1993.

'So how about you don't retire, but take a year out?' he suggested. 'Everyone's a winner. You'll get a rest; I'll get a better driver when you come back after a year; Formula One will have the old Jenson Button back.'

I had to admit it was worth thinking about. After all, what if I did change my mind? What if Ron was right and a rest was exactly what I needed? A year hanging out with Brittny might be the recipe for getting my head together.

His next idea was that I become an ambassador for the team, which was also an attractive proposition, given that it allowed me to keep a foot in the door. I liked the idea of keeping things open-ended. Just in case. We shook on it.

And so, at Monza, on 3 September, I announced that I'd be retiring from driving but staying on as ambassador, so you won't be getting rid of me that easily. Meanwhile, the team limped to the end of a fairly inglorious season. I was fifteenth but beaten by Fernando who was tenth. Overall, we were sixth in the Constructors'. Hardly surprising, then, that major changes were afoot, and I watched from the sidelines when at the end of the year Ron was ousted after a battle with shareholders.

As I've said, we weren't exactly great friends, but I had huge respect for what he'd achieved. Under his guidance, McLaren had won ten Drivers' World Championships with the likes of Niki Lauda, Alain Prost, Ayrton Senna, Mika Häkkinen and Lewis Hamilton, as well as seven Constructors' titles. To see him effectively get the boot was sad. It certainly felt as though some kind of line had been drawn beneath an era of McLaren. I had definitely chosen the right time to take a back seat.

That said, I know the team will rise again. They are, after all, 'my' team, and when I think of them I picture those rows of gleaming trophies and that factory full of winning racing cars. McLaren might be struggling right now, but there's too much history and too much passion there for it to be anything other than a temporary state of affairs. They'll be great again, you mark my words.

The last race of the season, Abu Dhabi, was my farewell, and I went into it surrounded by family and friends. Mum was there, Natasha, Richard and Caroline, Chrissy, James, Mikey, Brittny and my lovely PA, Jules.

On the morning of the race we ate breakfast together. Big smiles. There was a strange, unique atmosphere, as though everybody was focused on me. After that, I got ready as normal, and then, as I was about to make my way to the garage, I walked slap-bang into a huge guard of honour that had formed up while I was getting my massage: family, friends, everybody from the team, so many familiar faces lining the route, cheering and clapping. It stretched all the way from the outside of the drivers' area to the garage, and I walked it in a blissful dreamlike state, wishing I could stop, hug, shake hands and thank everybody who had turned out, and trying at the same time to really savour the moment.

On the track Fernando greeted me with an embrace. Alain Prost, who doesn't normally come out on to the grid, appeared. 'I'm here for you. I'm here to watch your last Grand Prix,' he told me, and I was already choked up, but I almost lost it then.

As for the race? Well, I retired with suspension failure after twelve laps. But you know what? It was for the best, because rather than reach the end and join the celebrations for Lewis and Nico, I got a moment all to myself, stopping in the pit lane, waving to a cheering crowd and then embracing the team before dashing off to join my family and friends for more hugs and tears.

Surrounded by them all it struck me that most people when they leave work get a pint at lunchtime and a whip-round on their last day.

Me, I got a guard of honour, Alain Prost, a cheering crowd, and best of all, a room full of the people I love.

EPILOGUE

Do I miss it?

Tough one, but the answer's no.

I mean, I still love it. God, I still love it. And I still think it's the *coolest* thing.

But as for missing it? No, I don't think so, because as someone said on the weekend of my last race, 'You arrive with dreams, you leave with memories', and I've got a wealth of those. Besides, I drove once more at Monaco 2017, when Fernando was given leave of absence to race elsewhere and McLaren called me in as a replacement. I qualified ninth, which I was very happy about, but for the race itself, I was a DNF. I didn't come away from the experience feeling like I wanted to go back and prove myself.

'But the lifestyle,' people say. 'Why would you want to give that up?' And the answer is that even the best job, a boyhood-dream job, can be something you grow… well, 'bored of' is probably not the right expression. 'Jaded by' might be more accurate, or perhaps 'out of', because while you're a pampered hamster and it's a pretty bloody brilliant treadmill, at the end of the day you're still a hamster on a treadmill.

Bear in mind that I raced in Formula One for seventeen years and in other categories for years before that. That's almost my whole life with all days off and holidays dictated by a racing calendar.

And as for a home life… I'd based myself in Monaco but I was never there, always travelling. Show me the person who doesn't love seeing the world and I'll show you a very dull person indeed, but even so, there comes a time when you just want to settle down; you want to stay in the same place for more than three weeks at a time; a place that's yours, surrounded by things and people you love. You want to put down roots.

At the beginning of this year I moved to LA to live with Brittny. I love it there – I'm thirty-seven and I'd never decorated a place before, but it turns out that decorating your own place is one of life's great pleasures. Who knew? We have dogs – Storm and Rogue, a pair of lovely Pomskys. We chill out, cook, train together, watch films. For the first time in seventeen years I'm not spending nine months of the year going to a different country every fortnight. I loved racing and I loved Formula One, but you know my new philosophy? Taking time to live life, savouring each moment? I get to do that for real now.

In the meantime, I've been offered drives in Formula One but I'm not interested, although I will race in the future. Now that I'm no longer contractually forbidden I'm free to race in other categories. I enjoyed that rallycross experience, I've already dipped a toe in Super GT and I'd love to do Le Mans at some point – there's so much out there.

Just not Formula One. Not without Dad.

Last year, during the week before the Monaco Grand Prix, a group of us recreated one of Dad's favourite drives by taking his Ferrari 550 and other beloved cars up the coast from Monaco to Alassio. There for the trip were me, my sisters and their partners, as well as Chrissy, Richie, Brittny, Mikey and Jules.

It was a gorgeous day when we reached Alassio, the seafront twinkling in the sun as we sat and had a little drink, toasting his memory. After that my sisters and I took a boat out into the sea, where even though we weren't able to grant his wish of sliding sideways into his grave in a cloud of tyre smoke, we did the next best thing. We scattered his ashes into the water and let the urn sink.

He would have liked that, all his children gathered at one of his favourite places in the world. It was the least we could do for him.

Most of all, though, he would have loved what he left behind: his legacy. He would have loved the fact that he and I had come from Frome, burst our way into Formula One and turned our dreams into wonderful, unforgettable memories, and best of all he would have loved the fact that we did it together, side by side as father and son.

I know that he would have understood my retirement for the simple reason that I'd fallen out of love with Formula One, and that for him was the best reason to walk away; he would have practically insisted upon it. And I would have listened to him because I always listened to my dad.

After all, I never forgot his words at Clay Pigeon in 1988 when he grinned and told the TV cameras that it was his hobby.

I was just the pilot.

ACKNOWLEDGEMENTS

A son couldn't wish for a better Mum and Supporter! Whether I've won a Grand Prix or ended up in the tyre barriers you've always been able to find something positive to say and find a way to make me feel better about any given situation. Whether you've been at the track or watching from home I know you've been with me every step of the way. I love you, Mum.

To my family – I'm so incredibly lucky to have you all and not a day goes by when I don't realise that. We've been through so much together, the highs and the lows, but because of you all the highs are unbeatable and the lows are all conquerable and, no matter what, it's all made us as close and as strong as we are today even though we live so far apart. I love you all greatly and look forward to making up for lost time thanks to my new schedule, and especially look forward to my first 'I can weigh what I want' Christmas with you all!

RG, 'The God', Richard Goddard – I can't thank you enough, from our friendship to you being kinda a big deal when it comes to management! The journey we've been on for the last thirteen years is quite incredible and I'm so lucky to have had you by my side through it all. In fact, a lot of the time it wasn't by my side, it was leading from the front, breaking through walls for me and rewriting the rulebook along the way. Knowing you have my back means the world to me. Love you big guy!

Jules Gough, the world's greatest PA – I would LOVE to be able to work out some facts and figures that demonstrate how much you've done for me over the years. I'd probably cock it up though and you'd end up doing it for me, so, instead of giving you work to do, I'll just say thank you, from the bottom of my heart. Thank you for taking it all in your stride, even when I've called you from the other side of the world and have massively miscalculated what time it is in the UK! Thank you for everything you do.

Mikey 'Muscles' Collier – when we met, if someone had asked me how much time we would spend together, I would have given it three months, tops! Eight years on, and not only are we still speaking but you're one of my closest friends. Thank you for all your support over the years, and thank you to Harriet and the kids for letting you be a part of my travelling circus, you're a legend! I'll miss those magic hands ;-)

Richie 'Wee' Williams – the test of a true friend is one who's there no matter what, and, more importantly, one who will happily tell you when you're wrong! And that, my friend, you do brilliantly! We've literally grown up together, we've laughed and we've cried, and we've had an embarrassing amount of fun along the way. Thank you for just being you and a constant reminder of what's really important in life. Big love.

Chrissy Buncombe – you've been an amazing friend, an amazing training partner and you're pretty nifty behind the wheel yourself! My off-track teammate and brother I never had, we've been through so many ups and downs together. You're loyal to a fault and always willing to be the designated driver – what more could I ask for! There every step of the way from the karting days to my last race in F1, thank you. Much love.

James Williamson – my PR man, the master of keeping the good in the press and the bad out! Thank you for not only being my PR guru but also more importantly being a great friend and a big part of 'Team Button'.

To my Frome boys: Brad, Fraser, Spud, Paolo, Yogi and James 'T-Rex' Thurston – over the years we've flown the Somerset flag with pride! True friendships stand the test of time and you boys are very special to me. I've been lucky enough to find a job that has allowed me to experience some amazing things over the years but it's being able to enjoy so much of it with you that's made it truly special. Thank you for always being there for me.

To my lovely girlfriend Brittny – thank you for your support and putting up with me for my last year in F1, which was emotional to say the least. I can't tell you how excited I am about sharing the next chapter of my life with you. Love you, Miss Ward.

Storm and Rogue – the best doggies anyone could wish for. Thank you for the unconditional love and endless face licks!

On the book front, a massive thanks to Andrew Holmes, the 'Ayrton Senna' of the page, who has put in an incredible shift. Thanks, too, to my literary agent David Luxton and my editor Matt Phillips, without forgetting all the other other people involved – Nathan Balsom, Karen Browning, Richard Collins, Naomi Green, Lisa Hoare, Oliver Holden-Rea, Justine Taylor and David Tremayne.

Finally, to the fans. You guys are simply awesome. We've been on such an insane journey together and I am continually overwhelmed by the support I've been given year on year throughout my entire career. Thank you for standing by me through thick and thin and for that I am eternally grateful. You made great moments even more special and I can't wait to celebrate with you during the next stint of my career – because it's far from over!

INDEX

(Key: GP = Grand Prix; JB = Jenson Button)